Community-Engaged Scholarship

COMMUNITY-ENGAGED SCHOLARSHIP

Reflections from Netter Center Alumni

Edited by Rita Axelroth Hodges
and Michael Zuckerman

PENN

UNIVERSITY OF PENNSYLVANIA PRESS

PHILADELPHIA

Published by
University of Pennsylvania Press
Philadelphia, Pennsylvania 19104-4112
www.pennpress.org

Printed in the United States of America on acid-free paper
10 9 8 7 6 5 4 3 2 1

A Cataloging-in-Publication record is available
for this book from the Library of Congress.

Hardcover ISBN 978-1-5128-2763-7
Paperback ISBN 978-1-5128-2765-1
Ebook ISBN 978-1-5128-2764-4

CONTENTS

FOREWORD

John L. Jackson Jr.

For more than thirty years, the Netter Center for Community Partnerships, under the leadership of Ira Harkavy, has been building mutually beneficial partnerships between the University of Pennsylvania and West Philadelphia. In so doing, the Netter Center has become a powerful model for democratic engagement between universities and their local communities.

Academically Based Community Service (ABCS) courses are at the heart of the Netter Center's mission, engaging Penn students and faculty with our neighbors as they advance research, teaching, and learning across our campus and our community. Teaching an ABCS course on urban ethnography, I experienced firsthand the power of these courses to bring students together. Penn students and West Philadelphia high school students worked with and learned from each other, collaboratively developing original research projects and media productions. The Netter Center fosters sustained, trusting relationships with our local schools and the West Philadelphia community, creating a cycle of mutuality that encompasses students, instructors of ABCS courses, and the many citizens who are partners in this work.

In addition to ABCS courses, the Netter Center is a powerful catalyst for community-engaged scholarship at Penn. Recently, I participated in a group of scholars convened by the Center to think deeply about community-engaged research, teaching, and learning. What do these values mean to us? How do they transform intellectual work? How do we ensure that they continue to be valued across the wide range of disciplines at Penn? The Netter Center helps Penn attract scholars who understand the value of this work and want to do it, yet even these scholars find that it fundamentally transforms the way they understand being an academic. I have heard numerous colleagues, students, and alumni speak about how their community engagement experiences at the Netter Center changed their lives and inspired their careers.

These meaningful personal narratives form the heart of this book. I am especially pleased that the volume includes one of our inaugural Provost's Graduate Academic Engagement Fellows at the Netter Center, a signature initiative designed to make Penn a leader in training PhD students as community-engaged scholars. As Penn's thirty-first provost, I look forward to continuing to help community-engaged research, teaching, and learning grow and thrive on campus. We aim to advance knowledge for social change by educating and engaging Penn students as ethical democratic citizens and improving the quality of life and learning across our community. As the stories in this volume illustrate, the impact of such community-engaged scholarship does not end here. The ripples can be felt far and wide.

PREFACE

Rita Axelroth Hodges

I share many things with the authors in this volume. Like most of them, my personal and professional trajectory was profoundly shaped by studying with Ira Harkavy, working with what is now known as the Netter Center, and learning from and with West Philadelphia partners as a Penn student. In my student days, I never imagined that twenty years later I would be part of the leadership team of the Netter Center preparing for its thirtieth anniversary.

The Netter Center held a beautiful year-long anniversary celebration in 2022–2023 that included, among other activities, events with K–16+ partners at university-assisted community schools, an Academically Based Community Service (ABCS) and Community-Engaged Scholarship (CES) panel featuring undergraduate and graduate students, and a gospel concert at the church where Netter's community board chair serves as pastor.

Barbara Netter, whose 2007 naming gift with her husband (the late Edward Netter, Penn C53) propelled the Center's work to a new level, suggested holding a symposium during our anniversary year on core themes of our work. When Cory Bowman, Isabel Sampson-Mapp, and I—the Center's associate directors—began thinking about what such a symposium might look like, we focused on the many Netter Center alumni who are now in leadership positions throughout the country and around the world. Cory suggested we narrow our focus to alumni who had gone into careers in academia and related fields and had stayed in touch about the work they were doing in community-engaged research, teaching, learning, and practice. We wanted to bring these alumni together to help advance this work at Penn and beyond and to inspire current undergraduate and graduate students.

In an initial call with three alumni, we raised the idea of bringing them and others together for a symposium on Penn's campus. They responded enthusiastically, so we called a larger meeting. The energy in the Zoom room was palpable as alumni from across the country exchanged reflections on their experiences at Penn and the paths they had taken as a result.

On April 20, 2023, we hosted the Netter Center's Thirtieth Anniversary Alumni Symposium on Community-Engaged Scholarship on Penn's campus. Following opening remarks from Vice Provost for Faculty Laura Perna, a fellow Penn alum who has taught ABCS courses and championed CES, two panels involving a total of thirteen alumni engaged in animated and stimulating conversation about their experiences.

It is the stories of these alumni that comprise this volume. Their personal accounts make vivid the staying power of the lessons they learned and the values they developed through ABCS courses and other Netter programs that brought them in partnership with West Philadelphia neighbors. Many of them worked closely with local K–12 students, families, and teachers in university-assisted community schools, which remains a core strategy of the Netter Center that is aimed at mutual transformation of universities, schools, and communities. The continuous nurturing of democratic partnerships with local schools and community organizations, the growth and development of the Netter Center itself, and the vision and commitment of its leaders have made it possible for these individuals, and so many others, to have had such meaningful and impactful experiences.

The authors are a diverse group. They were Penn undergraduates as long ago as the class of 1987 and as recently as the class of 2008. Most of them went off to earn graduate degrees and faculty positions at other institutions. They also include two individuals whose engagement occurred as doctoral students at Penn, with one having graduated in 1997 and the other in 2020. They represent a range of academic fields—Africana Studies, anthropology, arts administration, data analytics, design, education, epidemiology, history, information science, law, marketing, and writing. But they all agree on the power of working in partnership with local community members to develop solutions to society's most complex and important problems. They all testify to Ira Harkavy's and the Netter Center's enduring influence on today's community-engaged scholars and practitioners.

Finally, some quick words of thanks: to the alumni authors for their thoughtful contributions; to Cory Bowman (C91) for his indispensable contributions to the Netter Center and help with this volume; to Mike Zuckerman (C61), editor extraordinaire; to Walter Biggins and Penn Press for believing in this project; and of course to Ira Harkavy (C70 and Penn doctoral graduate), the founder and Barbara and Edward Netter director of the Netter Center, for his tireless and inspirational leadership and mentorship of generations of Penn students.

CHAPTER 1

"Having a Real Impact": A Conversation About Community-Engaged Scholarship

Salamishah Tillet and Wendell Pritchett

For this special collection, University of Pennsylvania Law and Education Professor and former Interim President Wendell Pritchett and Pulitzer Prize–winning *New York Times* critic and Rutgers University–Newark Professor Salamishah Tillet had an in-depth dialogue about their philosophy and practice of university-based civic engagement. They are both Penn alumni, with Pritchett earning his doctorate in history in 1997 and Tillet receiving her bachelor's degree in English and African American Studies in 1996. They have also served here in other institutional capacities: from 2007 to 2012, Tillet was an assistant professor of English and from 2012 to 2018 an associate professor of English and Africana Studies. In addition to serving as the interim university president from February 2022 to June 2022, Pritchett was the university provost at Penn from 2017 through 2021. He joined the Penn Law School faculty in 2002 and later served as associate dean for academic affairs in 2006–2007 and as interim dean and presidential professor in 2014–2015. However, it was their formative experience at the Netter Center while they overlapped as students at Penn in the 1990s that inspired this conversation and influenced their respective approaches to community-engaged scholarship. Here, they discuss their initial attraction to Academically Based Community Service (ABCS) courses, the impact those classes had on their professional trajectories and the schools at which they've worked, and, most important, their shared interests in the role that universities have played and can continue to play as anchor institutions in their mutual city of Philadelphia and their respective Rutgers University campuses of Camden and Newark.

This conversation occurred in 2023, during the thirtieth anniversary year of the Netter Center. It has been edited for clarity.

Salamishah Tillet: I'd like to start with the moment we both discovered community-engaged scholarship. How did you learn about this approach?

Wendell Pritchett: I started my doctoral program in history in 1993, graduating in 1997, and I met Ira Harkavy through my dissertation adviser and history professor, Walter Licht. They were working closely together on community-engaged scholarship. Walter and I came up with one of the earliest ABCS courses, "Immigration and Migration to Philadelphia." We did an oral history project at a senior day-care center on 54th Street and Haverford Avenue in West Philadelphia, where the students did many of the interviews and we helped edit them. It was a fairly diverse senior center, with people from different backgrounds, from Eastern and Western Europe and South America, and obviously from the south of the United States. We were just figuring out what community-based scholarship was and trying new things. We were experimenting. I'm guessing that was similar to your experience figuring out this field.

Tillet: I was an undergraduate at Penn from 1992 to 1996, so you and I overlapped. During my first year, I met Ira, Cory Bowman, and Glenn Bryan while learning about their community-based programs as a work-study student in the Center for Community Partnerships, which later became the Netter Center. By my sophomore year, I became more involved by teaching Saturday classes to young kids at one of their partner schools, the Turner Middle School in West Philadelphia. It was such a critical moment for me because it was my first time teaching ever, much less my first time teaching African American Studies, which is now one of my main academic disciplines, and I had this core group of students with whom I connected. They enabled me to feel that I was part of their community, that same West Philadelphia community that I was a member of by living on Penn's campus.

Then, the following summer, I participated in another Netter program, piloting a nutrition curriculum and implementing it that fall. I was at Turner again, this time with Penn undergraduate students, Penn Medical and Nursing faculty, Turner Middle School administrators, and elementary school kids from West Philly. As part of that program, I was in a seminar with Ira on democracy and education, which helped me theorize and better appreciate what we were doing. I was introduced to John Dewey's writing in that course and became captivated by his idea of a twenty-four-hour school and experiential education. It was a unique experience because many of my peers weren't doing that kind of engaged scholarship, nor were they as concerned with their relationship with the city where we were. At the time, I was just trying to figure out my way as a young Black woman in a majority-Black section of a city that has a big African American population. I didn't just want to give back; I wanted to be a good citizen here in Philadelphia.

But, as a graduate student, you had far less time than I did to experiment with your course schedule and the type of teaching you did. It sounds like you wanted to do this kind of work all along.

Pritchett: We probably were in the same classroom at some point at Turner Middle School because I was there several times. I visited Ira's summer class, so it's funny that we were probably in the same room at the same time. But, back to your question, I did come to Penn to do this type of scholarship, and again, Walter Licht was the draw for me because I knew he wanted to do this kind of work, too. Before coming here, I had practiced real estate law and was interested in community development. I decided to go back to grad school because I wanted to be a professor, but I also planned to continue practicing law on the side and doing community-based work. That was my vision for my future, which I was privileged to be able to accomplish. I decided to do history because, in essence, I was trying to understand the history of cities to help use that knowledge to improve life today. Walter and I had talked about that from the beginning. I chose Penn mainly because I wanted to be back in Philadelphia, where I am from, and I was very lucky that Penn was a place that was engaged.

Tillet: That makes sense. It's interesting. I chose Penn because I wanted to be in a big city, but at the time, I didn't realize the responsibility of attending a college in an urban setting. I knew colleges were places of student activism and protests in the 1960s and 1970s. Still, I never thought about their relationship to the cities and communities where they resided until I lived on campus in West Philadelphia.

The Center for Community Partnerships was attempting to do deep work in the community, and that meant not just bringing West Philly students to Penn but encouraging Penn students to remember that we were also part of West Philadelphia. I didn't know that a university could think of itself as a good neighbor and that, too, was a profound political act. These values were important to me because I grew up in working-class and middle-class Black communities that weren't so different from the one that we were in then. I wanted to be as kind, generous, and compassionate a community member as possible. Now that I'm at Rutgers University–Newark, I can see how those early years at Penn shaped my current publicly engaged scholarship. I probably wouldn't be doing this work if I didn't have those experiences.

Pritchett: I think one of the things that's special about Philadelphia that Penn has helped facilitate but also benefited from is the community-based nature of this city. There are very committed and passionate people who've lived in neighborhoods for a meaningful amount of time, care about their neighborhoods, and have created organizations, some weaker and some stronger than others, to do that work. So Philadelphia has always been a good place to be a community-based lawyer.

But I also think about the good work that Penn was doing in the 1990s, which you and I are partly responsible for, and we were pushing it as students. If you and I had gone to other places and they were different types of universities, we still would have found a way to do this work. But I do give Penn credit for helping to accelerate this work. You and I benefited from Judith Rodin becoming president because she grew up in West Philadelphia and inherently understood why doing this work in those communities was important. In that sense, we

were in a good place, the right place at the right time. So, when
I reflect back, it was a great experience for us and our fellow
Penn students committed to this work. It is still a wonderful
experience for them. But my view on Penn then and now is
that it's a flawed institution. There is a lot of tension, with long
historical roots, with community members and neighborhood-
based organizations, regarding Penn and how it interacts with
the community.

The relatively easy part of engaged work is helping our
students. We take that seriously at Penn. In my opinion,
there's no better place than Penn to do engaged scholarship
because many faculty here have been thinking hard about these
questions over many decades and trying to make it a better
place in terms of its engagement with the community, which
also makes Penn a great place compared to other higher-
education institutions. But the real work and harder work is
to do engaged scholarship that has real impact on kids and
other people in West Philadelphia. I've always been drawn to
that, but I don't think we can say that we figured out how to do
that, certainly not at the scale that creates a stronger and more
equitable community.

Tillet: I'm also curious about how you, as an administrator and the
chancellor at Rutgers–Camden, approached institutionalizing
this philosophy. Was it easier to implement this practice at a
public university, particularly one in a smaller city?

Pritchett: I frequently say what you just said, which is that university-
based civic engagement is easier at a place like Rutgers–
Camden because the vast majority of the students come from
South Jersey, and they are more intimately related to both the
opportunities and the challenges the school has within the
community. I genuinely believe that. But this is only partially
true, because only a small number of Rutgers–Camden students
are from Camden. Over time, the institution has been more
successful in having more students from Camden, but almost
all of the students are from South Jersey. And, of course, there
is a similarly complicated relationship between the suburbs
of South Jersey and Camden that West Philadelphia has with
Penn. There is a fair amount of resentment between people who

live in Camden and people who live in affluent Jersey suburbs such as Cherry Hill, and of course very few of the faculty live in Camden. So, while the opportunities and challenges at a public university are different, they were also often similar because there are inherent tensions between higher education and underinvested communities.

Ira and his colleagues were very helpful to me at Rutgers–Camden. Nyeema Watson, then the head of community partnerships (now senior vice chancellor for strategy, diversity, and community engagement) at Rutgers, received her master's at Penn and was very connected to the Netter Center. So she, Andrew Seligsohn (who at the time was associate chancellor for civic engagement), and I took and adapted many of the templates that Penn developed for things like academically based community service courses. Penn leaders were very helpful because they had already tried out and polished many things we could adopt and adapt more quickly. The Rutgers–Camden engaged classes certainly were different from the ones at Penn because of the public nature of the university and its relationship with Camden, but we used a lot of the structures that they developed here, and that was very helpful. But I'm also very interested in your perspective on Newark.

Tillet: When I left Penn as a faculty member in 2018 to go to Rutgers–Newark, I was immediately struck by how central university-based civic engagement and community-based scholarship was to our administration. Our [then] chancellor, Nancy Cantor, and Ira are kindred spirits. They often work together, coauthor articles, and have a progressive vision of how the university should relate to and share power with the community in which it dwells. I am the director of Express Newark, a center for socially engaged art and design open to all community residents, K–12 students, and Rutgers students, staff, and faculty. It is an example of Rutgers–Newark's role as an anchor art institution in Newark, and Nancy conceived it as a third space that bridges the campus, the city, and the community.

We are developing ABCS-like courses through our Newark Free School, in which artists, Rutgers members, and Newark residents learn about and cocreate art around specific social and political topics like environmental injustice, racial equality, or gentrification. A few years ago, my administrative team and I went to the Netter Center and met with Ira, Cory, and Rita Hodges to better understand how to design a curriculum that encourages this collaborative approach in the community. Of course, we are using the arts, but the collaborative learning model holds.

When you were provost and president of Penn, how did you continue to do this work?

Pritchett: Being provost and working with Ira and many other Penn and West Philadelphia community members was very rewarding, and I believe we made meaningful progress. Again, we made more progress internally than externally. We were particularly focused on building up graduate student support for this work because undergraduates like you, and even more in 2023, come with a desire to have an impact. A lot of the work at the undergraduate level was just making sure courses were available and that students knew their possibilities and had basic training on how to be good community members. But at Penn and many universities, those are well-oiled machines to help undergraduates. However, universities are still trying to figure this work out at the graduate level.

One of the things we did was create a fellowship for graduate students, the Provost's Graduate Academic Engagement Fellowship at the Netter Center, where students who had shown a proclivity for academically based community service received funding to do that work as graduate students. In graduate school, a lot of where the rubber meets the road is what you get compensated to do, so we provided financial support, and that drew some talented students. We also created a committee of faculty interested in supporting graduate students. I think we've built a nice and growing cadre of graduate students who are doing good work at Penn and will, when they graduate, go out into the world at other universities and spread the gospel. So I feel really good about that.

But expanding the impact of the work on the broader community remains a challenge. As the university has become

even wealthier, the tensions and the pressures on the university
to do more are high. People say Penn doesn't do enough in West
Philadelphia. My response was always, "Yeah, you're right. What
else should Penn be doing? What do you think the university
should be doing?" Over the past decade, the university has
significantly increased its community contributions, including
more financial support for Philadelphia schools in West
Philadelphia and throughout the city. Many people thought
that was good, but many thought it was not enough. There's
a constant tension as we have more economic division in the
country and institutions like Penn get even wealthier. I think
the work is harder, and the expectations are higher, which they
should be. Again, I think the internal university work is fun
and relatively easy. It's the external impact that's a big challenge.
Nancy and other people like you have struggled with that at
Rutgers–Newark. How are you thinking about those questions
at a place with fewer resources than Penn?

Tillet: Nancy spoke eloquently about how to scale this work
throughout campus and the city and the many infrastructural
changes she made here at Rutgers–Newark to accommodate
this work. But seeing what's easily possible and extremely
difficult to implement has been pretty eye-opening. What's
challenging and exciting for me is running a center that is for
the community and supported by Rutgers but is also beholden
to the university's complex bureaucratic system. So we have
many difficult conversations and robust negotiations about
access, resources, and community needs that I imagine are
different at many other research centers at Rutgers. That might
be about how best to fund our community film and media
studio or how the security officers at the front desk interact with
the community members. For example, having a no-ID policy
to enter the building might seem like a little thing, but it's big
for us because we are the only place on campus to do so. Also,
we are in the building that was the former Hahne and Company
department store, a place that notoriously discriminated against
its Black customers. So if, today, we say that we are free, open,
and inviting to all members of the Newark community, we need
to reflect that in all ways, big and small.

But we also reflect on creating equity within our Express Newark systems to ensure that all the faculty-led and community-directed studios have access to the same resources and opportunities. So, as director, I've spent a lot of time finding new resources to support community-directed programs, particularly our Community Media Center, the only institution in Newark where video artists and filmmakers can learn how to make their own films and podcasts for free. To sustain Express Newark as a third space where community members and Rutgers students meet and make art for social change, we must have an infrastructure that treats everyone fairly but is well respected and resourced enough to do so. Oddly, I often feel like we are creating a community-based organization within the university, which means we must be flexible and responsive and balance our idealism and the practical realities of our highly bureaucratic university system.

Pritchett: I completely agree with you. There are so many layers. Let's be honest: these institutions have only been welcoming for a short time, so there's lots of history of exclusion here, and doing things like not asking for an ID is fundamental. There are many things that people within the institution need to consider. And, often, institutional leaders say, "Well, what's the big deal?" with something like the question of IDs. But actually it is a big deal. Then, I also think about the vital importance of approaching all the work with humility. We tend to celebrate things at universities, and that's good. It's okay to celebrate achievements. But we often present ourselves as having clear answers to really complex problems for which we don't have the answers: being humble means recognizing that many people outside of our institution probably know the answer to the question much better than we do. That's another part of the Netter Center's success. Being humble is in its DNA.

Tillet: What you're saying, or at least what I am hearing, is that we should have metrics that do not only measure the success of the Penn or Rutgers students but also account for the relationship to the community we're in. In other words, success must not be measured so much by how our university students are experiencing these collaborations as by how the residents are experiencing us. That shifts how you think about a university's role and commitment, and if that were a fundamental metric, it would also change how the university organizes and evaluates itself. What would it look like if our reputation was partly predicated on how we interacted with the people and places around us? We both say that our universities are doing good stuff, but we can do much more.

Pritchett: Well, there are some basic metrics. We use them at our institutions and places like Netter. Are we seeing meaningful increases in high school graduation rates in our community, and in the number of people who attend college, and in the number of good-paying jobs? These are some basic things, and we've made some progress on those things, not just at Penn but at other institutions. But the question you asked is really hard. I think about it as an urban historian. When I was in grad school, the context for American urban history was one of decline. Cities had been vibrant, but from World War II on, they declined. In the 1980s and into the 1990s, cities just had lots of problems. Cities have problems now, but there are a lot of differences and more resources in cities now—and many more wealthy institutions, such as Penn or even Rutgers–Newark.

When I started working on these issues, many people thought any development happening in West Philadelphia was good. Now, a lot of people do not think that. There's a lot of skepticism about who's benefiting from these investments, a skepticism which, in my view, is well taken. So how do we create a vibrant and equitable community today? It is a really hard question about which we have a lot of disagreement, and at the same time, there's an imbalance of power. Institutions like Penn have significant resources, while other institutions don't. So it's a hard one to figure out. I've spent much time thinking about this challenge in the last few years and don't have a good answer. Many other smart people like you also think about it, and we must figure it out together. But it's an even harder question when you have resources and have to figure out how to use them to benefit people who have not historically benefited.

Tillet: In Newark, there is ongoing anxiety about who's coming into the city and why. We have a lot of conversations about displacement and gentrification, so having a university trying to be a good developer is a noble cause. How do you create new projects that serve community members? Express Newark is in a recently renovated 500,000-square-foot mixed-use space of the Hahne Building. It is a start, and we are trying our best to contribute to the city's ecosystem. Still, we do so against the backdrop of the closing of many community art galleries and organizations in the city that Black and Latino artists primarily led. So we constantly ask ourselves, How do we best share our resources with our neighbors?

Pritchett: A lot of that work is qualitative. There are some quantitative measures, but how do you get a sense of the feel of the community and who feels like it's moving positively for them? I'm sure those are things you talk about.

Tillet: This is why I'm very grateful to continue to be in dialogue with Ira and the Netter Center; it informs the work I'm doing here. I wanted to push myself and the type of scholarship and engagement that I learned to do at Penn in the city that my mother grew up in and my children are now from. In other words, I wanted to learn how to have a bigger impact—in a city and on campus—in relationships of true partnership.

CHAPTER 2

Majoring in Harkavy: Linking Research, Policy, and Practice to Create Positive Social Change

Jacqueline Kraemer

I came to the University of Pennsylvania in 1983 already committed to working to address poverty and inequity. My dad was a union organizer, and my mom was a social worker; this gave me two very different lenses on the world. My dad looked at the world in terms of how to impact institutions of power; my mom looked at individuals and how to navigate structures and policies to aid them in their struggles. I had big dreams, but I was also very focused on making a difference for individuals.

My first foray into activism at college was to join a newly formed student group called the Political Participation Center (PPC). PPC had been created, it turned out, by the students in the inaugural Ira Harkavy–Lee Benson seminar on the role that universities can play in solving the challenges facing society by focusing on their own communities. PPC had grand ambitions: engage students in the work of democracy and activism. We registered students to vote (and convinced Penn to add registration forms to new student packets) and organized forums and actions around key issues. Disinvestment from South Africa's apartheid government was a rallying cry in the 1980s. The work was exciting, but even more exciting to me was the idea that the university and its students could be a force for change.

By sophomore year, I was enrolled in Ira's seminar. We studied the history of urban universities and their engagement—both through research and as employers and neighbors—with their communities; we looked at how these universities often remained walled off from the high-poverty neighborhoods they bordered. Even when faculty reached out to organize research in partnership with organizations, individuals, and institutions in their neighborhoods, the research was often short term, organized around a research question rather than the partner's priorities, and too isolated to have broad impact on the long-term trajectory of the community. The frame proposed in Ira and Lee's seminars was different: the challenge was how the university—via research, institutional engagement, and volunteerism—could help address key issues in the West Philadelphia community. The specific strategy was for each student to choose a partner and identify an issue for work on that partner's behalf, but the broader goal was for the individual efforts of students, faculty, staff, and the institution to cumulate into substantive positive change in the community. And the theory was also that this approach to research— engaging with practitioners and community members as partners and focusing financial, human, and research resources—would make the research better and help the university fulfill its mission of research and teaching to contribute to addressing challenges in society.

When asked what my major was in college, I often joke that I majored in Ira Harkavy's seminars. The seminars were grounded in history and a deep understanding of the context of the challenges we studied and tried to address. The ability to connect my interests in history, sociology, and policy to my passion to address real problems in my own community not only hooked me intellectually but also gave me a sense of purpose throughout college. I wasn't just doing work to get good grades. I was doing work that mattered. By junior year, I created an individualized major that pulled together these seminars and related classes across disciplines under some sort of long title about the history of community-engaged research. Ira Harkavy signed off on it.

My cohort of students in that first seminar had a broad set of partners ranging from church alliances to economic development organizations to Philadelphia public schools. We spent time in West Philadelphia, engaging with people who lived and worked there. The seminar not only introduced us to action research but also introduced us to the community we were living in. Before I was part of these seminars, I remember thinking that there was an invisible wall around the campus, bordering 40th, Market, and Spruce Streets; I do not remember venturing much past those borders. The seminars and projects exposed me to the vibrancy and history of those neighborhoods and to their stark needs, which presented a striking contrast with the well-resourced university campus and community.

For my project, I looked at two issues and saw an intersection: young people dropping out of high school and abandoned housing in the neighborhood surrounding the university. In the spirit of the seminar, I proposed engaging "at-risk" (to use an old term) youth in the work of improving their community by creating a program to train them in construction skills as they renovated abandoned housing in their own neighborhood. I saw a parallel: in the same way that we as college students were advocating for our university to focus on improving its community and empower its students to help in that work, we needed to advocate for the same kind of opportunities for students in public schools. The task of education is not just to accumulate knowledge but also to learn how to apply it and to develop skills to learn independently to address the problems one confronts in work and in life. Providing contexts to do all three things is what a world-class education does.

The work of what was then called the Office of Community-Oriented Policy Studies (OCOPS) and now the Netter Center was, to my recollection, reshaped in response to terrible tragedy during that first year I was involved. It was 1985, the year that Philadelphia police bombed a city block occupied by members of the MOVE movement in West Philadelphia. The resulting fire destroyed the block of houses and killed eleven people, including five children. The West Philadelphia Improvement Corps (WEPIC)—which focused the university's programming and work on the West Philadelphia schools—was born of this fire. The image on the hundreds of WEPIC T-shirts we would eventually distribute was of a phoenix rising from the ashes of a fire.

For me, immediately, the MOVE bombing led to two things. First, it enabled me to become part of the first cohort of students who spent time working at Bryant Elementary School around the corner from the city block the MOVE fire devastated to build what became known at Penn as a university-assisted community school. We saw schools as the best community institutions around which to organize support for children and families in that neighborhood and to address broad neighborhood challenges. The schools were neutral hubs and could bring people together. And second, it provided a chance to turn a proposal I'd presented in an undergraduate paper into a reality. Ira Harkavy saw the moment for what it was: an opportunity to get core funding to start to build the kind of university-community partnerships he had long envisioned.

For the next few years, as I finished undergrad at Penn and then deferred graduate school to stay and work on these projects, I helped build the early WEPIC programs at Bryant and then at West Philadelphia High School, Lea

Elementary School, and Turner Middle School as well as expand what is now known as Academically Based Community Service (ABCS) courses at Penn. I also continued to organize and run a youth apprenticeship program in construction trades at West Philadelphia High School to renovate housing on the block of houses destroyed by the MOVE fire. I still have a photo album of the celebration when the first house at 6009 Osage Avenue was completed and sold at cost to a neighborhood family.

For me, it was a heady time. The WEPIC program was expanding rapidly, the program I proposed in a seminar paper was a reality, and I was able to play a lead role in helping to oversee all of these developments right out of college. I felt like I was engaged in the work of change, still idealistic about what we could do but also beginning to appreciate the complexity and challenges of implementing real and lasting change in communities. I was also positioned to see the links between research, policy, and practice, working as I did with faculty and students from Penn; with funders; with city, state, and federal officials; and with community organizations, school leaders, and teachers.

I began to appreciate the key role that Penn as an institution was playing in initiating, developing, facilitating, improving, and expanding programs. I saw the university in the role of what is sometimes called an intermediary organization. It was providing the focused manpower, coordination, and conduit for additional resources and ideas that community-based programs often sorely lack, hampering their ability to fully realize their goals. Penn was more than a mere intermediary organization in this role. With its extraordinary intellectual, institutional, financial, human, and workforce resources, it was a supercharged intermediary. It was not just its resources that provided the supercharge; the difference was that Penn too was part of the community it was trying to change, so it had a real and lasting stake in the success of the work.

As Penn's model of university-assisted community schools developed, Ira and the OCOPS office attracted the attention of national foundations. One of these was the German Marshall Fund, which at that time was funding projects to share knowledge about social and education policy in the United States and Europe. The fund supported a trip to France, Germany, England, and Sweden for WEPIC teachers and leaders along with Penn faculty to look at community schools and other programming that supported youth and to introduce policymakers in those countries to the Penn model.[1]

I participated in a planning trip for the project, and for me this was a pivot point in my professional development. What I saw in these countries was a policy structure very unlike that in Philadelphia, Pennsylvania, and the United States. The commitment to supporting all children universally and the structures to engage communities in shaping policy were utterly different and sparked in my mind key questions that would shape my graduate work and eventual professional work. Why, I wondered, was policy so different outside of the United States and what could we learn from it to inform what we do in the United States and in West Philadelphia in particular? And why has all the "research" in education and community change done in the United States yielded so little insight into how to fundamentally change the trajectory of the communities we are most concerned about?

I took those questions with me to my graduate program in public policy at the John F. Kennedy School of Government at Harvard and then to the organization I have worked with for the past twenty-some years, the National Center on Education and the Economy (NCEE) in Washington, DC.

In graduate school, I studied the history of social policy in advanced economies to try to understand why and how they developed very different kinds of education and social policies than did the United States. What was striking was the idea that education and social supports were seen as key to building the nation. Many of those policies were put in place in Europe to encourage population growth after the decimation of World War II. Many more, also aimed at educating the population, fueled the birth of world-class economies in Korea, Singapore, and other Asian nations. And the story repeated itself in Estonia and other former Soviet satellites after 1990. A crisis in each country opened a window of opportunity to rethink the system in place and create a consensus around a goal of rebuilding the nation through investment in its people.

The United States, on the other hand, created its mass education system piecemeal in the early part of the twentieth century, in service to the needs of an industrial society untouched by globalization, the digital revolution, and new thinking about learning. And with its commitment to states' rights and local control in education, the governance of education in the United States is more marked by incoherence than anything else. Most innovative work in social and education policy is done despite the governance system in place rather than supported by it. The United States is known internationally for being an incubator of innovation, but the nation lacks capacity to implement these innovations at scale.

All of my graduate study and NCEE work leads me to consider the "West Philadelphia story" in a different light. As in many of the countries I studied, there was a crisis (the MOVE fire) that provided an opportunity to do something new. But in West Philadelphia, the university acted as an instigator and sustainer of reform efforts. Successfully addressing West Philadelphia's challenges was in Penn's best interest, giving it an incentive for ongoing participation and expansion of the work. In some sense, what it did paralleled the "nation building" I saw in European and Asian countries; in this case it was neighborhood building. And for Penn, it was also institution building, as the action research it supported through its university-assisted community schools yielded more reliable and more actionable research. ABCS made Penn a better research university, not just a better neighbor, based in a better neighborhood.

Another key thing that my colleagues and I have observed in successful education systems is a core focus on both careful implementation of policy and continuous improvement. These systems have structures in place to keep abreast of trends in work and learning and to adapt their policies and practices to respond to an ever-changing context. This agility seems key as our world grapples with climate change, the promise and perils of advancing digital technologies, and threats to democracy, among other challenges. Positioning universities as integral partners in the work, not by studying discrete problems in society from a narrow disciplinary perspective but as laboratories to incubate, refine, and scale policy and programs to transform whole communities, may be a way for the United States to create the innovation infrastructure we need to advance change.

In addition to what I learned—and continue to learn—about policymaking in successful systems, I always keep West Philadelphia and Penn's work there in mind as we shape projects and partnerships. I draw particularly on the commitment to creating sustained (but evolving) partnerships to reorganize how policies get made and improved for the long term.

In the early 2010s, I started work on a project aimed at what I often think of as a forgotten sector in education: providers of alternative high school diploma programs, including GEDs. These programs exist in a space in between employment training and education, with both benefits and drawbacks. Increased flexibility to adapt to their target population is likely the biggest benefit; lack of support and disconnection from professional communities is high among the drawbacks. We saw this isolation as a sign that no matter how good the materials, coaching, and support we might provide, it was unlikely to have a lasting impact unless this community was connected to an institution that would continue to support it and inspire it to continue learning, improving, and problem-solving.

Our team broadened its work to include this as a goal. We connected the providers with school district professionals as well as with local universities to provide resources, ideas, and opportunities for reflection and improvement. These linkages weren't a full answer to the many challenges the programs faced, but they began to build the infrastructure and ecosystem to make the work of communities the work of researchers and to ensure their partnership. We also saw that the providers had much to teach others, with their targeted and personalized teaching approach and emphasis on engaging students in just-in-time learning.

This is just a small example, but I think the point is big. The idea of creating the infrastructure for continued implementation, innovation, and learning has been a key consideration in all of my work and one deeply influenced by my early experiences at Penn. Universities are uniquely positioned to take that role; the very close connections between universities and ministries of education and schools in the countries we study in our benchmarking work at NCEE are striking. It is part of how many high-performing systems work. In Estonia, for instance, universities support the new teachers they train even after those teachers are on the job. In this way, universities operate as an extension of the schools. They improve their own programs based on deeper understanding of the schools where their graduates work, and they provide better support for those schools by organizing preparation and assistance that is responsive to school needs. This partnership extends to research, which is often organized as a partnership with the schools that the universities already work with and know well. They also work closely with the national ministry, helping to connect and align policy, research, and practice.

As I reflect on my experience at Penn in the 1980s, there are two aspects of the Netter Center's work that stand out as particularly significant and especially notable and relevant today: the unique role that university students play and the ability of university-assisted community schools to build bridges and transformative partnerships between people of different ages, backgrounds, and perspectives.

The ABCS model positions students to play roles that are different than typical volunteers. They provide needed support, but they also bring new ideas and thinking into schools and community organizations. They are unthreatening because of their youth and their deference to the expertise of those they are supporting. They can ask out-of-the-box questions and propose out-of-the-box solutions, which infuses a very different sense of the possible into the work. And they are taken seriously, which is empowering for young people and provides them the kind of leadership opportunities they need to take on the challenges ahead for their generation.

Beyond this, the university-assisted community school model itself is a key strategy to build partnerships between people who often do not work together or even interact in meaningful ways. The work provides a context for them to think, act, and problem-solve together in a mutually beneficial way and to have the dialogues that build understanding, connections, and new visions of what is possible. Working on something together—even a small project—may be the most productive way to build community and, at the same time, preserve our democracy.

Note

1. William E. Nothdurft, *Schoolworks: Reinventing Public Schools to Create the Workforce of the Future* (Washington, DC: Brookings Institution, 1989).

CHAPTER 3

Calling Philosophy Down from the Heavens: The Moral and Civic Imperative of Engaged Philosophy

Michael Vazquez

Since antiquity, philosophers have offered contrasting ideals: the philosopher's vocation as a life of theoretical contemplation or as an active life in politics; an aristocratic conception of philosophical competence as the possession of a select few or an egalitarian view of philosophizing as a widely shared human impulse; philosophy as a rationale for retreat from the vicissitudes of social life or as an antidote to them. As these long-standing tensions make clear, proponents of "public philosophy" (if we may so call them) are as old as the discipline itself. Often, but not always, proponents of public philosophy conducted their most impactful work *outside* of formal institutions of higher learning. This was the case, for example, with the prominent French philosopher Jean-Jacques Rousseau, with protofeminist pioneers such as Mary Astell and Mary Wollstonecraft, and even well before the rise of the modern university as we know it with Socrates in Greece and Cicero in Rome. There is an interesting story to be told about the commonalities shared by these otherwise ideologically diverse figures. But the focus of my chapter is on the other side of the contrast I originally presented, on a democratic impulse that works *in and through* formal institutions of higher learning. I will focus in particular on what Ira Harkavy has called the "democratic civic university," whose primary mission is "*advancing democracy democratically* on campus, in the community and across the wider society."[1] I was first introduced to this vision for university engagement by the Netter Center as an inaugural Provost's Graduate Academic Engagement Fellow (PGAEF) at the University of Pennsylvania. That encounter was formative and significant but never uncritical. It gave me a new vocabulary with which to articulate my own commitment to public philosophy, which draws primarily from my work as a historian of ancient Greek and Roman philosophy. In what follows, I set out my philosophy of engagement as I came to see it during and after my time at Penn.

PGAEF: A Formative Experience at Penn

With respect to public engagement, the discipline of philosophy has seen encouraging trends in recent years: increased institutional support from higher levels of administration, shifting hiring and tenure norms, and even graduate training that promotes public-facing work among rising generations of scholars. In this respect, the department of philosophy at Penn was ahead of the curve; it has for many years challenged traditional academic and disciplinary boundaries. One particularly notable example is Karen Detlefsen's Project for Philosophy for the Young, which began when I was a graduate student and has grown into an impactful outreach program that extends the reach of philosophical education across the Philadelphia community.[2] I can vividly recall my first opportunity to practice philosophy with high school students at the after-school Philosophy Club at Philadelphia Futures. I facilitated a session on knowledge and reality using Plato's famous Allegory of the Cave. We had an absorbing conversation about the nature of reality and the ways in which social institutions shape and stymie our ability to think about the world. That experience jolted me from my academic slumbers by reminding me that philosophy ought to be—and was for most of its history—a *public* phenomenon. After all, Socrates spent his days of philosophical activity in the agora, conversing and debating with folks from all walks of life. This simple truth is easily forgotten in our increasingly siloed university system, even among humanists, and even by a scholar of ancient philosophy like me. At this stage in my graduate career, I began to think that the university's business of knowledge production must be tethered to an equally important civic aim: production of knowledge for the public good and for the betterment of society.

The semester following my work with high school students, I helped run a philosophy discussion series with seventh-grade students at Benjamin B. Comegys School in West Philadelphia, one of the Netter Center's comprehensive university-assisted community schools. In particular, I served as a teaching assistant for Karen Detlefsen's new Academically Based Community Service (ABCS) course, "Philosophy and Education: Philosophy in Middle School." My primary task was to conduct research into philosophical pedagogy in middle schools and to present this material to the Penn undergrads who were designing developmentally appropriate lesson plans for fifth-grade students at Comegys. I was struck by the enthusiasm and interest these conversations generated. When philosophical discussions are framed thoughtfully, young students do not need to be convinced about the importance or relevance of philosophy. Without any jargon or elaborate theories, folks of all ages immediately recognize that philosophy is already part and parcel of their thinking about the world.

Community engagement became a regular fixture of my weekly schedule in graduate school, ranging from serving as a coach for teams competing in the first-ever Philadelphia Regional Ethics Bowl to facilitating "Philosophy and Film" at the Sadie Tanner Mossell Alexander University of Pennsylvania Partnership School. Eventually, as a fourth-year PhD student, I applied for and received the inaugural PGAEF fellowship at the Netter Center.[3] As part of this project, I was able to design and teach my own ABCS class, "Public Philosophy and Civic Engagement," working alongside the talented Mr. Griffin Pepper at Mastery Charter School–Shoemaker Campus, another university-assisted community school, to integrate ethics into a twelfth-grade civics and economics course. By attending meetings off campus with experienced engagement practitioners such as Netter Associate Director Cory Bowman, I learned firsthand how to forge lasting and meaningful community partnerships—partnerships that promise to enrich the lives of all involved and that speak to expressed interests and needs in the community. We dubbed our discussion program at Shoemaker the "Ethics Think Tank." With an emphasis on active and inquiry-based learning, we explored quintessentially philosophical themes such as moral equality, obligations to distant strangers, individual and collective responsibility for climate change, and the philosophical rationale for prisons as a form of punishment.

Befitting a course centered on the idea that university-based partnerships can revitalize democracy, our seminar received a welcome visit from Penn's then-president, Amy Gutmann. In addition to discussing an excerpt from her book-length treatment of deliberative democracy, we discussed President Gutmann's 2004 inaugural speech introducing the Penn Compact, a plan for Penn that articulated a vision for equitable and impactful engagement locally and globally: "I propose a compact—a Penn Compact—that expresses our boldest aspirations for higher education. A compact based on the shared understanding that 'Divided we fail. United we flourish.' By honoring this Penn compact, we will make the greatest possible difference in our University, our city, our society, and our world."[4] Notably, the third pillar of Gutmann's compact is *engagement*. In the context of my course on public philosophy and my year as a fellow at the Netter Center, her words struck a new chord: "No one mistakes Penn for an ivory tower. And no one ever will. . . . Effective engagement of these values begins right here at home."[5]

President Gutmann's visit was, for me, more than a nice bonus. It marked the culmination of an intellectual trajectory that I now see, in the rearview mirror, as continuous and logical. My inklings about the distinctive character of ancient philosophical practice, sometimes referred to as "philosophy as a way of life," crystallized into a set of guiding principles for public philosophy:

1. *Universal Access*: Philosophy is within the purview of every human being and every human community. Philosophy belongs in schools, in the workplace, and in community spaces that reach folks across the lifespan, especially those who are often deprived of the opportunity to engage in philosophical reflection.
2. *Distributed Expertise*: Inasmuch as philosophizing is a natural human impulse, the distinctive value of philosophical expertise is that it helps people refine a skill that they already have some degree of acquaintance with. No socialized human being needs to be initiated into philosophy ex nihilo.
3. *Social Reasoning*: The paradigmatic case of reasoning is not solitary reflection but dialogue with others. To philosophize is to enter a shared space of reason-giving in which we are genuinely open to changing our minds and in which we strive to make progress toward truth.

In coming to articulate these ideals, I was also struck by an insight that connected the disparate threads of my research and my engagement work. I was at the time working on a dissertation on ancient Greek and Roman Stoicism, a tradition best known today for its therapeutic methods aimed at eliminating the disturbances that arise when we let our judgments and our emotions be guided by external events and things that are not "up to us." One other important strand in the Stoic tradition is egalitarianism (or something like it), which is difficult to spot if we focus on the Stoics' unyielding rigor and moralism. The egalitarian insight hidden in plain sight is that all humans have a natural, inborn aptitude for truth and virtue, and it is the task of lifelong philosophical education to get us there. While the ancient Stoics did not draw out the radical, democratic implications of these ideas, others later would.

The Stoics were also opposed to any form of ivory-tower escapism. They emphasized our degree of dependence on other humans and the obligations that flow from this fact. The Stoic Seneca once enjoined his addressee Lucilius: "Let us hold things in common, as we are born for the common good. Our companionship is just like an arch, which would collapse without the stones' mutual support to hold it up."[6] The Stoics maintained that humans are fundamentally sociable, which finds expression in a moral imperative to a life of *action*: "Moreover, learning about and reflecting upon nature is somewhat truncated and incomplete if it results in no action. Such action is seen most clearly in the protection of human interests and therefore is concerned with the fellowship of the human race. For that reason this should be ranked above mere learning."[7] In marked contrast to the Epicureans, the Stoics considered it a moral obligation to serve one's state, one's community, and humanity as a whole. In their commitment to serving the human race and to honoring our specific social roles and relations, Stoic altruism is not so far from Harkavy's modus operandi of working to address "universal problems manifested locally."[8] I began to see that this connection between Stoic philosophy and a life of engagement was likely what attracted me to begin doing the unconventional work of community outreach in the first place.

The Stoics were, in a nutshell, inheritors of a Socratic tradition of philosophy. In my titular passage, Marcus Tullius Cicero reports that "Socrates was the first to call down philosophy from the heavens and to settle it in cities, and even to bring it into homes, compelling it to ask questions about life and morals and things good and evil."[9] It would be a mistake to say that Socrates's great act was to enlighten the world with his expertise, like the philosopher king who descends back into Plato's cave in order to educate those in the grip of ignorance. That would be to miss the point—not least the point of Socrates's frequent reminders that the only thing he knows is that he knows nothing at all! Socrates's excitement about the prospect of conversing with others was partly driven by his hope that *they* had something to offer *him*. Instead, I found in Socrates's legacy a basis for maintaining that university-based community engagement—which one might be tempted to view as an asymmetric relationship in the mold of Plato's descending philosopher king—is an intellectual feedback loop. When we cultivate spaces of inquiry for folks who have not been given the opportunity to think about philosophy in an intentional way, those voices expand the breadth of philosophical inquiry in new and critical ways. All parties stand to benefit, as do the prospects of our collective pursuit of the truth.

Furthermore, the passage above tells us something about the character of Socratic philosophy in contrast to the esoteric philosophy he inherited. The questions he posed looked different; they had more practical import and normative significance; they spoke to human interests and concerns and to the way we live our lives individually and collectively. That is not to say that all philosophy must be "useful" (here I find myself breaking ranks with dyed-in-the-wool pragmatists). Part of the joy and appeal of philosophical reflection lies in its *uselessness*—that its spaces can be free from political maneuvering, that its questions and answers take a spontaneous course not dictated by this or that project of social change and that it is, frankly, unproductive. So when I take Socrates as a model, I by no means denigrate "thinking for its own sake." In my view, which I gather is uncommon among engagement practitioners, philosophy and other humanistic forms of inquiry provide an important counterweight to the tendency of socially driven projects to instrumentalize learning—even, or especially, for well-meaning and noble ends. Even so, Socrates's legacy shows us how "useless" inquiry must be conducted if it is to be humanizing. First, we should philosophize in community with others. The impetus for doing so is intellectual humility: a recognition of the limitations of what we know and could ever come to know on our own. Second, philosophy is not just a set of abstract principles or doctrines, but a way of orienting ourselves that has palpable implications for the way we think about the world and the way we conduct our lives. It therefore ought to be written and spoken in an attractive and intelligible style so that it can move the hearts, as well as the minds, of its listeners.

These are some of the very themes and passages that were racing through my mind at the time. I certainly did not resolve all of the tensions they presented, but I began to see a thread that linked my own study of ancient philosophy with Ben Franklin's vision for a humanity-serving education that promotes self-governance,[10] with Dewey's vision of democracy as a "way of life"[11] that is as much about culture and ethos as it is about electoral mechanisms, and finally with Gutmann's Penn Compact and her deliberative theory of reciprocity and mutual respect. The formerly inchoate reasons for which I pursued a fellowship at the Netter Center in the first place were suddenly crystal clear, and I owe a very great debt to Ira Harkavy and the University of Pennsylvania for helping me get there.

Enduring Lessons from Netter

After defending my dissertation in May 2020, I began my first academic post as a teaching assistant professor of philosophy at the University of North Carolina–Chapel Hill and as the director of outreach at the Parr Center for Ethics. In my instructional capacity, I continue to teach and design experiential education courses with community engagement ranging from a high school Ethics Bowl to intergenerational philosophy with older adults.[12] My experience with ABCS at Penn showed me how these courses can normalize community engagement within a department culture and within a disciplinary course sequence—making them not exceptional or one-off experiences but a regular part of student formation. In my administrative capacity at the Parr Center, I work to form community partnerships with the goal of promoting philosophical and ethical reflection across the state of North Carolina. In any given semester, I offer community-based programming in K–12 schools, community colleges, libraries, prisons, juvenile detention centers, museums, professional workplaces, retirement communities, and more. My experiences as a Netter fellow gave me a vocabulary for articulating the narratives that my outreach efforts resist (for example, that young children and older adults cannot contribute to philosophical inquiry or that philosophical knowledge is the province of a select few). It also gave me a vocabulary for articulating a positive vision for that work, which I have since codified in the mission of the Outreach Program in Philosophy:

1. to help people in the community think carefully and clearly about a broad range of ideas, commitments, and practices that shape their lives;
2. to expand the scope and breadth of philosophical inquiry by bringing new voices into the fold; and
3. to promote the university's mission to produce and disseminate knowledge for the public good.

I have come to believe that public philosophy can contribute to a flourishing and autonomous human life and to a vibrant civic sphere, that we owe community members the opportunity to be exposed to the joys and challenges of philosophical thinking, and that we owe them the opportunity to cultivate the habits of mind that will empower them to reflect on and pursue their own conception of the good life. Immanuel Kant famously summarized the zeitgeist of the Enlightenment with the Horatian slogan "*sapere aude!*" (dare to know). Institutions of higher education are uniquely well positioned to realize Kant's vision of democratic self-governance by creating public and lifelong opportunities for critical reflection. Crucially, one assumption that stands behind this egalitarian vision is the idea that engaged philosophy is mutually beneficial for the university and the community. Our philosophical thinking and research are enriched to the extent that we conceive of the philosophical community in the broadest and most expansive terms. I am convinced that in order to achieve this, we must build *intergenerational* spaces that break down the barriers that prevent people of different ages and generations from sharing their wisdom and lived experiences and from engaging with one another as moral and political equals.

In addition, the habits of mind that philosophy cultivates and sustains play a crucial political function in our "democracy of discussion." Consider a metaphor Plato once offered to describe people and their government: governing a city or any political association is like steering a ship.[13] Plato used this image to argue that democracy is the worst form of government, destined for ruin by incompetence, demagoguery, and internal strife. I think our democratic experiment has proven Plato wrong, but we can still appreciate the underlying lesson: if our ship of state is going to avoid shipwreck, then the individuals that make up our democratically governed society— that is, all of us—need the right skills for the job. Those skills include not only technical know-how but also social and civic dispositions to deliberate about public problems and a moral compass to guide the way. What follows from this is a program of universal democratic education; attempts to restrict access to the core competencies and skills that philosophy offers come at our collective peril.

University departments of philosophy can perform this vital civic function only by forging sustainable community partnerships. The process of doing so, I learned from my time at the Netter Center, is nonlinear and iterative. There is no simple algorithm or predictable path for university-based community partnerships. This lesson served me well when trying to build an engagement portfolio from the ground up in North Carolina during a global pandemic. It helped me think creatively alongside the North Carolina

Department of Public Safety (NCDPS) to launch a statewide Philosophy by Mail program in adult prisons at a time when face-to-face encounter was not possible, resulting in hundreds of letters sent between state prisons and Chapel Hill's campus. It propelled my efforts to extend, in an unprecedented way, our philosophy programming with NCDPS into the domain of juvenile justice education, leading to multiple grant-funded initiatives that included a high school course on Plato's *Republic* at Cabarrus Youth Development Center and an intensive weekend seminar at UNC open to all juvenile justice educators across the state. PGAEF gave me the tools to identify areas of interest and need in conversation with the community. One of those issues was, for me, the marginalization of the old and the social barriers (all too common in college towns) that prevent students from forming meaningful relationships with older adults in the community. To begin to address this problem, I forged a new partnership with the Orange County Department on Aging wherein the department of philosophy at UNC regularly offers a free, semester-long intergenerational philosophy course at a local senior center. I could not have predicted the success and overwhelmingly positive reception of that course, which has now grown into a flourishing community of lifelong learning on and off campus. Netter taught me the rewards of a collaborative posture, which extends to on-campus collaboration just as much as it does to off-campus partners. Aided by my burgeoning view that the university, and especially the humanistic disciplines, must provide integrated and holistic experiences for students, I formed an unprecedented network of partnerships with the Society for Classical Studies, Carolina Public Humanities, Humanities for the Public Good, and several departments at UNC to host a semester-long series of intergenerational events that culminated in a stage reading of Seneca's *Medea*—a campus- and community-based program that has now become an annual collaboration centered on ancient tragedy.[14] I did not have these ideas worked out from the start, nor did I discover and pursue them unilaterally. We arrived at a shared vision because of our readiness to engage in an iterative process of collaboration and experimentation.

The iterative approach to community partnerships is the only way to figure out "what works"—and there is a lot packed into that phrase. "What works" can be what solves or mitigates tangible social problems. But it can also be what contributes to individual and social flourishing in less visible ways, for example, by allowing Medea's story to be an occasion for reflection on human fragility and the role of emotions in our moral lives. It "works" when it helps people across the lifespan develop civic habits, such as deliberative readiness, open-mindedness, and humility. It "works" when it breaks down social and spatial barriers that prevent older and younger people from getting to know one another. And it "works" when it gives people the opportunity, too often reserved for a select few, to ask life's big questions. It took some time for me to realize that humanities programming can "work" in this subtle way. We have good reason to think that philosophy's value lies not so much in the content that it conveys to the pupil as in the habits of thought and talk it fosters and the sense of belonging its communities promote.

Countless stories testify to the transformative impact of public philosophy programming, but we should be prepared to ask whether these anecdata are supported by our best empirical and social sciences. My quest to answer this question in a rigorous way has led me to new collaborations with colleagues in psychology to assess the impact of philosophy instruction on learners' intellectual and civic virtues, especially in the context of discussions about ethical and political questions.[15] It has led to research projects that have, most recently, been supported by grants from the John Templeton Foundation and from the Institute for Arts and Humanities at UNC–Chapel Hill. I believe these studies can help us understand how to promote virtues that are bulwarks of democracy, especially in our age of distrust and antipathy. It is more important than ever that folks across the lifespan cultivate the dispositions that allow them to engage in open-minded, charitable, and respectful dialogue about issues of public concern.

One example of this work centers on the Parr Center's signature outreach program, the National High School Ethics Bowl (NHSEB). In NHSEB, students work in teams to analyze ethically challenging scenarios. The goal is not to crush opposing views under the weight of superior arguments but to engage in respectful and supportive dialogue.[16] Competition scoring criteria thus discourage adversarial debate and reward depth of thought, responsiveness to the other team, and thoughtful consideration of diverse perspectives. The moral and civic aims of the program are clear, but how successful is the program at realizing them? A collaborator and I conducted the first-ever longitudinal study of NHSEB in pursuit of the answer, focusing on outcomes such as intellectual humility, prosociality, and affective polarization.[17] I also continue to work with K–12 teachers to implement pedagogical resources that draw from the same wellspring of philosophy and Ethics Bowl pedagogy.

For example, in partnership with TED-Ed, I have been working with philosophers at UNC to create a series of videos that develop an "ethical toolkit," a set of concepts and distinctions that give people a vocabulary for thinking through dilemmas and deliberating in the face of disagreement. I also work with these same partners to assess the impact of our programming on an ongoing basis, both for the purposes of program design and for the production of socially useful knowledge about education. Here I continue to find inspiration in the spirit of provisionality that permeates the work of Dewey, Gutmann, and Harkavy. We want to know what works and what does not work so that we can revise our plans, which were only ever provisionally set down. We must, therefore, be open to following the evidence wherever it may lead, even if it takes us in unexpected directions.

It is perhaps unsurprising that an organization like the Netter Center would lead me to develop an interest in the questions that comprise the scholarly subfield known as "philosophy of education." Working with the Netter Center helped me to see that life is coextensive with learning and that learning is not exhausted by what happens within the walls of formal institutions of education. These insights brought greater coherence to my teaching, research, and service and, thereby, to my identity as a professional philosopher. I continue to develop this interest in my teaching at UNC and as a lecturer for the Mid-Career Doctoral Program in Educational Leadership at Penn Graduate School of Education. In recent years, I have hosted numerous professional development seminars and workshops that create opportunities for K–12 educators and educational leaders to reflect on the philosophical and normative dimensions of their practice. With all the clarity of hindsight, I can now say that this aspect of my development as a scholar and engagement practitioner was predictable. The public character of higher education and the experience of forming community partnerships are liable to make one reflect on the foundations of education, as Plato, Dewey, Franklin, Gutmann, Harkavy, and so many others have done. For my part, I began to ask three questions more directly: What are schools and universities *for*? How, in a pluralistic and multicultural society, can we educate for civic and participatory readiness? What role should the humanities, and philosophy in particular, play in the lifelong education of free and equal citizens? My own provisional answers to these questions continue to shape my teaching, service, and research in ways I could not have anticipated years ago, before my consequential encounter with the Netter Center.

Notes

1. Ira Harkavy, "Dewey, Implementation, and Creating a Democratic Civic University," *Pluralist* 18, no. 1, (2023): 49–75, quotation on 53.

2. Dustin Webster, Stephen Esser, and Karen Detlefsen, "Bringing Philosophy into Philadelphia Classrooms," in *Intentional Disruption: Expanding Access to Philosophy*, ed. Stephen Kekoa Miller, 131–48 (Wilmington, DE: Vernon, 2021); Jacqueline Mae Wallis and Karen Detlefsen, "Philosophy, Academic and Public: Lessons from the Graduate Certificate in Public Philosophy at the University of Pennsylvania," *Precollege Philosophy and Public Practice* 4 (2022): 91–109.

3. Kristina García, "The Inaugural Provost's Graduate Academic Engagement Fellowship Cohort," *Penn Today*, Feb. 11, 2020, https://penntoday.upenn.edu/news/provost -netter-center-fellowships.

4. Amy Gutmann, "The Inaugural Address," *University of Pennsylvania Almanac* 51, no. 8 (Oct. 19, 2004), https://almanac.upenn.edu/archive/volumes/v51/n08/inaug_ag _speech.html.

5. Gutmann, "Inaugural Address."

6. Lucius Annaeus Seneca, *Letters on Ethics*, trans. Margaret Graver and A. A. Long (Chicago: University of Chicago Press, 2015), 377.

7. M. T. Griffin and E. M. Atkins, eds., *Cicero: On Duties* (Cambridge: Cambridge University Press, 1991): 59–60 (slightly modified).

8. Ira Harkavy and Matthew Hartley, "Integrating a Commitment to the Public Good into the Institutional Fabric: Further Lessons from the Field," *Journal of Higher Education Outreach and Engagement* 16, no. 4 (2012): 17–36, quotation on 19.

9. Marcus Tullius Cicero, *Tusculan Disputations* 5.10. Translation from *Cicero: On Life and Death*, trans. John Davie and ed. Miriam T. Griffin (Oxford: Oxford University Press, 2017).

10. See Paul Guyer, "Freedom of Reason," in *The Autobiography of Benjamin Franklin: Penn Reading Project Edition*, ed. Peter Conn, 150–53 (Philadelphia: University of Pennsylvania Press, 2005).

11. John Dewey, Creative Democracy—the Task Before Us (1939), reprinted in *John Dewey: The Later Works, 1925–1953*, vol. 14, ed. Jo Ann Boydston, 224–30 (Carbondale: Southern Illinois University Press, 1976), quotation on 229.

12. See Michael Vazquez, "Deliberating Across the Lifespan," in *The Ethics Bowl Way: Answering Questions, Questioning Answers, and Creating Ethical Communities*, ed. Roberta Israeloff and Karen Mizell, 91–100 (Lanham, MD: Rowman & Littlefield, 2022).

13. Plato, *Republic*, Book 6: 488a–489d.

14. For details about the inaugural collaboration, see Kari Lindquist, Delaney Thull, Michael Vazquez, and Aurora Yu, "The Future of Humanities Is Public," *EducationNC*, Mar. 21, 2023, www.ednc.org/the-future-of-humanities-is-public/.

15. See, for example, Michael Prinzing and Michael Vazquez, "Does Studying Philosophy Make People Better Thinkers?" *Journal of the American Philosophical Association* (2024): 1–22, https://doi.org/10.1017/apa.2023.30.

16. Alex Richardson and Michael Vazquez, "Looking for a Better Way to Disagree This Election Season? Look No Further Than Your Local High School," *EducationNC*, Nov. 7, 2022, www.ednc.org/perspective-looking-for-a-better-way-to-disagree-this -election-season-look-no-further-than-your-local-high-school/.

17. Michael Vazquez and Michael Prinzing, "The Virtues of Ethics Bowl: Do Pre-College Philosophy Programs Prepare Students for Democratic Citizenship?" *Journal of Philosophy in Schools* 10, no. 1 (2023): 25–45.

CHAPTER 4

The Transformational Power of Community and Culturally Sustaining Education: Reflections from Two Netter Center Alumni

Jeff Camarillo and H. Samy Alim

We distinctly remember the narrative when we began our undergraduate academic careers at Penn in the mid-1990s:

"You should really never cross 40th Street."
"If you want to stay safe at night never venture past 42nd Street."
"Penn has increased its security presence at the 40th Street corridor to ensure the safety of our student community."

I (Jeff) heard messages like these repeatedly during my first year at Penn. As I rode the SEPTA trolley from the Penn campus down Baltimore Avenue toward 59th Street—the "green line," as Philly heads called it—those messages somehow made me feel like I was taking a risk by venturing so far west of campus. If I am completely honest, the way West Philly and its predominantly Black community were discussed at Penn often echoed European colonial discourses of "the dark continent." Decidedly dangerous, essentially off-limits. Reflecting now, all these years later, I see that Ira Harkavy and the Center for Community Partnerships (as it was known at the time) provided me a much-needed space to encounter realities beyond these distorted depictions. They set me on a lifetime of building genuine, reciprocal, working relationships with those communities based on mutual trust, care, and respect.

In the summer after my freshman year, in 1998, I participated in a program through the Netter Center's Penn Program for Public Service Internship, teaching world history and Spanish to a group of rising seventh graders from Southwest Philly. As University City faded around 44th Street and gave way to the cultural vibrancy of West and Southwest Philadelphia, I remember, as a nineteen-year-old, feeling something transformational bubbling inside my spirit and my intellectual soul. When I got off the trolley, ready to launch the first day of my "teaching" career, I studied my surroundings and embraced the opportunity I was ready to embark on.

As the young people of Southwest Philly made their way into my classroom and settled into their summer school program, I began to realize the fallacy of the narrative with which I had been presented during my orientation to Penn. I started to understand and embrace the vision that my mentor and professor, Ira Harkavy, shared in our seminar about the potential for learning that comes through academically based community service. By the end of the first week of the Netter Center–Turner Middle School summer program, I was struck by several realizations that ultimately became guiding forces in the trajectory of my career as a teacher and educational leader post-Penn:

1. There are transformational learning opportunities within the cultures of historically marginalized communities.
2. There is more to learn about community, society, democracy, justice, and equity at 59th and Baltimore in Southwest Philly than there is at 34th and Walnut at Penn.
3. Teaching and learning from and with vibrant young people and families was and still is the most gratifying, joyful, and transformative part of my life.

But I was still far from seeing, in that summer of 1998, that my venture beyond the elite bubble of the Ivy League institution I was privileged to attend would transform my vision of my future and ultimately set the course for a quarter-century (and counting) of community and culturally sustaining educational work.

At the culmination of my summer internship experience, I wrote a research paper and a proposal for the creation of a literacy-based after-school program at Turner Middle School. My mentor during my internship had been an older Penn student, H. Samy Alim, who had already worked extensively with the Netter Center and the Southwest and West Philly communities and schools. He'd helped guide me through my teaching experience. Now he worked with me on my research and in crafting my proposal to continue my work at Turner Middle School. With his support, I developed my vision of centering the creativity and brilliance of my Southwest Philly students and their cultures and identities through Hip Hop and R&B music.

Little did he and I know at that time, but Samy's work with me that summer laid the foundation for what he and Django Paris would later expand and theorize as *Culturally Sustaining Pedagogies*. He led me to consider what he and Paris would later say more elegantly in their book, "that schooling should be a site for sustaining the cultural practices of communities of color rather than eradicating them."[1] Such pedagogies seek a liberatory learning that can "sustain and support" students who have been marginalized within the education system.[2] This is the aspiration that was implanted in my educational DNA in the course of my experience at Turner and the Netter Center. This is the commitment that catapulted me through the remaining three years of my undergraduate career.

I learned constantly, not only in the praxis work I led at Turner Middle School with incredible students and other Penn undergraduate volunteers whom I helped recruit, but also in Dr. Harkavy's seminars where we examined the theoretical frameworks of democratic schooling and equitable educational approaches. My vision for my future became clearer.

Fast-forward twenty-five years from the summer of 1998 and that first transformational experience. I am now one of a small team of leaders of color of Stanford University's Teacher Education Program (STEP), one of the most renowned teacher preparation programs in the world, preparing future educators to teach for racial justice and educational freedom through a focus on community and culturally sustaining pedagogies that seek to elevate and center the narratives and voices of historically marginalized students and families. Calling upon my experiences at Penn, and as a California urban school teacher and leader, I designed a new course at STEP titled "Race, Culture, Identity and Intersectionality in Diverse California Communities." This course is driven by the research and scholarship of one of the world's leading researchers on Hip Hop linguistics and culturally sustaining pedagogies, my mentor from my first teaching experience at Penn and in Southwest Philly in 1998, Dr. H. Samy Alim. The course looks to disrupt misguided narratives and misconceptions about communities of color and, instead, pushes Stanford graduate students and future teachers to ask questions such as

- How do we embrace and lift up the power of intergenerational knowledge, wisdom, and cultural assets of historically marginalized communities, students, and families?
- How can we further evolve as culturally sustaining and community-oriented practitioners through continued learning about cultural history, intersectional identity, and community contexts?
- How can we translate course learnings into decisions and practices that reflect culturally sustaining pedagogies?

My arrival at Stanford University to lead this critical, restorative, and academically based community educational work came after serving in historically marginalized communities of color for over two decades as a teacher, principal, and school founder.

As a middle school teacher on the west side of Compton, California, for seven years, I called upon my experience at Turner Middle School daily to center Hip Hop pedagogies for my students. At every turn, I sought to accentuate and honor the cultural gifts and wisdom of their community and allow the students to see their potential and their greatness.

As an assistant principal transitioning from classroom practitioner to developing school leader in East Palo Alto, I found myself in a community of color that has a troubled relationship to Stanford very similar to the relationship that West and Southwest Philly have to Penn. East Palo Alto Academy High School is a university-community high school founded by Stanford. An important part of my work there was to lead university-community partnership efforts to involve Stanford undergraduates in the power of academically based community service.

As a principal and school founder in East San Jose and East Oakland, I led the creation of two community and culturally sustaining charter high schools that elevated and centered the cultures, identities, languages, and communities of the students and families they served to disrupt the historical inequities of schooling in two of the Bay Area's most culturally vibrant and historically marginalized communities of color.

In Compton, East Palo Alto, East San Jose, and East Oakland, the seeds that were planted in me at the age of nineteen, through my work at the Netter Center and in the heart of Southwest Philly, have now blossomed into a flourishing forest of critical hope and community-centered educational freedom dreams.

There is rarely a day that passes where the learning and values instilled in me through my work as an undergraduate at the Netter Center do not make their way into my educational praxis and leadership. Every time I assign my Stanford graduate students a reading from Alim and Paris's *Culturally Sustaining Pedagogies*, I think back to our shared trolley rides down Baltimore Avenue in 1998 and the trajectories of our paths, the interconnectedness of our journeys, the dialectical and reciprocal nature of culturally sustaining education, and the transformative impact that Samy and I have had on educational institutions, communities, and schooling.

*   *   *

I (Alim) remember them trolley rides well, Jeff. And it's an honor that you would even refer to me as your mentor, since I learned at least as much from you as you learned from me, if not more. But let me take it back for a minute, because I came under the tutelage of Dr. Harkavy with a strong interest in Black language, what folks were calling "Ebonics" at the time, right around the time of the "Oakland Ebonics Controversy" in the late 1990s. In short, in 1997, the Oakland Unified School District had proposed using the language patterns of their African American students as resources in teaching them so-called standard English—and for a whole host of complicated reasons having to do with racism, classism, and widespread ignorance about language and education, all hell broke loose.

In my senior thesis that same year, I asked in all earnestness, "Is it not time to begin developing pedagogies that provide new and innovative approaches to stimulate and motivate our students to mobilize toward educational excellence? How can we begin using pedagogical approaches that value and preserve the many languages and cultures Americans bring to school?" As a Hip Hop head—bumpin *Wu-Tang Forever* all day every day (while Jeff was busy bumpin E-40 and all that Bay Area rap)—I advocated passionately for the use of Hip Hop language and culture in the classroom. Dr. Harkavy helped guide some of my earliest research questions. When I wrote my honors thesis, "Teaching 'Standard English' in the Inner City," I was driven by the opportunity, as Harkavy would often say, "to put educational scholarship to work for the people." From that day onward, throughout my entire career, I have strived to do just that. At the same time, I became acquainted with some of the paradigm-shifting scholars whose ideas form a pedagogical basis for much of the work that Jeff and I continue to do under the rubric of community and culturally sustaining education: Carol Lee, Gloria Ladson-Billings, and of course, Geneva Smitherman's revolutionary conceptualization of Black language in America.[3] Back in the days at Turner Middle School, Jeff and I joined the call for educators to build on the cultural-linguistic practices of our students for academic success in the language arts classroom and *beyond*. In using Hip Hop pedagogies to teach and learn from fifth- and sixth -graders at Turner, we came to view Hip Hop culture (that is, the latest manifestation of African American expressive cultures) not just as a "bridge" for academic success but also as a complex and creative culture that had the potential to transform the schooling and life experiences of many of our students. As we both found out, no matter *what* some people tried to tell us, "these kids" could not only write. They could *write their asses off!* And they produced issue after issue of *Da Bomb!* Hip Hop magazine and became locally known in their neighborhood!

Needless to say, Jeff and I were incredibly proud of our young students. This wasn't about "pedagogical theory" for us at the time; this was about young people, their families, and communities. Yes, we were centering culture in educational theory and practice, but we centered students *first*. Teaching was always, for us, about relationships. Dr. Harkavy modeled that for us. He built genuine, caring relationships not only with his students but also with everyone he worked with in many Philadelphia communities.

I'd like to add four final thoughts about what we've been writing here as "community and culturally sustaining pedagogies" as a way to consider the centrality of communities in our work. And in the tradition of Dr. Harkavy, I'd like to conclude with some questions for us to consider as we continue to do this community work and as we continue to put communities *first*. As I write in my most recent statement on culturally sustaining pedagogies, with Django Paris and Casey Philip Wong, "CSP is a critical framework for centering and sustaining Indigenous, Black, Latinx, Asian, and Pacific Islander communities as these memberships necessarily intersect with gender and sexuality, dis/ability, class, language, the land, and more."[4]

My first final thought takes me back to the classroom with Dr. Harkavy where this work began. In the literature, we used to talk about "cultural mismatches" and the need to use students' culture to bridge those mismatches or those "gaps." That's how things were talked about, in large part, when I began doing my work. And as the next generation of scholars came onto the scene, I knew that we needed to go beyond that and argued for, and implemented, critical language awareness, which was a European tradition, here in the

United States. I wrote about this in *Educational Researcher* nearly twenty years ago, in "Critical Language Awareness in the United States: Revisiting Issues and Revising Pedagogies in a Resegregated Society."[5] The idea of using students' culture and language as a way "to move them from point A to point B," right, or "to get them from here to there, or to some presumably better place," was actually reproducing the kind of nefarious white supremacist ideologies that sometimes even well-meaning teachers held. As Django and I have written, the field desperately needed to produce the kind of truly transformative research that would *redirect the object of critique away from our children and communities and toward the oppressive knowledge systems that relentlessly frame them as deficient, pathological, and so on.* But since that early time, I have consistently pushed the field to move beyond uncritical, conformist, and assimilationist models of language pedagogy and pedagogy in general.

My second final point has to do with culture. As we looked to develop state-of-the-art pedagogical theory, a big part of what we needed to do was to look inward. What are we doing as communities of color, as people of color, surviving and thriving over generations and decades and centuries? Those cultural forms are not just pedagogies. They survive and have value "as goods unto themselves." And Carol Lee spelled this out very clearly in her chapter in our 2017 *Culturally Sustaining Pedagogies* book: the cultural practices of communities of color, as sustaining pedagogies, have value.[6] If, as she says, Black and Indigenous folks have been surviving for centuries under the most brutal of conditions and in the most brutal of contexts, horrific situations, then what was the community pedagogy like that enabled generation after generation to survive that context and those circumstances? Again, that's asking yet a different question. We're thinking about pedagogies as ways to survive these contexts and these situations and not just to survive them but to do so much more than that, to create movements, to create new worlds, new futures, to imagine new ways of being and then make them happen. And so those kinds of questions that I ask above have led to huge developments in that time.

Third, I think that focusing on *organic* forms of culturally sustaining pedagogies is key. While the analogy is not exact, you can think of Antonio Gramsci's organic intellectuals not as individuals but as communities that develop organic pedagogies in homes, street corners, community-based organizations, houses of worship, and so forth. In my chapter in *Culturally Sustaining Pedagogies* with Adam Haupt about our work in South Africa, we talk about *organic forms of culturally sustaining pedagogies.*[7] I cannot emphasize this point enough, and I'm an anthropologist, so I'm bringing these points from that perspective. Look at the communities and the organic forms of pedagogies that are already present. That's where the work, for me, begins. To dig in the crates is not just a technical Hip Hop term for DJs. It is also about archiving, giving new life to these cultural forms that have given *us* life. That's what DJs were and are doing. And so when I talk about digging in the crates in this way, I mean, going back not just to our scholarly traditions but also through community traditions and ways of teaching and learning which have been absolutely pivotal and necessary, and even more critical in these times where we are faced with rising fascism and repression all over the world (right here at home with attacks on African American Studies, any curricula that discuss race, gender- and sexuality-affirming education, and the like).

My fourth final thought has to do with a redefinition of culture in educational scholarship that has happened in the years since we began this work with Harkavy. Again, I'm speaking as an anthropologist. I think when some educational researchers began talking about culture, they were talking about cultural practices. And for some people, that was where it ended. *But you can't have practices without practitioners.* And that means when you focus on culture, you focus on people, right? Not individual people, but communities. So with culturally sustaining pedagogies, as I mentioned, we now talk about them as a critical framework for sustaining and centering communities. So when we enter communities, we don't have an essentialist, race-based notion of culture or a national origin–based understanding of culture. We ask, What is going on in these communities right now? What do they face in terms of gentrification, settler colonialism, police brutality, and other forms of state violence? What is going on and how are people responding? All of those forces and factors are forming culture. So we're talking about communities as central.

As Dr. Harkavy taught us, we must work in partnership *with* communities. These are lessons that have stayed with us for nearly a quarter century now, as we both continue to carry on the Harkavian tradition.

Somewhere in Philadelphia, we hope Dr. Ira Harkavy is smiling.

Notes

1. Django Paris and H. Samy Alim, eds., *Culturally Sustaining Pedagogies: Teaching and Learning for Justice in a Changing World* (New York: Teachers College Press, 2017).

2. Paris and Alim, *Culturally Sustaining Pedagogies.*

3. Geneva Smitherman, *Talking and Testifyin: The Language of Black America* (Boston: Houghton Mifflin, 1977).

4. H. Samy Alim, Django Paris, and Casey Philip Wong, "Culturally Sustaining Pedagogy: A Critical Framework for Centering Communities," in *Handbook of the Cultural Foundations of Learning*, ed. Na'ilah Suad Nasir, Carol D. Lee, Roy Pea, and Maxine McKinney de Royston (New York: Routledge, 2020), 261–76.

5. H. Samy Alim, "Critical Language Awareness in the United States: Revisiting Issues and Revising Pedagogies in a Resegregated Society," *Educational Researcher* 34, no. 7 (2005): 24–31, www.jstor.org/stable/3699797.

6. Carol Lee, "An Ecological Framework for Enacting Culturally Sustaining Pedagogy," in *Culturally Sustaining Pedagogies*, 261–73.

7. H. Samy Alim and Adam Haupt, "Reviving Soul(s) with Afrikaaps: Hip Hop as Culturally Sustaining Pedagogy in South Africa," in *Culturally Sustaining Pedagogies*, 157–74.

CHAPTER 5

Threads: Reflections on Engagement

Margo Shea

I am sitting in a small room on the "TLC" floor of a nursing home nestled into hills that hug the Connecticut River where New Hampshire, Vermont, and Massachusetts converge. My father is in a good mood. At ninety-three and living with Alzheimer's disease, this is increasingly rare, and so I savor it.

When people ask me if he knows who I am, I ponder the limitations of conventional understandings of recognition. Can he name me? No. Does he understand that I am his daughter? I don't think so. And yet he never gives me the wary smile he delivers to the staff. He allows me to get close, to touch him, even at his most obstreperous. He relaxes. My father knows me, even if he doesn't.

I read to him "Ode to Ira," which ran in the *Pennsylvania Gazette* in July 2023. While I often read to him, this is different. For reasons I can't explain, mention of Penn strikes something in his brain. For my dad (C55, Law58), Penn is something of a touchstone. While the details do not register, there is a thread, a shared thing between us, that he grasps and holds. As I read him the story of Ira Harkavy's long history with Penn and West Philadelphia and the thirtieth anniversary of the Netter Center for Community Partnerships, he nodded along. Was there a shadow of a memory, I wondered?

It was Parents' Weekend, my first year at Penn. We were standing in Carney's bar, at the corner of Chestnut and 37th Street, next door to what now houses a WaWa.

> "Oh my God, Billy Shea. Is that really you?" Marie Carney came out from behind the bar and wrapped my father in a hug. "I can't believe it!"

"Hello Marie," my dad smiled his widest grin. "It's been a long time."
"Thirty years? Or more?"

At the time, it seemed utterly confounding that my dad could pick up a conversation with a woman he had worked for decades before. As a teenager, time's elasticity and the power of place and memory had yet to reveal themselves; nonetheless, I absorbed his stories and recollections of the past as we walked around campus and through the streets of West Philly.

He pointed out the parking office, which was the home of the Urban Studies Department when I was at Penn. That building was, in his memory, his second home in Philadelphia. He parked cars for special events throughout his undergraduate career and as a young law student, an experience so formative that, many years later, when I asked him for a six-word story that defined him, he smiled and said, "Always keep it between the lines."

*   *   *

There is no big bow with which to tie up and contain decades of personal and professional exploration and effort that began in College Hall as my father and I listened to Ira Harkavy talk about the history of Penn's relationship with West Philadelphia and what the future could look like. My path from Penn to public history and academe was circuitous and did not adhere to a simple narrative.

Instead there are threads. In this essay, I examine threads that I can trace to my years of engagement with Ira Harkavy and what is now the Netter Center for Community Partnerships, threads that have become over time central to a tapestry of engagement, teaching, and scholarship that I have labored on, mostly lovingly, for almost thirty years. Tapestry is an apt metaphor. A key to transformation is marshaling people with diverse, even divergent skills, gifts, and goals. The work is messy, uneven. It is almost impossible to see how all the components fit together, and yet faith drives the process. Faith in the intertwined fate of all the parts, faith in the contributors, faith that the outcome, though unknowable, will yield something new, vibrant, necessary. The work I do now, as a public historian and as a professor, mentor, and facilitator of relationships between heritage organizations and Salem State University, continues the weaving of important threads that originated all those years ago.

Soon after I arrived at Penn, the ugly and destructive realities of American racism and inequality came to my doorstep. The murder of my first-year dorm floormate, Tyrone "Bear" Robertson, when he went home to Chester, Pennsylvania, for winter break, was both a shock and a wake-up call. His mom and dad came to campus to meet their "Sugar Bear's" friends. Being in the wake of their grief was eviscerating. Up to that point in my life, my own privilege was normalized in so many ways, and like a lot of white middle-class kids, I took it for granted. In the aftermath of Bear's death, I was humbled by this fact, by my privilege, by the awareness that different rules, different possibilities, different expectations surrounded me. The meritocracy was a crock.

Once seen, this could not be unseen. The normal and normative preoccupations of my fellow students at Penn rang a little hollow. More, the question of "what will you do to be a force of change?" became unavoidable and central to my emerging identity. I declared Urban Studies as my major and registered for one of Ira's year-long courses on the history of Penn and West Philadelphia. This was one of the most transformative experiences in my learning and growth. Ira invited us to find our passion, to be passionate—about our ideas, our actions, the praxis between action, reflection, observation, change. In an era of the blasé, the unruffled, the cool, Ira invited his students to care, to get excited, to get angry and then to do something about it.

He'd walk into class, staggering under the load of hundreds of pieces of paper, all going in different directions. He read to us from former students' papers. He handed out theory pieces, op-eds, maps, narratives about community organizing in Chicago, arguments about learned helplessness and the school-to-prison pipeline. We learned about relationships between Columbia University and Morningside Heights during Seth Lowe's reign, the Highlander Folk School, Dewey's schools for democracy, Freire's derision of banking models of education. Everything was connected, radically, unapologetically multi- and transdisciplinary. He taught us about community-based research, participatory action research, pedagogies of liberation.

Learning by doing and practical problem-solving grounded Ira's pedagogy. My experiences at the Turner Middle School in West Philadelphia—teaching ice skating, assisting law students in a "street law" course for seventh-graders, helping with model airplane-making at Saturday school, and serving as a counselor for a summer nutrition program—engaged me in myriad ways. I made friends. I encountered people who led by example and insisted on creativity and resilience; they enacted an asset-based model of neighborhood development before the term was coined. In a culture awash in narratives of urban decay, my time at Turner taught me that, given resources and allies with access to those in power, people in Black, working-class neighborhoods could and did solve problems and find solutions. I also discovered that every community has its "doers," the people who show up, roll up their proverbial sleeves and work hard with joy and energy; they don't seek attention or kudos. They can run a program with no money and feed a congregation out of ingredients they have sourced from their own kitchens. Learning to see, to acknowledge, and to find those people has served me in communities in Northern Ireland, Tennessee, and throughout New England.

Things were not always sanguine, and the work of being troubled and working through my own discomfort and confusion was central to my experience with both Ira Harkavy and the Center for Community Partnerships. Over the years, I have come to appreciate what Julia Flanders has called "productive unease."[1] A few examples highlight this learning.

I had a work-study position at the West Philadelphia Improvement Corps. The work was administrative—filing, collating data, providing assistance in grant writing and grant reporting. Another work-study student from Penn was there as well. He was pledging Kappa Alpha Psi, one of the oldest and most prestigious Black fraternities in the nation. My roommate had pledged the year before, so I knew the pledge process was grueling. Still, I bristled when I found my fellow work-study student sleeping on the couch in the office or frantically catching up on schoolwork while I did data entry and addressed labels on mailings. I became fluent in exasperated side-eye. It didn't seem "fair." The director, Rae Lynn Jones, noticed. She called me into her office one day and provided a "teachable moment."

You've probably all seen this lesson in meme form. It's about equal conditions versus fair conditions. She schooled me on fairness. The pledge process was temporary. The other work-study student would be back to work soon. Fairness meant giving him what he needed in that situation. It was another critical peeling back of the layers of institutionalized racism, of unlearning and relearning about what was actually fair within the context of centuries of injustice, within the reality of that moment. People often say that white women in particular are antiracist until someone calls us out personally for our racism, and then we get reactive, defensive, churlish. I admit that I got all of those things, but I didn't walk away. Ira Harkavy often quoted Marx, although it was not fashionable then and is even less so now: "From each his ability, to each his need." I learned that lesson and I continue to learn it. Being humbled by one's privilege is not always easy or comfortable. I stayed at my job at the West Philadelphia Improvement Corps. Over time, the lesson I learned there became a part of how I understand equity in education, in the workplace, in the world.

Dynamics of power and privilege presented themselves in other ways. While I was at Penn, the university hosted a conference of the Participatory Research Network. This was probably my first conference. And it was fiery. I remember the Canadian adult educator Budd Hall getting angry about the ways that academics from elite institutions were taking over the conversation. Antagonisms abounded. There were invisible fissures, hard-to-identify animosities in the room. Authenticity was policed, and virtue-signaling had an intensity that I could not make sense of at the time. Lines were drawn—Canadian/US, newcomers/old hands, perceived dilettantes, dreaded expropriators. Until this event, I did not know that university-community relations had a political economy, that power dynamics and hierarchies were part of every setting.

In these ways, Dr. Harkavy's courses and the work of the Netter Center provided important "firsts." Encountering the complexities of naming, seeking to understand and trying—in small ways—to address complex, systemic inequalities in cities and in American life more broadly was meaningful not simply because we were taking classes on these issues. Being in a setting that provided space for active and critical reflection, some guidance, and a community of peers interested in the same questions was critical, at least for me. As we navigated supposed dichotomies—university and community, doing good and doing well, theory and practice—the structure and space to think, to read, to write, to argue, to examine invited us to put aside simple black-and-white questions and answers and to embrace the gray, the in-between, the both/and as opposed to the either/or.

Engagements with the Center for Community Partnerships and with Dr. Harkavy invited us into a practice that resisted those oppositions and actively celebrated the spaces of overlap, intersection, and productive unease. That led us to explore, interrogate, work with and around these kinds of categories. Stark oppositions, we learned, could be limiting. Struggling to find a way through them, we learned not only to *have* experiences but to navigate experience from the vantage point of learning. And that meant listening, paying attention, being open, being prepared to be wrong, and being committed to trying again.

When I left Penn, I wanted to continue to try to weave the threads of engagement that were central to my undergraduate career. I set my sights on direct action. I wanted to do practical things. Directing a supportive housing residence for otherwise homeless people with HIV and AIDS in the city where I was raised and serving as assistant director of a small nonprofit community loan fund in New Haven, Connecticut, offered myriad opportunities to learn and grow. The work was both meaningful and soul-crushing. Working with activists and social workers, bureaucrats and ministers, people who had fought their way out of poverty and others who had never known want opened my eyes to the hard work of collaboration and the art of compromise. I gained a much better understanding of Bismarck's adage that "politics is the art of the possible."

After several years, I found myself craving more space for reflection and increased opportunities to interact with students and academics as well as community activists, philanthropists, and people who worked in local and state government. I took a position at the Walt Whitman Center for the Culture and Politics of Democracy at Rutgers University, working to implement programs designed to instill democratic values and principles through reflective community engagement as envisioned by the center's director, the late political theorist Benjamin Barber. Barber, along with Harry Boyte at the University of Minnesota and Ira Harkavy, were all working on harnessing resources at research universities in order to envision, plan, and implement social, economic, and political change. Barber and Boyte worked from the public university–land grant model to make the argument that universities should provide ample opportunities for young people to learn to be active, engaged, thoughtful citizens. Service was central to this model.

As coordinator of a federal (Learn and Serve America Higher Education) grant with fifty institutions of higher education implementing service-learning initiatives as subgrantees, I dove deep into the "business" end of things. What does a project need to be successful? How do we evaluate success or effectiveness? At that time, the urge to quantify was strong. Were the number of hours served, the number of children tutored, the number of elderly visited in nursing homes, and so on really the most reliable indicators of effective campus-community programs? If not these criteria, then which ones? How might one quantify meaningful engagement?

My colleague Kevin Mattson, a historian, and I worked to bring the best elements of academically based public service to the cocurricular and extracurricular service programs that were popping up everywhere in the late 1990s. AmeriCorps. City Year. Public Allies. We worked with dozens of community-service programs and wrote a manual: *Building Citizens: A Critical Reflection and Discussion Guide for Community Service Participants*.[2] The guide aimed to help busy and overworked program coordinators move away from front-loaded training and episodic reflection that offered few opportunities for critical self-examination, critical deliberation, or space to rethink and recommit to the opportunities and vulnerabilities present at their service sites.

Ira and the Center for Community Partnerships had been deeply invested and engaged in building a model with a solid infrastructure on a foundation of university support as well as investments from philanthropists and government agencies. As a result, the university-assisted community schools model and the concept of academically based community service were central to their focus, necessarily limiting other frames. Working at the Whitman Center enabled me to explore competing concepts of service and social change and to invite others to ask big questions even as they worked day to day to make a difference. In *Building Citizens*, we included readings and developed discussion questions aimed at teasing out threads that both held and ensnared the experience of service and engagement. Was service moral or immoral? Did it build or destroy communities? Was it a calling, activism, or a profession? Was it therapeutic, empowering, or damaging? Who defined the terms? Who got to decide whether or not service mattered or was of use? How might service be liberated from a power dynamic in which those doing the serving were seen to possess the solutions to pressing community challenges and needs, while those "being served" were passive beneficiaries?

I was deeply involved in the work of community engagement and academically based community service in 1998, when the people of Northern Ireland voted overwhelmingly to pass the Good Friday Agreement, also called the Belfast Agreement, the first blueprint for peace since the Troubles had broken out in 1969 that all parties had found acceptable. I had spent a summer as a camp counselor at a "peace camp" for Catholic and Protestant youth when I was in high school. I had never returned to Northern Ireland, but the peace process compelled me. Through chance and luck, I was able to travel to Derry/Londonderry in 1998 as a visiting fellow for community engagement at Magee College, a campus of the University of Ulster. It was in Northern Ireland that my interests in community, memory, and ordinary people's capacity to marshal the past in the service of the present and the future came together. In Derry, I began to think like a public historian.

I trace my interest in public history to a conversation held at a wobbly little table in a small trailer that served as the community space for a public housing project, or "estate," known as Tullyally, on the Waterside of Derry/Londonderry in 1999. It was long before I had ever heard the term "public history." As part of a broader effort to improve community relations through local heritage projects, I was helping to facilitate a meeting of the Tullyally Young Loyalists—kids ranging from ten to seventeen who had identified themselves as committed to their community and to their heritage as Protestants and as unionists. They had a stake in celebrating, communicating, and perpetuating the history of Ulster and Northern Ireland as an integral and important part of Great Britain. The young people with whom we met lived in a small publicly subsidized residential community that was predominantly Protestant and unionist-loyalist in a city whose demographics had leaned overwhelmingly Catholic and nationalist since the 1850s. They represented the sticky and difficult realities of cultural and political conflict in post-Troubles Northern Ireland, and we were there to explore how heritage, long a vehicle for conflict, could also be a way out of it.

During this particular meeting, we talked about stereotypes. The kids were like most of us—eager to believe the stereotypes about the "other" while adamant about the incorrectness of stereotypes directed at themselves. Yes, Catholics were priest-ridden and brainwashed and bred like rabbits. No, Protestants were most definitely not domineering, dug-in, narrow-minded bigots. As we began to peel back the anxieties and suspicions that lent weight to invective, it occurred to me that many of the stereotypes were historically rooted. When asked about the histories that had shaped and directed sectarian relationships in Derry/Londonderry, in Ireland and in the United Kingdom, responses were scattered, often incorrect, always incomplete. The young people knew history passionately but only partially, unevenly. Investments in their identity shaped the ways people interpreted and understood the past. History mattered only insofar as it explained the present and cleared a path toward the future; in that sense, it mattered very much indeed.

I didn't think much about this interaction until several years later, sitting at another table, this time in a graduate seminar in public history in a leafy western Massachusetts town. We were discussing Robert Archibald's book *A Place to Remember*, specifically, a vignette Archibald told about Tony Lucero, a member of the Pueblo of Isleta, and the tribal narratives he recounted about the arrival of Spaniards in the valley they called home, just south of what is now Albuquerque, in the mid-sixteenth century. When asked by an academic historian what the tribe recalled about this encounter, Lucero replied, "My people got on their horses and ran for the mountains because they were afraid."[3] The historian was quick to discount the story, insisting that there were no horses before the Spaniards came because the Spaniards had brought the horses. (I've always imagined that a derisive "duh" was silent. Also, this assumption has been proven false as evidence of horses predates the arrival of the Spanish.)

How do we evaluate whose narratives are valid? On what grounds? Does the incorrectness matter if the story is successful at its aim—in this case, to bolster and bond a community? Should the story that "worked" be discarded because it is inaccurate? Are alienated minorities the only people prone to editing the past, or do those in positions of power and authority do the same—and if that is the case, how much faith can we invest in the accuracy of the "historical record" when silences and power imbalances shape the very sources that historians pore over in search of the past? What happens when overly simplistic accounts of the past are weaponized? Is there such a thing as truth?

Beyond positivist or constructivist perspectives, these kinds of questions introduced me to the complex, occasionally frustrating, and always engaging world of public history. What continues to excite me most about public history has been its insistence on a both/and rather than an either/or approach to both historical truth and its commitment to the processes through which individuals, communities, and societies construct and communicate knowledge about themselves and their pasts.

Public historians recognize that history itself is more than an intellectual pursuit and acknowledge that history is always processual, despite its appearance as a thing, an entity, a product. By trying to build and sustain frameworks that engage myriad publics in many pasts while at the same time endeavoring to make meaning about our social, political, and cultural investments in the past through an exploration of those very engagements, public historians take seriously the ideas and questions that shape and are shaped by public engagements with the past. Public historians are committed to working with and being a part of the public even as we interrogate and challenge the assumptions and motivations that drive the public (including, sometimes uncomfortably, ourselves).

I have come to understand that we do not need more passive consumers and armchair critics of the histories with which we are presented. Shared authority is a shared responsibility. It is challenging to implement, difficult to assess, and often opaque in both theory and practice. And it is necessary. It allows us to connect the present to the past and to inspire and safeguard rich, complex, and participatory histories for the future. My experience at Penn had taught me to distrust dominant narratives, but it did much more than that. It taught me to excavate and seek to understand narratives from a place of engagement and connected involvement. It taught me to see myself both passionately and dispassionately. It taught me that structure and agency both matter, that the process and the product can never really be disentangled. It also taught me that entangled relations were somehow at the root of my curiosity.

My time in Northern Ireland invited me to consider the resonance of divided histories and the power of memory. While I returned to service-learning work after coming back to the United States in 2000, intellectual questions started to bubble. I started to take courses in public history at the University of Massachusetts while continuing to work full time as a service-learning coordinator at Berkshire Community College. It was a rich and exciting time. Community college students were deeply rooted in their towns and neighborhoods. We were no longer involved in "helping others." Service learning was an opportunity for students to find ways to connect their own preoccupations and investments in community to their educational and career aspirations. I credit this paradigm switch with helping me to understand the potential of public history to engage diverse people in histories that mattered deeply to them.

Eventually, graduate school took me back to Northern Ireland, to Derry. As a doctoral student conducting research, my training at Penn and the University of Massachusetts prepared me uniquely to enter into spaces where researchers had a reputation for swooping in, assuming they knew best, and leaving with knowledge and insights that never really made their way back to the people who had served as guides, gatekeepers, and resources. I was determined to be a different kind of scholar. What did that look like? For starters, I immersed myself in community life. I delivered meals-on-wheels and went to a weekly tea dance for senior citizens, where I danced and served tea and sandwiches. I joined writing circles and performed at poetry slam sessions. I did Zumba and volunteered for a group that brought children from Kosovo and Bosnia to Derry. I tried to understand the city from its own points of view.

I am not sure I always succeeded. I am also not sure humility and a desire to share authority served me particularly well in Derry or academia. My dissertation ultimately became a book. *Derry City: Memory and Political Struggle in*

Northern Ireland came out during the first year of the pandemic and dropped with a thud. It was not widely reviewed, and Derry did not celebrate it in the ways I had hoped. Still, when I try to assess success or failure in terms of the book, the praise from people who were raised in Derry and Northern Ireland has mattered to me more than awards. Two examples, from people I've never met, may illuminate the ways my training at Penn and beyond shaped my sense of what matters when it comes to academic outputs. Emily Cargan wrote of my book, "Her account compels me not just because of my own history as a child of the Troubles, but also because of how it reinforces Shea's uniqueness as an historian who gives ordinary voices their due."[4] Paula McCafferty, who left Derry in the early 1970s, wrote, "Every page evokes memories and gives me insight into people and events that I knew and knew of. I wasn't very politically aware when I was young; I was more interested in finding a man than equality, but I still knew what was going on and had all the preconceptions of my fellow Catholics. Reading this book isn't just a matter of turning pages; it's reliving an experience. It's also seeing what happened through new eyes. It's surprising how very right Shea, as an outsider, gets things."[5]

While I certainly made mistakes in the book, which is in many ways a local history of Derry, these assertions that I held space for ordinary people and presented their worldview with empathy and a fair amount of accuracy are the best evidence I can marshal that my training shaped a set of perspectives, sensibilities, and values that have enabled me to collect and share stories in responsible ways. Local people are using my research in their own projects and exhibitions. I would be lying if I said the response from scholarly peers was not a disappointment, but I am proud to have labored on a project that ultimately is returning a history to a community that was separated from it for various reasons.

This stood me in good stead when I served as a Mellon fellow at Sewanee: The University of the South. With my students, I created a crowdsourced cultural atlas of the "mountain," a space shared by people with very different experiences and perspectives. The result was over six hundred stories of places that mattered to local people plotted onto a huge map that now hangs in the South Cumberland Visitors' Center in Monteagle, Tennessee. My students and I also delivered free walking tours of the famed Highlander Folk School original site. We held space for the varied histories of the site and the organization's long trajectory after it was forced to move to the Knoxville region. While all of this work mattered deeply to me, this comment from one of the very few local students to attend Sewanee mattered more. "You were the first person at Sewanee who made me feel like it was OK to speak with my actual accent. So, really you were the first person who showed me it was OK to be myself."[6]

I have long felt like a unicorn as an academic and a professor. Twenty-five percent of historians have parents who were professors. My mom didn't go to college, and my dad was the first person in his family to do so. I went to a public university and not a particularly prestigious one at that, for my MA and PhD. I started graduate work in my thirties. All of these things made it highly unlikely that I would land a tenure-track job, let alone in the part of the United States I love and call home.

Salem State is known to be the most diverse university in the public system in Massachusetts. Our students are first-generation college students, veterans, returning adults, kids who have not excelled in school and don't always know how to. Some of our students have been all but written off when they arrive. Many have been minoritized by a society that applauds the meritocracy but systematically writes off people of color, people with disabilities, people with unconventional life trajectories. Many of our students are determined, hungry, and highly motivated. Some speak three languages and navigate complex cultural and political identities. What I learned about Penn and West Philadelphia was a kind of microcosm of the narratives and structures that shape and constrain my students' lives and then lie to them about who is to blame. My students have said that meritocracy is a lie designed to make the large majority of people who can't succeed in this phase of post-industrial capitalism blame themselves for not making it. I do not disagree with them. Everywhere we turn, things seem to be fragile or on the verge of breaking apart. Maybe we are finally awake to injustice and to the consequences of our actions—or it is possible that things have become more fragile, more breakable.

There are constraints on my capacity to deliver on the expectations I had when I began this journey into academia. I have a heavy teaching load (4/4 for those in the know) with no teaching assistants or graders. If we want to go on a field trip or work in the community, we have to walk or carpool. There are decreasing numbers of students who want to major in history. Between identity politics and the dictates of capitalism, it seems neither useful nor compelling to study the past.

And yet holding space for possibility and for different narratives to emerge is a central legacy that I carry today from my time at Penn. The highlight of my professional life is working actively to create experiences that students and I can share with the broader world. These projects are extremely modest.

I like to think they have the same kinds of impact that my learning with Dr. Harkavy and the Center for Community Partnerships had on me. Creating things through collaborative work, sharing ideas and bringing them to fruition together. Allowing students to be active agents in their own learning while also encouraging them to see that their ideas and actions have ripples and consequences in their communities and the world they inhabit is important to me.

My students have collected and exhibited hundreds of six-word memoirs from their fellow Salem State students. They have researched, written, designed, and distributed a cookbook as a way to raise needed funds for our campus food pantry. They have interviewed refugees and immigrants, some of whom are university employees, about precious objects they carried from home. They have worked with nonprofit organizations on social media, historical interpretation, and activity planning at historic sites. They have hosted conversations with activists from the 1960s and current student activists. The community around them has been their classroom. Through this work, many have become more confident, engaged, and passionate students and citizens.

I had a quote from Gandhi on my wall in college. Not the famous one, "Be the change you wish to see in the world." The one I loved was, "In a gentle way, you can shake the world." Ira Harkavy taught me to start where I am, to believe in my own capacity to make change, and to be humble and open to learning, making mistakes, and trying again. Through his example, he taught me not to give up, not to get hung up over who gets and takes credit for work in the world, to stay the course. While I may never have as deep or as broad a reach as Ira has had, I hope that my efforts are an echo of the lessons learned all those years ago at Penn and in West Philadelphia.

When my niece Emily graduated from Haverford in 2019, she settled in West Philadelphia. We took my dad to Philly for her graduation, and the three of us posed for pictures with the statue of Ben Franklin on a bench on Locust Walk. Raised in Russia, she now walks the streets that my father and I walked. She is involved and engaged in her community. Her interests are in material culture, a cousin of public history. Emily, raised by Jewish and Catholic parents, would agree with the quote by Rabbi Tarfon: "It is not your responsibility to finish the work of perfecting the world, but you are not free to desist from it either." The threads continue. I am glad for the opportunity to witness the compelling tapestries that emerge.

Notes

1. Julia Flanders, "The *Productive Unease* of 21st-Century Digital Scholarship," *Digital Humanities Quarterly* 3, no. 3 (2009), www.digitalhumanities.org/dhq/vol/3/3 /000055/000055.html.

2. Margo Shea and Kevin Mattson, *Building Citizens: A Critical Reflection and Discussion Guide for Community Service Participants* (New Brunswick, NJ: The Walt Whitman Center for the Culture and Politics of Democracy at Rutgers University, 1998).

3. Lucero is quoted in Robert Archibald, *A Place to Remember: Using History to Build Community* (Lanham, MD: AltaMira, 1999), 91.

4. Emily Cargan, "Giving Ordinary Voices Their Due: A Review of Margo Shea's Derry City," *The Typescript* (February 27, 2021), accessed May 20, 2023, thetypescript.com/.

5. Paula McCafferty, personal correspondence with author, Oct. 10, 2020.

6. Amber Layne, personal correspondence with author, Dec. 1, 2021.

CHAPTER 6

The Journey of a Data Scientist: How a Local Crisis Bridged Machine Learning, Community Engagement, and Social Entrepreneurship

Eric Schwartz

An Overview of the Journey

Over the twenty years since my first day as an undergraduate student at Penn, two threads of my experience have woven together in a way that I can only describe as ideal.

In one thread, I experienced the challenges of addressing important social problems by working to nurture community-university partnerships in West Philadelphia. As a Netter Center volunteer, I connected with students and educators at Sayre High School and the McMichael School. In student government, I advocated for—and practiced—problem-solving learning in the undergraduate curriculum.

In the other, I spent time dreaming up ways to apply math and statistics to understand and solve problems in the world that I found both interesting and meaningful. I dove into my math major coursework and even deeper into my undergraduate research in applying quantitative methods to market-ing problems in business ("data science," before the term was popularized to describe that work). This quantitative journey laid the foundation for a career exploring methodological advances in machine learning and new data.

As my academic interests in marketing evolved, through my PhD and beyond, I yearned to connect those threads, to make deeper, more meaning-ful applications of those methods. And soon enough, the opportunity to do so arose, in a way that would have seemed like fantasy to my Penn undergrad brain: as a young professor at the University of Michigan, I found myself collaborating with students, fellow faculty, community members, and public officials in Flint, Michigan, to address the nation's most-discussed water crisis, a symbol for environmental injustice in America, by using data science.

Together, we developed a model using machine learning to predict the chance that each address in Flint had lead pipes. The city then used those predictions to direct resources and send construction crews to dig up and replace lead pipes where new pipes were most needed, using limited funds efficiently in order to reduce the time residents were living exposed to lead and especially to look out for those most vulnerable.

This morphed into far more than a research project. It brought me to several City Council meetings, to writing an affidavit to be used in a federal court judge's ruling,[1] to advising Michigan's state regulator and over a dozen state regulatory agencies, and ultimately to working with the Environmental Protection Agency (EPA) and being invited to the White House.[2] The novelty of our application of machine learning, to identify hazardous infrastructure that was buried or otherwise costly to inspect, spurred a regulatory transformation accepting and encouraging these methods. The EPA cited our work in its official guidance to a new rule in 2022 that opened the door for states to follow.[3] Now fifteen states have accepted the use of predictive modeling to find lead pipes. At the same time, interest in our work ignited a surge of companies offering new software and consulting services to water utilities.

The seed that we started as a collaborative student-faculty research project blossomed into the establishment of BlueConduit.[4] This social venture, which I cofounded with an academic colleague, now employs twenty individuals and draws significant philanthropic support. Our company specializes in providing advanced software and services to water systems in more than three hundred cities and towns across the United States and Canada. The founding principles of BlueConduit were heavily inspired by the values of the Netter Center, emphasizing community engagement and university partnerships. These principles are deeply woven into our organizational culture. BlueConduit's data-driven technology empowers communities to prioritize health and sustainability, starting with universal access to clean drinking water and a lead-free future.

In this chapter, I illustrate the impact of my personal experiences with the Netter Center—its staff, faculty, students, partners, and courses—on the trajectory of my professional career. I draw a throughline from my work in Academically Based Community Service (ABCS) courses and from curriculum advocacy in student government to all that I have done since: my academic research, teaching, and student mentorship; my work impacting policy and business; even my cofounding of a social enterprise.

Statement on Flint Water Crisis

This chapter is not meant to be an account of the Flint water crisis. I recognize that the protagonists and heroes of the crisis are community organizers, advocates, public health experts, and those with power who made a difference. Instead, in this chapter, I want to highlight contributions that are small in the broader context of Flint's crisis but have had a wide-ranging and surprising impact well beyond Flint. That would be a university-community collaboration that spurred activities. And these have not been detailed before.

Lasting Lessons

My story reflects the lasting impact of the Netter Center on my professional and personal life. There are key themes in all of my experiences in Flint and starting with BlueConduit that have their origins in the work that I did with the Netter Center. I highlight that impact through three lessons.

Lesson 1: Global Motivation for Local Problem Solving—Doing Data Science for Good

One lasting lesson has been the dual importance of solving global problems locally and of motivating participants with a sound theoretical objective.

During my junior and senior years at Penn, I participated in two ABCS courses with Ira Harkavy and Lee Benson. All through those courses, I kept asking myself why we were spending all that time talking about Dewey? What was the value of such theoretical framing of work that was ultimately so practical? For instance, we were managing the logistics of an after-school program guiding first-year high school students through the process of exploring their options in higher education. This involved classroom management, coordinating with teachers, and arranging transportation for us. How did that really have anything to do with participatory democracy and theories of education? How were we making the world a better place in those hyperlocal moments?

In retrospect, I now understand what role these theoretical ideas played. It was something I didn't appreciate enough in the moments sitting around the table in the seminar room. The theoretical foundation and values all motivated me and my classmates. By saying "We are dedicated to making access to education more equitable," we were able to grasp how our immediate activities, however local and however challenging logistically, fit into a broader and more compelling project.

This has taught me the importance of articulating my motivation with the underlying objective and theory. This is what motivates people participating in the research project or the organization. This is what makes them active participants and not mere recipients of knowledge.

The power of highlighting a common purpose is that it not only motivates an individual but also attracts talent to collaboration. And collaboration expands impact. As my Netter Center experience revealed to me, connecting the limited local work with my larger motivation and my underlying objective elevates the importance of the work directly at hand.

What brought students to engage with us as we embarked on our project in Flint? It was the meaning they sought in a project with bigger implications for environmental justice and racial equity, all while applying the methods of data science. Descriptive framings alone—"doing data cleaning," "running machine learning models," "writing code to create software"—are devoid of much meaning. We do not use them. Instead, we speak of more resonant and motivating objectives. "Use data science for public good." "Use machine learning to enable communities to live healthier and more sustainable lives." "Prioritize resources for the biggest bang for limited bucks and do so equitably." This is the basis for the mission and vision of BlueConduit. It is the reason why the organization continues to attract top data-science talent in competitive markets.

The Netter Center's approach taught me the power of creating models to be used as repeatable frameworks. One after-school program is a model for other programs; one elementary school is a model for others in Philadelphia; ABCS courses are models for other courses at Penn; Penn in West Philadelphia is a model of university-community partnerships around the world; and so on. This Harkavian and Bensonian approach unites the local and the global, linking the practical to the theoretical. It defined my approach to seeking an impact in our work beyond Flint. By 2019, it was clear that we had a strong example and that it ought to be a model for other cities to follow. Suddenly our work in Flint became that model of how to use data science for good to find lead service lines. As the effort matures, we have grown and adapted so that the granularity of the scale also expands. Now we talk about data science to find lead pipes as a model to use data science to identify hazardous infrastructure of all sorts, be it lead paint, other water contaminants, or aging bridges. The bigger vision interacts with the specific in just the ways we integrated the theoretical teachings of Dewey with the humbling realities of working in West Philadelphia schools.

DEVELOPING A THEORETICAL ORIENTATION
FOR MY OWN PROFESSIONAL PROJECT

I can now define my own broad professional project as aiming to do data science for good. That clarity has come through a journey influenced by the Netter Center's approach.

Through my quantitative educational experience, I developed a new way of seeing the world through underlying processes that generate data. Wharton Professor Peter Fader did more than merely open my eyes and encourage me to be curious and creative. He motivated me to ask questions in ways I had not before. Above all, he led me to look for similar statistical patterns across domains that seemed on their face to be distinctly different and to wonder whether those deep similarities might point to common underlying processes. Instances of such similarities abound and tantalize. The pattern of customers repeatedly purchasing from a given retailer is mathematically analogous to the pattern of baseball relief pitchers successfully closing games (which continued to fuel my passion for sports analytics). Mathematical models capturing customer behavior in subscribing and canceling subscriptions are quite similar to those characterizing school attendance and school dropouts. The seeds that Pete Fader planted were there to apply a lens of data and models of patterns of data to make better decisions in unexpected places.

The quantitative side of my undergraduate experience not only provided me with that lens, but it also trained me to have comfort with uncertainty and deep curiosity, which dovetailed perfectly with my problem-solving learning with the Netter Center. Facing uncertainty, I was empowered. I recall a moment sitting across the desk from Pete Fader, asking him how I should get through a particular mathematical challenge. He paused, then delivered the empowering line coming from one's mentor, a chaired professor, "I don't know. You figure it out!" The mix of enthusiasm and encouragement was infectious. I bring this up to highlight the way that ABCS courses through the Netter Center both tapped into the spirit of traditional academic inquiry— which is not unique to any discipline—and served as a phenomenal comple- ment to the unstructured.

I was in a rut in research. Thinking about the ways I could contribute to the world through data science for good motivated me and brought me out of that rut.

HOW DO WE BALANCE OUT TOO MUCH THEORY?

If the presence of a theoretical foundation and objective motivated me in some ways, I also had doubts that I had to address. With all this theoretical talk of the biggest problems in society, how could I seriously make a differ- ence? I recall asking, What difference am I really making in the massive soci- etal problem of access to college? How could we do that as just a group of students in our privileged seats in a Penn classroom? We are merely reading research about access to higher education (by Dr. Laura Perna, who has since become Penn's vice provost) for the first time, so what do we know? This is where the local engagement made the difference. We could look narrowly, for the moment. We did not look at West Philadelphia as a whole, just at one local high school in the neighborhood, Sayre High School. And we did not look at Sayre High School as a whole, just a group of twenty students who were first-year high schoolers in the Netter Center's after-school program in the 2007–2008 school year. How could I contribute, in some small way, to their access to information about college and vocational schools? That I could wrap my head around. At that level of granularity, the personal experiences of connecting with community members one-on-one was most transformative. That personal connection not only made the theoretical framing real but also highlighted why we must bring values of empathy, trust, humility, and open- ness to all of our interactions.

Lesson 2: Engaging with Community Members as Partners

Another major theme that I trace directly from the Netter Center's activities in West Philadelphia to my engagement in Flint, and subsequently hundreds of other cities, was engaging with communities in real partnership.

The relationship between the University of Michigan campus and the city of Flint bears some similarities to the relationship of the University of

Pennsylvania and West Philadelphia. In fact, the University of Michigan has campuses in both Ann Arbor and Flint (as well as Dearborn). This connection was the very reason we got involved in the first place.

By the spring of 2016, the international news media had come to and left Flint. The US president and presidential candidates had visited Flint. Yet for very good reasons, there was still great distrust among community members. A fuller community-centered account of the crisis in Flint is in *Flint Fights Back* by Dr. Benjamin Pauli.[5] Briefly, the causes of that distrust were many and significant. The spark of the crisis occurred in April 2014, when the city of Flint switched the source of its drinking water from Detroit's system, which drew its water from Lake Huron, to the Flint River. The Flint River was locally understood to be polluted from decades of auto manufacturing in the city. Through eighteen months of mounting public outcry, documented health issues, and visual evidence of changes in the water, local and state governments largely denied the problem. Only after the research and courageous advocacy of Dr. Mona Hanna-Atisha was confirmed in a separate study by the *Detroit Free Press* did officials acknowledge that lead exposure was disastrously high.[6] And even then the crisis continued. Indeed, it continued long after the point when parts per billion of lead in drinking water fell below the maximum level allowed by federal and state laws, which was in late 2016.

Beyond massive issues of distrust, we also had to deal with the overwhelming complexity of the stakeholders of the city. Initially we spoke with folks at the University of Michigan campus in Flint. Then we met with a local community nonprofit and with people working for the city itself. Then there were contractors. Residents. Community group leaders. Some community groups disagreed with others; some managed to be universally liked and trusted. There were City Council people. There was the Public Health Department, which was sometimes at odds with City Council and sometimes not. There was the Public Works Department, also sometimes at odds with the council and sometimes not. There was a mayor and the mayor's staff. Through it all, we were able to identify people to stay engaged with. Eventually, someone introduced us to the person who reported directly to the mayor and the governor and who was appointed to oversee the exact question that we were trying to answer: which houses should you go to next?

Channeling my experiences with the Netter Center, I sought to build long-lasting relationships and trust. I admired how the Netter Center staff and faculty were partners with folks in West Philadelphia. They had real relationships with people as allies in doing good work together. As we began sitting down with Flint residents and officials, this approach remained top of mind. My Netter Center experiences imbued me with values of humility, empathy, and openness in each conversation. I also kept in mind what I desperately worked to avoid: falling into the path of a "savior," a white privileged male professor swooping into the community in the name of "impact" and then flying off, leaving it no better or even worse. With that cautionary archetype, I did the opposite. My colleagues and I spent time building trust. And there's no shortcut to that. Trust is built over time. Trust is earned by showing up. Building trust meant using language that signaled our purpose. I recall that in early meetings I made sure to ask the people we were working with what they wanted to get done, what goals they had, and what they couldn't do or didn't have time to do but would love to see done.

By June 2016, we formed a close partnership with the mayor's Flint Action and Sustainability Team (FAST) Start initiative. We identified a small niche, a little wedge, where we could offer our assistance to stakeholders to better enable them to achieve their own goals. We could help them decide which houses to visit and what to do on those visits.

The goal was to reduce the time that residents of Flint were living exposed to lead risk in their drinking water. If the city sent its contractors and their equipment to excavate at a home, often closing the street as they dug in the street or at the sidewalk, and if the contractors then discovered there was no lead pipe buried, then the city's resources had been misspent. They could have been directed to removing a lead pipe at another home and replacing it with the safer copper pipe.

We created a point of connection between our faculty-student group and the FAST Start team by helping to design the process of gathering and storing data. The FAST Start team needed to ensure that the right information was collected by each contractor at each home where service line work was performed. The team had initially planned to provide paper forms and clipboards to all contractors to input information about both the service line pipe and about the residents of the home. We asked whether there was concern about compliance in filling out these forms, and we discovered a key incentive: the contractors would not get paid unless they submitted these forms, completed fully. In fact, how they answered some of these questions would determine the pots of federal funding from which the contractors would be paid by the city. Knowing how critical this information was and how logistically challenging it would be to have to deal with digitizing paper records, we immediately stepped in.

We devised a system that digitized the data collection process from the outset and ensured a strong foundation for data collection for years to come during this critical moment in the FAST Start program. In just forty-eight hours, an exceptional team of students worked to build this digitized process. We provided just enough technology to enable a closed-loop system: with our current information, we provided predictions and recommendations to the FAST Start team; the team then assigned those specific addresses to contractors, who went to inspect the service lines at those locations; the contractors then replaced whatever lead they found and used the online form to update our current information. And we repeated this process. This data collection also set up the opportunity for better transparency and making the information easily auditable. Further, it enabled us to perform exactly the kind of analyses that we sought to provide. Based on the information coming in from the field via these electronic forms, we could answer and continuously update the answer to these questions: how many of the homes that have not yet been visited are likely to have lead, and where do we expect those homes to be located?

But simply providing the technology would not have been enough. Managing stakeholders and meeting them where they were was critical. At one point, as a few new contractor firms began working with FAST Start, I met with them all in Flint to give them a hands-on tutorial about the workflow and to ensure that the collection of information was easy for them. That allowed me to communicate with the people who were literally digging holes in their own community members' homes and to help them understand the value of the information that they would be feeding back to us. I appreciated not only the challenge of the work at hand but also the great pride that the contractors took in their work and the meaning they found in contributing to their community in a time of extraordinary crisis.

As a team of data scientists, made up of two professors, a few graduate students, and some undergraduates, our goal was far greater than just building an information-gathering system for the city of Flint. Yet doing that alone signaled our recognition of the importance of our partnership with the city; we were willing to do anything to see that partnership succeed. And in fact, that very attitude, I believe, allowed us to demonstrate tangibly the value we could provide. We showed with our actions, not just our promises, that we were invested in doing the work to contribute to the project. And we proved our commitment to our partners even before we began using the data science and machine-learning models we were all trained on and eager to apply, which would ultimately generate the prediction of lead at every address.

One aspect of my approach to collaborating with people in different organizations in Flint was to understand how we could plug into our partners' existing workflows and communication channels instead of trying to recreate new ones. For instance, we collaborated with the Healthy Flint Research Coordinating Center, which coordinated any research related to Flint, engaged community members in that research, and organized a research ethics review board. Linking up with this group also allowed us to better connect with faculty and university projects between our campus and other ones.

As we sought to build trust, I attended events in Flint whenever possible. Flint City Council meetings were especially critical times and places for these discussions. After one such meeting, an elderly woman approached me and asked, "When are you coming to fix my pipes?" This was a poignant reminder of who was most affected and the importance of communicating the limits of what we could do. It was also a reminder that these one-on-one experiences are transformative, just as I discovered in the schools of West Philadelphia.

This moment in Flint City Hall changed my perspective. While I had been working closely with public officials and the contractors performing construction services, I had lost touch with the group most affected: residents of Flint. This experience shifted my focus to transparency and accessibility for *all* stakeholders, especially residents of the broader community not actively working for the city. My experience speaking with residents after City Council meetings was the experience that transported me back to the Netter Center and my experiences in West Philadelphia. While I spoke with a range of residents and listened to their concerns, I felt as if I was accompanied by the support of the Netter Center faculty and staff, with their decades of experience collaborating with community members as partners. The Netter Center's influence continues to reinforce the importance of working with community partners as longtime colleagues and friends and not as subjects of study. That's what I sought to emulate.

When we started BlueConduit, we knew that we had a moral imperative to focus energy on finding communities like Flint that were underserved yet had lead. And we did just that. Some of our first work out of Flint was with the philanthropic support of the Rockefeller Foundation, which provided funding to subsidize the cost of BlueConduit for four cities: Detroit and Benton Harbor, Michigan; Trenton, New Jersey; and Toledo, Ohio.[7]

While the work in these cities subsidized by Rockefeller was successful, we knew that coordinating with community partners, in addition to public water systems, would make our work even more impactful. The next time we had an opportunity to ask for funding, we did it differently.

We explicitly wrote community groups into the grant. In our grant proposal to Google.org, we requested that funds go not only to our BlueConduit Charitable Fund but also to the grassroots nonprofit organizations that were supporting environmental justice and doing drinking-water advocacy in each of the communities where Google.org would fund our work. For instance, we received funding to work with Richmond, Virginia, so a local environmental justice nonprofit in Richmond also received funding. To choose which city-specific organization should get that funding, we also enlisted the help of trusted national nonprofit organizations, Natural Resources Defense Council and We ACT for Environmental Justice, both of which specialize in working with local environmental justice groups. In fall 2021, Google.org granted us and our partners $3 million to work with four more cities—Richmond, Virginia; New Orleans, Louisiana; Buffalo, New York; and Jackson, Mississippi.[8]

The Google.org grant also funded BlueConduit to build free software tools for transparency and compliance. We are creating a free, open-source tier of our software platform accessible to all community water utilities and subsidizing the price of extra services to disadvantaged environmental justice communities. As part of this, we are also designing a nationwide map of all states and all water systems, providing estimates of how much lead each one has. In another part of this work, we will enable cities to easily generate and publish user-friendly maps of their lead pipes, simply by uploading data to our free platform. This transparency will strengthen public communication and help meet the EPA's new Lead and Copper Rule Revisions and Improvements.[9]

Lesson 3: Importance of Empowering Students to Engage

STUDENTS FOUND MEANING ENGAGING IN FLINT

I cannot overstate the importance of students in all of this endeavor. Flint would not have had its lead pipes identified as efficiently as it did without their work. And the impact of that student work now stretches far beyond Flint, extending into the language used in the EPA's new rules about lead pipes and even into the details of how predictive models can be used. I recognize that we did not replicate an ABCS course in Flint, but the spirit of ABCS was central throughout all of the students' engagement.

For me to best express the role of students in this work, I will go back to describe how all of this started: a student organization, a bus trip, and a hackathon. In the winter of 2016, Google.org, the philanthropic arm of Alphabet/Google, reached out to the University of Michigan–Flint computer science department to see how Google could provide funding and talent to help. The Flint campus invited our Ann Arbor campus's computer science department to participate. Our computer science department quickly reached out to the Michigan Data Science Team, a student organization of undergrad and grad students excited about learning and developing their data science and analytics talents (which I will describe in more detail later). The student group was advised (and created) by my close colleague and coauthor, then-Michigan computer science professor, Jake Abernethy. He had recently invited me to join him in coadvising this student group.

By the spring of 2016, the students of the Michigan Data Science Team organized a trip to Flint for about thirty volunteers. Jake and I helped coordinate with our initial contacts in Flint and with the students to make the visit meaningful for everyone involved. The students (and we) met with staff from the university's Flint campus, with the Community Foundation of Greater Flint (a local nonprofit), and with a mix of city of Flint employees from public health, city planning, and economic development. The students also met the person who managed the city's geospatial data, who would later prove instrumental by sharing data with our team. The range of people who were open to students and faculty was encouraging. I quickly saw an opportunity to build relationships to form partnerships in Flint.

One scene stays with me clearly from this trip when I think of the students feeling empowered to solve some of the hardest problems of the world. It is a scene from the auditorium in Flint City Hall. Students were posing questions to public officials to better understand this sizable crisis happening in real time around them. The students were curious and respectful. Some questions had clear factual answers that the city representatives could provide. But then there were other questions that were challenging in part because of their simplicity. "How many homes have lead contamination?" The officials managing the crisis didn't know. "If the lead pipes are the source of the contamination, how many homes have lead pipes?" Again, the officials didn't know.

Uncertainty was everywhere. This was not a classroom where the students were uncertain and the professors understood the reality. We, the professors, knew no more than the students did. All of us quickly confronted the reality that the very public officials managing the recovery of the crisis, which would require the replacement of these toxic lead pipes, did not actually know where those pipes were located.

In that auditorium, the students' questions led to a transforming appreciation of the opportunity for student skills in data analysis to have an impact. Their curiosity had revealed another dimension of the crisis in Flint. To be sure, it was an environmental justice crisis. And an infrastructure crisis. And a political crisis and a crisis of trust. But it also was an *information* crisis. There was so much uncertainty and there were so many unknowns that it was incredibly difficult to make informed decisions. And information crises are exactly the kind of difficulties that good data scientists help people deal with.

The day after the trip to Flint, the students held their hackathon, an all-day activity where students formed small groups to dig into the available data. Critically, the choice of problems to explore during the hackathon itself was among the most important parts. Jake and I mingled among the groups, providing help where we could. For me, it was challenging yet fascinating to grapple with my own high level of uncertainty while guiding the students through their reckoning with that uncertainty. At the end of the hackathon day, the student groups presented their discoveries to the main body of students and pointed directions for future analysis.

One group addressed a public statement by the governor's office that seemed misleading. The students analyzed a graph posted on Twitter and recreated it with the raw data, which they now had thanks to our visit to Flint, to display information in a more accurate way. Another group looked specifically at how the water test data, which was publicly reported online by the state, was spread geographically across the city. In their analysis, they separated the results of the water test—how much lead was detected—from crucial issues of selection. How were certain characteristics of households represented or not represented in that sample of households who had voluntarily asked for a kit to perform water tests in their own home?

But one line of questions that emerged from the hackathon changed the course of our research and the entire collaboration between our team and Flint. A couple of students asked about the materials of the pipes themselves. After the visit, they had gained access to a dataset that specified those materials, according to older city records. These old records, which indicated where people thought lead might be in the pipes, had been digitized by faculty and students at the University of Michigan–Flint earlier in the year.[10] Our students noted that these records, like previous reporting, suggested that 10 percent to 20 percent of Flint homes had lead pipes. But our students also noted the incompleteness of the old records. In that hackathon, they documented what was known about those materials and, more critically, what was still uncertain. The students recognized the potential value of filling in the gap in our knowledge of those materials by building a predictive model of pipe material, which would capture patterns of association of housing characteristics and greater incidence of lead.

In the same conversations with students, we also realized that the old records themselves were not reliable enough to be treated as "ground truth" in a model. We would need at least some physically verified materials of pipes before we could extrapolate to those that had not yet been verified. Unfortunately, out of the fifty thousand parcels of land in Flint, the material of the service lines had been physically verified at just thirty-six homes by April 2016.[11] That alone was not going to be enough data on which to build a machine-learning model to predict the likelihood of lead.

Meanwhile, the FAST Start team had begun digging where they knew lead pipes were almost certainly buried underground. They'd found lead pipes in 96 percent of the first two hundred homes they investigated.[12] A visiting graduate student, Jared Webb, took a particular interest in this finding and decided to dedicate his summer to the possibilities it presented. He became the leading student on the project and worked closely with me and Jake as we aimed to provide the newly formed FAST Start team with recommendations on where to dig next. One urgent question was, What percentage of homes actually had lead throughout the city? Surely not 96 percent. But not likely as little as the 10 percent to 20 percent that had been presumed previously. What should we do to simultaneously find out the true scope of the prevalence of lead pipes and give recommendations to help the FAST Start team locate and remove as much lead as possible?

After examining the data where those digs occurred, our student confirmed that the homes verified to that point through replacement attempts were not representative of the broader set of all homes in Flint. A problem was that we did not have access to the verified materials from a representative sample of the city's service lines. A bigger problem was that no one did. Collaborating with this student, we devised a semi-representative sampling approach that considered some of the information we had seen so far, including old records and water test results, and also included some randomly selected addresses. The goal was to generate a dataset from which we could make a better preliminary estimate of the incidence of lead pipes in Flint. By the fall of 2016, the three of us had just that. We provided the city evidence that about 40 percent of the homes likely had lead pipes.[13] We achieved that estimate with fewer than four hundred digs. Now, in 2024, after nearly thirty thousand homes have had their pipes excavated, the proportion of homes found to have had lead pipes is, in fact, about 40 percent.[14]

Thereafter, the three of us focused on using our predictive model to indicate addresses with the highest chance of having lead. Our student wrote the code for the foundation of the model, and Jake and I continued to advise. Our predictions shaped the city's direction of precious excavation resources and enabled the city to be remarkably efficient. When contractors dug up a service line that was identified by the model to have a high chance of lead, they found lead around 85 percent of the time, far more than they would have done had they been digging purely at random or following the old records.[15]

This was a novel application of machine learning to public health and safety. But the students wanted to do more, and they wanted to do scholarship too. For the next two years, as we continued to refine the work in Flint, students published two academic articles in the top applied machine-learning conference proceedings in the field, Knowledge Data Discovery (KDD).[16] In 2018, the students presented a paper at the KDD Conference in London, which covered our work predicting the materials of the pipes and selecting addresses for subsequent visitation using a type of data-collection algorithm known as active learning.[17] The paper won the Best Student Paper Award in Applied Data Science KDD 2018. I felt tremendous pride as our student authors received that award.

While this chapter is largely about the impact that the Netter Center had on my life, I must mention the impact that our work in Flint has had on the lives of the undergraduate and graduate students who were most integrally involved in it. One of those graduate students has never stopped working with us. His one summer looking into the materials of pipes in Flint turned into two more years as a research assistant, updating the model, and then into a full-time job for the social venture we would go on to start together. He is the founding chief data scientist at BlueConduit, and he remains with the company today, doing data science for good and mentoring junior data scientists to do the same.

Other students have continued down professional paths greatly influenced by their experience applying data science to Flint's crisis. One computer science major graduated and went to work at an urban infrastructure analytics company, very much inspired by the work he had done on our projects. Soon after, he joined BlueConduit to work as a software engineer and worked with us for two years. Another completed his PhD in physics and then went on to do a postdoc at a top data-science university with a leading and robust program called Data Science for Social Good.

HOW OUR WORK STILL ENGAGES STUDENTS

Even beyond the direct work in Flint, students have been involved in this work in a number of ways over the years at Michigan. Students were critical to the founding of BlueConduit, and we have kept the company closely connected to them and to the action-based learning projects we do with them.

It is fitting that, given my Netter Center background, I would find myself a tenured professor at the Ross School of Business. Michigan Ross is the leader in action-based learning among American business schools. Its pioneering course, "Multidisciplinary Action Program(MAP)," is required for all MBA students. The course sets groups of five or six students to work with a company or organization somewhere in the world to solve a problem. It is the only course that the students are permitted to take during the fourth quarter of their first year.

In recent years, this action-based learning design has expanded to other programs (other master's programs, undergraduate programs, and more) and to other formats. One format is a semester-long (or optional year-long) course, "Living Business Leadership Experience," in which the student teams very nearly become part-time employees of the sponsoring organization.

Another such format was just emerging exactly as we considered forming BlueConduit. Michigan Ross had just launched the Business+Impact initiative, which was going to house a wide range of activities that used business for good to improve the world. The centerpiece program was to be known as the Impact Studio, a course open to students across campus (not just in the business school) that I would describe as a problem-solving learning course.[18] As the faculty director prepared for the program's pilot semester, he shared with me its mission, to take ideas from research at the University of Michigan and find ways to have the greatest impact in the world. The vehicle of that impact could be a business or a nonprofit, a center at the university, or open-source software. Impact was the goal. Students would have to figure out the most appropriate vehicle.

Impact Studio captured the challenge we faced perfectly. We had this research and practical experience in Flint. We knew that other cities were struggling with similar problems, and we had already been approached by a large water utility that needed help too. We understood that it would be a challenge to balance the needs of disadvantaged communities with the building of a sustainable enterprise.

So, in 2019, I became part of the pilot project of the Impact Studio.[19] This started before we started the company. It was an exciting moment in my journey through the world of problem-solving learning. I was no longer the student or even the faculty member advising students; I was part of the company, the client, the outside representative of the "real world," whose messy, hairy problem the students had to solve. One prominent recommendation that the students had for us in that term was that we appreciate the importance of transparency and trust. They recognized that the crisis of trust that we had dealt with in Flint would be repeated elsewhere (they were right) and that transparency in local governments and water utilities would be a critical step to build and restore that trust (right again). Since then, BlueConduit has continued to engage with student groups from Michigan Ross. We have sponsored projects across the full range of action-based learning formats—Impact Studio, MAP, and Living Business Leaderships Experience—that the school offers.

These activities have not gone unnoticed by others around the school. Those in admissions and fundraising have leveraged the story of our work in Flint and the involvement of students in BlueConduit's founding days. I have been asked to speak to groups of alumni in Detroit about it, and I've even been asked to present to the alumni Board of Advisors. It is gratifying to learn that admissions officers and development representatives have shared details of my work with prospective donors and prospective students and their families.

Throughout all of my experiences engaging with students, from that initial bus trip and hackathon to the student projects connected to Blue-Conduit, an additional lesson continues to resonate. Students are motivated by meaning and purpose; the activity itself is secondary. I am impressed by what students are willing to do when they see the bigger purpose and find it personally meaningful. That was true for me and my classmates in West Philadelphia, and it is truer than ever for me now that I've seen it from the other side as well.

Looking Ahead

As I prepared to write this chapter, I went back to look at other reflections on my Netter Center experience that I had occasion to write down. One was an especially meaningful moment for me. As a college senior in 2008, I was asked to reflect on the work of community partnerships at a dinner at President Gutmann's house celebrating the gift of Edward and Barbara Netter. I was humbled and honored. The concern of that speech was much like the concern of this chapter: how has the Netter Center made an impact on me personally?

What stood out from that evening was less the content of what I said and more the feeling that stuck with me about the event. I was being taken seriously. I felt like a respected equal. One aspect of the impact that the Netter Center had on me came outside of the classrooms and even outside of the class activities across West Philadelphia. It came through the faculty and staff of the Netter Center treating me as a peer. I was—and critically, I *felt* like I was—a partner in a broader project to improve the world through the resources and talents of the university. The staff and faculty of the Netter Center nurtured my own leadership skills and empowered me to do more than I could have imagined.

The Netter Center and my undergraduate experience exploring problem-solving learning continue to influence my academic and professional journey. As I reflect on that journey, there are some distinct phases that emerge, which inform where I would like to go next.

As I transitioned from idealistic undergraduate to jaded graduate student, I started to experience a gulf between my graduate studies in data science and my passion for social impact. I felt, unfortunately, that I had to put aside my interests in community-engaged work because it just wouldn't count toward my PhD or the way my field values research publication. This was difficult to swallow since I had spent years critiquing such arguments by graduate students and researching faculty who said just that to me.

I knew that I wanted something deeper and more meaningful, to help others and improve the world. I was sure that there was a bigger reason to be learning these quantitative methods, and I wanted to face those challenges. But I did not see many examples of scholars in my discipline doing quantitative work in active pursuit of social good. The few I saw, who were rarely well-established academics, were doing so for a course but not for their primary research program. At best, doing good was for them a side project.

I took up my appointment at Michigan, but I fell into the rut of assistant professor life: teaching a couple of hundred students a year, publishing, and competing. I was not feeling particularly moved or motivated by the usual challenges of my academic research at the time, as I hoped to find more meaning in my research but did not know how to find it.

After three years, that changed dramatically. The first lesson from my Netter Center days—the power of meaning and a bigger purpose to motivate me and others—resurfaced in the Flint water crisis. My engagement in that crisis marked the start of a new phase of my professional life, one that felt like a return to the Netter Center and all its values.

Now that I'm eight years into this work, I am ready to move forward to a new phase. In this next phase, I want to turn my attention to enabling students to have even more of the kinds of transformative experiences solving problems that the Netter Center affords its students. To me, this involves my teaching and mentorship along with my research.

In this next phase, I expect that undergraduates will play a markedly greater role than graduate students. I have personally experienced the pull during a PhD program to stay within disciplinary boundaries and maximize traditional training. And that is perhaps appropriate for graduate studies, which may be the time to lean further toward a discipline. But in the undergraduate experience, there is an opportunity to better balance two pieces: "Learning to think within a discipline and using complex problem-solving learning are complementary components in an undergraduate education. Each component makes the other more purposeful and effective."[20] So I commit to working with undergraduates in ways that I understand I will not be able to work with most graduate students. (Needless to say, I will gladly work in those ways with any graduate students who can make the time and have the passion for such work.)

Also in this next phase, I commit to doing what I wished others had done. I will integrate my impact-focused social-good research into my primary research program rather than treating it as a side project. I hope to enable students to be a part of that research. I plan to use my privilege and authority to legitimize the meaningful work they will then do. These are not huge risks for me anymore. But thinking back to my undergraduate days, goals such as these were just what we were talking about.

Some of the lines from my time at Penn to my current activities are astoundingly direct. Here's a powerful one. In 2007, moved by the two ABCS courses with the Netter Center that I had taken by then, I led an initiative of the Student Committee on Undergraduate Education (SCUE) to put forward a proposal about problem-solving learning. We wrote

> The most effective strategy to cultivate problem-solving learning through courses and other academic programs across the undergraduate education is to establish student-faculty collaborative research groups, each focused on solving a particular problem. We propose a concrete, replicable model of student and faculty collaborative groups to effectively integrate courses, research, and extra-curricular activities in order to best align resources towards solving a particular problem. These collaborative research experiences are ends in themselves. . . . These experiences enable students to contribute to an academic discipline and to improve the conditions of the world beyond that discipline through their research. These collaborations [are the best way] to develop new courses and extra-curricular programming structured around solving particular problems.[21]

And to put a finer point on it, we proposed four examples of such student-faculty collaborative research groups, and one of them was "social enterprise":

> This would represent a large collaborative group of Penn undergraduates and faculty working together solving local and global problems through business. . . . This student-faculty coalition will be able to develop a new research center that will be dedicated to social entrepreneurship and will support a number of "Social Enterprise Scholars" who will engage in a four-year track of solving problems in this field. Recognizing this student-faculty Social Entrepreneurship group as the nucleus of Penn's institutional effort to solve global problems through business knowledge will align Penn's intellectual resources—students and faculty—in the most effective manner.[22]

Those proposals shaped recommendations in Penn undergraduates' 2010 SCUE White Paper.[23] It is incredibly meaningful to know that my experiences with the Netter Center guided me to plant these seeds seventeen years ago. Then twelve years later, I would form my own social enterprise, which I continue to run with many of the same Netter Center values.

As a business school faculty member, I have always engaged deeply with the impact-oriented activities of my school and have always engaged in action-based learning. Now I want to do still more. I envision a collaborative research group, initiative, or center focused on Data Science for Good, which reflects my vision as an undergraduate and is informed by my experiences as a faculty member. Such a center will both engage and partner with communities and advise students in their own problem-solving learning journeys. It will be an engine for community partnerships and bring technically oriented students from disciplines like data science, math, artificial intelligence, computer science, and statistics into the world of doing good with business and data. This vision also aligns with many of my colleagues' views of the evolving role of business education. It aligns with a shift in the attitudes of students attending business schools. And it aligns with my desire to engage as a partner with local communities. I'm delighted to have the privilege of exploring these possibilities, as I carry the Netter Center's spirit one more generation forward.

Notes

1. Declaration of Eric M. Schwartz, PhD, Concerned Pastors for Social Action, et al., v. Khouri, et al., case no. 16.10277, 2:16-cv-10277-DML-SDD, ECF No. 203-4, filed Oct. 1, 2018, US District Court, Eastern District of Michigan, www.nrdc.org/sites /default/files/declaration-eric-schwartz-flint-20181001.pdf.

2. "Biden-Harris Administration Announces New Actions and Progress to Protect Communities from Lead Pipes and Paint," White House, Jan. 27, 2023, www .whitehouse.gov/briefing-room/statements-releases/2023/01/27/fact-sheet-biden -harris-administration-announces-new-actions-and-progress-to-protect-communities -from-lead-pipes-and-paint/.

3. "Lead and Copper Rule Revisions Service Line Inventory Guidance," Revised Lead and Copper Rule, Environmental Protection Agency, last modified Aug. 4, 2022, www.epa .gov/system/files/documents/2022-08/Inventory%20Guidance_Final%20080322_1.pdf.

4. BlueConduit, accessed Feb. 14, 2024, blueconduit.com.

5. Benjamin J. Pauli, *Flint Fights Back* (Cambridge, MA: MIT Press, 2019).

6. Mona Hanna-Attisha, *What the Eyes Don't See: A Story of Crisis, Resistance, and Hope in an American City* (New York: Penguin Random House, 2019).

7. "The Rockefeller Foundation Commits $1M to Expand BlueConduit's AI-Based Solution to America's Lead Pipe Challenge," Rockefeller Foundation, July 7, 2022, www .rockefellerfoundation.org/news/the-rockefeller-foundation-commits-1m-to-expand -blueconduits-ai-based-solution-to-americas-lead-pipe-challenge/.

8. "Google Grant Advances BlueConduit's Mission to Identify and Remove Lead Service Lines," BlueConduit, Sept. 28, 2021, 83

-blueconduit-s-mission-to-identify-and-remove-lead-service-lines/.

9. "EPA Revised Lead and Copper Rule," Environmental Protection Agency, www
.epa.gov/ground-water-and-drinking-water/revised-lead-and-copper-rule.

10. "UM-Flint GIS Center Mapping Flint Water System's Lead Service Lines,"
UM-Flint News, Jan. 28, 2016, news.umflint.edu/2016/01/28/10668/.

11. Schwartz, Declaration.

12. Schwartz, Declaration.

13. Schwartz, Declaration.

14. Flint Pipe Map, last updated June 2022, flintpipemap.org.

15. Schwartz, Declaration.

16. Alex Chojnacki, Chengyu Dai, Arya Farahi, Guangsha Shi, Jared Webb, Dan-
iel T. Zhang, Jacob Abernethy, and Eric M. Schwartz, "A Data Science Approach to
Understanding Residential Water Contamination in Flint," Proceedings of SIGKDD
Conference on Knowledge Discovery and Data Mining, Halifax, NS, Canada, Aug. 2017.

17. Jacob D. Abernethy, Alex Chojnacki, Arya Farahi, Eric M. Schwartz, and Jared
Webb, "Active Remediation: The Search for Lead Pipes in Flint, Michigan," Proceedings
of SIGKDD Conference on Knowledge Discovery and Data Mining, London, Aug. 2018.

18. "Now Open: The +Impact Studio at Michigan Ross Is Taking on Society's Greatest Challenges," *Michigan Ross News*, Oct. 14, 2019, michiganross.umich.edu/news/now
-open-impact-studio-michigan-ross-taking-societys-greatest-challenges.

19. Angelina Little, "Ross Launches +Impact Studio for Cross-Campus Collaboration on Social Issues," *Michigan Daily*, Sept. 22, 2019, www.michigandaily.com/news
/business/ross-launches-impact-studio-cross-campus-collaboration-social-issues/.

20. Christine Massey, "Deep Learning: Problem Solving Learning and Intellectual
Development During the College Years," *University of Pennsylvania Almanac*, Apr. 25,
2006, almanac.upenn.edu/archive/volumes/v52/n31/tatl.html

21. Student Committee on Undergraduate Education (SCUE) Proposal for Problem-
Solving Learning at Penn, Penn Student Government, Dec. 2007.

22. SCUE Proposal.

23. 2010 SCUE White Paper, *University of Pennsylvania Almanac*, Feb. 16, 2010,
almanac.upenn.edu/archive/volumes/v56/n22/pdf_n22/SCUE2010long.pdf.

CHAPTER 7

Relational Research and Cultural Humility: An Interdisciplinary Academic Journey in Community-Engaged Scholarship

Bernice Raveche Garnett

Introduction

It is with profound gratitude that I offer the story of my interdisciplinary journey in community-engaged scholarship. My journey was catalyzed by my transformative experiences as an undergraduate in the Academically Based Community Service (ABCS) courses I took at Penn. I value deeply this opportunity to practice critical self-reflexivity within the professionally nurtured space of this Thirtieth Anniversary Alumni Symposium on Community-Engaged Scholarship. I am deeply honored to play a small part in a larger movement to celebrate three decades of sustained Netter Center work to "develop and sustain democratic, mutually transformative, place-based partnerships between Penn and West Philadelphia."[1]

As an interdisciplinary public health prevention scientist, my research agenda is informed by a diverse array of methodological approaches, disciplines, and theoretical frameworks, all of them grounded in community-based participatory approaches and all of them seeking to support educational and health equity through collaborations, with schools, community-based organizations, and state social service agencies. I am currently the Adam and Abigail Burack Green and Gold Association Professor of Education in the College of Education and Social Services at the University of Vermont (UVM). I also have a secondary appointment in the College of Nursing and Health Science at UVM, which provides me structural support for my interdisciplinary teaching, service scholarship, and engagement with the undergraduate public health sciences program. Broadly, my research agenda sits at the nexus of public health and education, focusing on school- and state-level policies and programs that seek to promote positive youth development, school climate, and educational and health equity. I have taken from my formal graduate training in public health the same core values that inform my scholarly activities: primary prevention, social justice, multi-stakeholder partnerships, and interdisciplinary and place-based collaborations.

My academic career in public health was precisely informed by my undergraduate engagement with ABCS courses through the Netter Center. In those courses, I was exposed to the ideals of public health—primary prevention and social justice—through the Center's commitment to democratic, place-based, and mutually transformative partnerships between Penn and the West Philadelphia community. Schools have been the primary organizational context of my professional career as they represent a community asset for education, well-being, democracy, and cross-cultural and intergenerational connections and resilience. My long-term interest in and passion for school-based public health programming and policy development stemmed from my undergraduate ABCS course assignments and critical service-learning activities in the West Philadelphia public schools.

To date, most of my research has been connected to restorative practices implementation, school health policies and programs, community schools, and school climate. Restorative practices and the ethos in which this paradigm is situated are relational in orientation. They value sharing one's personal story. The indigenous protocol as written by Fania Davis in *The Little Book of Race and Restorative Justice* "invites us to introduce ourselves through ancestors, lineage and land."[2] Of course, my own positionality, lived experiences, biases, and privileges are important to name explicitly at the outset, as they affect the ways in which I approach community-engaged research, teaching, and service. I am a white, able-bodied, heterosexual, cisgender female with educational and class privilege. I was raised literally on a university campus. The vibrancy and intellectual stimulation of campus life were omnipresent in my childhood. My parents were both academics and university administrators with long, illustrious careers, one in physical engineering, the other in immunology. Work ethic, education, and family-first were core values of my upbringing. I come to this narrative with a deep sense of cultural humility, operationalized as a "lifelong commitment to self-evaluation and critique" to redress power imbalances and develop mutually beneficial and nonpaternalistic partnerships with communities.[3] I want to complicate the widely established academic language of expertise as I am dedicated to "resisting the tyranny of an expert" in my professional career, a dispositional outgrowth of cultural humility.[4] I recognize that my worldview is limited and that the work, my work, is never done. There is no singular truth, and our realities are reinforced and shaped by sociohistorical position factors and not equally legitimized. Embracing Donna Mertens's critical question, I reflect constantly on "which version of reality provides an understanding that can lead to changes in the status quo that will lead to furthering social justice."[5] I do my best to interrogate the ways in which my voice may be unduly loud and thereby consume and even silence other voices.

Now that I have briefly introduced myself, I want to thread key learnings that I experienced as an undergraduate at Penn that have shaped my professional persona in profound ways. Most notably, I want to highlight the developmental impact of ABCS courses on 1) kick-starting my journey toward critical consciousness through cultural humility, 2) my disciplinary orientation toward public health and educational equity, 3) my passion for community-engaged scholarship, 4) my place-based orientation toward schools as an organizational context for positive youth development and community resilience, and 5) my commitment to advance the role of institutions of higher education in generating mutually transformative, reciprocal, and equitable partnerships with local school communities. My learnings are not linear or finite. I continue to grapple with crises of self in relation to power, privilege, oppression, and marginalization and with the larger social-political context[6] that I experienced as a nineteen-year-old on Penn's campus through my ABCS courses and Netter Center engagements.

Developmental Impact of Penn ABCS Courses on Personal and Professional Trajectory

ABCS courses are one of the Netter Center's hallmark strategies for creating mutually beneficial transformative partnerships between Penn and West Philadelphia. Ira Harkavy has written extensively on the mission and work of the Center and described ABCS courses as "credit-bearing academic courses in which students and faculty work with the community to improve the quality of life and focus on what might be termed universal problems, such as poverty, social justice, poor schooling, inequality in healthcare."[7] These courses reject service-learning models that perpetuate power imbalances or frame communities from a deficit perspective.[8] They are designed to ensure that partnerships are mutually beneficial and mutually transformative by 1) bridging academic and community expertise, 2) using "collaborative local problem-solving to improve the quality of life and learning in the community and the quality of learning and scholarship in the university," 3) fostering "structural community improvement (e.g., effective public schools, neighborhood economic development)," and 4) emphasizing "student and faculty reflection on the service experience."[9]

Through my ABCS course involvement, I discovered my passion and connection to the discipline of public health, which at that time was a field reserved for graduate students. Still unaware of the languages of social justice, structural inequality, and the social determinants of health, I was curious and confused about issues of access and racial equity. I experienced my first exposure to "community based" and "community engagement" through ABCS courses at Penn in which partnerships with West Philadelphia schools and community members were central. ABCS courses were a pivotal and developmentally critical exposure to a different way of knowing, learning, and being that I had not yet experienced in my educational trajectory. Concretely, my engagement with ABCS courses influenced my undergraduate degree as I majored in health and society and double-minored in anthropology and nutrition. I added the minor in nutrition during my junior year at Penn as I was really interested in learning more about improving the health of our communities, in particular the health of children and families. The early 2000s was a time in which the country was ringing alarm bells about the childhood obesity epidemic. I was taking ABCS courses through the Department of Anthropology in partnership with the Netter Center's Urban Nutrition Initiative (UNI) and its community fitness program and school gardens, which gave me incredible opportunities to support health promotion activities in our West Philadelphia school communities.[10] I cotaught a semester-long community aerobics class at University City High School open to all members of the West Philadelphia community. I worked alongside UNI's "Food Soldiers" program manager and University City High School students to cultivate a school garden and use its produce to prepare meals of culturally responsive nutrition.[11] I collected street data on the variation in the price of milk between corner stores and larger grocery retailers in a block-by-block canvass of West Philadelphia, exposing place-based structural inequities before I had any knowledge of geospatial determinants of health. I supported a diabetes education pilot curriculum implementation through the Netter Center's collaboration with multiple Penn community partners, including medical providers. This was my first time interacting and collaborating with medical providers outside of my own clinical care and seeing the ways in which the medical community could partner on primary prevention of deleterious health outcomes focusing on nutrition education, for example, public health promotion! As stated by Frank Johnston, a professor of nutrition and early academic partner of what is now called the Agatston Urban Nutrition Initiative, "Obesity is the greatest public health failure of the twentieth century. The Agatston Urban Nutrition Initiative seeks to reverse that failure by attacking the cause, not the result."[12] This is the love language of public health—primary prevention and focus on upstream determinants of health outcomes and health disparities. I was swimming in the waters of the social determinants of health during my Penn undergraduate ABCS course engagement.

My ABCS courses exposed me to a new approach to learning that unraveled my sense of self and forced me to unpack my social positions of power and privilege. As a recipient of the transformative potential of place-based experiential learning as a nineteen-year-old, I was immediately drawn into this new way of learning and engagement with community that I had never before experienced in my educational journey. It remains a critical component of my ABCS educational legacy that directly impacts the ways in which I approach my own teaching in undergraduate and graduate courses connected to public health, school climate and violence, research methods, and educational equity. The course-based reflection and the partnering with West Philadelphia public school communities revealed my ignorance of my internal sense of privilege and power. They fired up a developmentally appropriate muddling of my sense of who I was and who I wanted to be. They spotlighted the scantiness of my understanding of structurally based inequities outside of textbooks and class readings. I wanted to know why the price of milk was so drastically different in certain locations. I was confused, even bewildered, that my own grocery experience in West Philadelphia, right on the outskirts of Penn's campus, was so little like my neighbors' experience of the corner stores that I surveyed to understand the nutritional landscape. I was an off-campus resident in West Philadelphia. Why was my experience in this community so incredibly different? Up until this point in my life, I was blind to my implicit biases and privileges and the ways in which my whiteness influenced my opportunities, and I was complacent about my blindness.

Through all these ABCS courses, I was a white, well-intentioned under-graduate entering into and working alongside communities of which I was not a part and that were predominantly Black. I was most certainly engaging in white saviorism and racial commodification of communities of color for the benefit of white students like myself without knowing it or intending to do so.[13] Despite the Netter Center's core principles of ABCS courses described above, careful course design and partnering will not completely avoid white heroism and the implementation of "white-serving service learning," given the power imbalance and racial dynamics between Penn and its West Phila-delphia community.[14] I distinctly remember one undergraduate class assign-ment connected to an ABCS course on community nutrition in which we engaged in mapping of differential prices of milk across various food retailers in Philadelphia. This assignment was eye-opening to me on several levels. First, I explored parts of West Philadelphia that I was told to stay away from as they were too close to dangerous parts of town. Moreover, I interacted with local businesses that I otherwise would most likely never have set foot in. I saw stark racial and place-based disparities in access, opportunity, and community development through this assignment, which further forced me toward an internal understanding of my own privileges. Through all of my ABCS courses, I often felt frustration as I wanted to be a part of a solution to urban poverty, community health, and health equity but was uncomfortable working with a community I was not a part of. I wondered how I was received and perceived by the University City High School students I worked along-side as we prepared meals connected to the Food Soldiers program. Was the consciousness-raising that supported my own internal growth merely self-serving? Was I really having an impact? For whom? How do I harness this new energy, learning, and passion to reduce structural and health inequities among communities of color in ways sustainable, mutually transformative, and reciprocal, given my own racial and educational positionality? I have floundered and I continue to flounder on these questions to this day, but I will briefly outline how my "changed awareness of my own social position-ing" and my growth in cultural humility have guided my academic journey thus far.[15]

I want to situate my academic career in the commitment to *sustained transformative* community-engaged scholarship and community-based par-ticipatory research (CBPR) and the devotion to mutually beneficial demo-cratic place-based partnerships that took root in my ABCS courses. I use a definition of community-engaged scholarship articulated by the ad hoc faculty committee on community-engaged scholarship for the provost of the University of Pennsylvania: "Community engaged scholarship entails working in partnership with the community in a relationship of transparency and trust in order to draw on the expertise of the partners to address a pressing real-world problem."[16] Additionally, my academic career is methodologically grounded in CBPR, "which embraces collaborative efforts among community, academic, and other stakeholders who gather and use research and data to build on strengths and priorities of the community for multilevel strategies to improve health and social equity."[17] My addition of *sustained* and *transformative* to community-engaged scholarship reflects my commitment to embedding community-engaged scholarship in *long-standing partnerships* so as to avoid doing harm by one-off service-learning courses that benefit university students at the expense of school communities or by symbolic community-engaged scholarship that does not build internal capacity, facilitate structural change for partnering school communities, or prioritize community knowledge and expertise. I have engaged in symbolic community-engaged scholarship during my career, and when I have done so, I've felt the same internal quaking I did in my undergraduate days, wondering if my learning and growth in critical consciousness were coming at the cost of my partnering school communities. This is the Achilles heel of community-engaged scholarship, particularly when there are stark racial and socioeconomic power imbalances among the stakeholders involved. How do we define success? Whose progress, learning, and growth is measured and prioritized? Whose reality and history are legitimized? How do I ensure that my engagement in service-learning courses remains critical and does not actualize "white-serving service-learning," given my situation in a predominantly white-serving institution of higher education?[18] How do my community partners experience our community-engaged scholarship? Is it meeting their needs? These burning methodological and professional questions were lit internally in my undergraduate ABCS courses and have remained fiery for more than two decades of my interdisciplinary public health academic journey.

What Sustains and Challenges Community-Engaged Scholarship: Social-Ecological Approach

As a public health prevention scientist, I apply theoretical and conceptual frameworks to parsimoniously address complex social phenomena. "The gift of theory is that it provides conceptual underpinnings for well-crafted research and informed practice."[19] As Kurt Lewin said, "There is nothing as practical as a good theory."[20] I approach my own work through a theoretically informed lens, applying the social-ecological model as an anchoring framework.[21] There are individual constraints, assets, skills, and dispositions that may attract or repel community-engaged scholarship as a modality of academic being manifested across teaching, research, and service.[22] However, individual agency to engage in *transformative sustained* community-engaged scholarship is fundamentally constrained, influenced, and shaped by proximal and distal peer and social networks, institutional structures and policies, and sociocultural community norms. The social-ecological model in public health draws from the seminal work of Urie Bronfenbrenner and his transactional model of child development.[23] It is critical to name and work toward *changing the context* to support sustainable individual behavior. The context in my situation is institutions of higher education, more specifically the professoriate, and the individual behavior that I am seeking to maintain, sustain, and institutionalize is transformative community-engaged scholarship to avoid individually based deficit narratives rooted in white supremacy and meritocracy that do not recognize structural determinants to academic faculty resilience and sustainability.[24]

Interpersonal Skills Necessary for Community-Engaged Scholarship: How I Try to Do the Work

There are critical interpersonal mindsets, values, and dispositional skills necessary for critical community-engaged scholarship.[25] I will list the core values and interpersonal skills that guide my approach to my work. All of them germinated in my ABCS courses at Penn, where my service-learning experiences changed my awareness of my social position, which resulted in greater cultural humility and ultimately in the cultivation of greater critical consciousness.[26]

Centering of Relationship-Building, Earned Trust, and Relationality

This is a "research approach that is based on relations with research partners."[27] It honors indigenous research methods and decolonizes ways of knowing.[28] I am critically conscious of the ways in which my position as a white faculty member with multiple advanced degrees connected to the signature land-grant university in my home state may initially win me "unearned trust" (trust based on my title or role rather than on direct interaction), but hopefully I move toward proxy trust (working together with partners because someone who is trusted invited them to work together) and ultimately to "critical reflective trust" (trust that allows for mistakes and where differences can be talked about and resolved).[29]

Flexibility and Embracing "Slow Food" Research

Community-engaged scholarship does not generate immediate or fast-turnaround manuscripts and other outlets for academic dissemination, as this methodology requires centering community needs, expertise, and dissemination above and beyond self. This requires me to show up for my community partners without asking for anything—no funding, no data, no papers. Instead, I need to live my values by "putting people over papers," which leads to critical reflective trust and sustainable long-term partnerships. For example, I and my colleagues in the College of Education and Social Services at UVM have been since 2016 in a community-based research project with the Burlington School District (BSD) to support the evaluation of restorative practices implementation. During the early years of our partnerships, we were in deep in building relationships with the BSD. This required lots of active listening, face-to-face meetings with various school partners, and a long process to develop a memorandum of understanding (MOU) that would guide our partnership, particularly as it relates to data-sharing, academic publications, data ownership, and acknowledgments. We have just recently revised our MOU to specify the expectations of both the BSD and UVM's College of Education and Social Services. The first MOU took almost two years to complete. The slow build of our relationship with the school district was necessary and contributed directly to the long-term success of our partnership. It was possible only because both my UVM colleague and I had recently earned tenure and thus had more agency and institutional space to push back on unrealistic expectations for academic productivity that do not align with the values and timelines required for sustained transformative community-engaged scholarship.

Commitment to Cultural Humility

This is a lifelong dedication to "self-evaluation and critique, to redressing the power imbalances ... and to developing mutually beneficial and non-paternalistic partnerships with communities."[30] My draw toward cultural humility stemmed from my young adult experiences in my ABCS courses in the West Philadelphia public schools, where I was forced to engage critically with my own white privilege and educational positionality. I was an outsider. I was doing my level best to support the UNI's school garden and Food Soldiers programs. And I had critical life lessons to learn. I had to sit with and see my racial identity in ways that I had not yet done as a young adult. Those lessons were monumental in my own development and professional journey. I needed and continue to need to stay humble and to recognize the ways in which my presence in communities that are not my own can be damaging, self-serving manifestations of white saviorism. I needed and continue to need to appreciate the ongoing tensions in my professional academic work as I seek to advance educational and health equity for marginalized students and families. I use data to drive social change, but I recognize that my teaching, knowledge, and academic identity are secondary to community knowledge and lived experiences. "True equity-oriented research must upend traditional power dynamics where university researchers are viewed as apex knowledge producers. Democratizing the knowledge production process to recognize the valued and essential contributions of both the researcher and community partners is essential for creating equitable research collaborations."[31] This mindset is the antithesis of the prevalent values of research-oriented universities and of the standards by which academic tenure-track faculty are often evaluated. It is at ironic odds with my professorial need to be an "expert" and often to introduce myself as an expert in my professional spaces. It necessitates sharing myself with my community partners with vulnerability rather than wrapping myself in a mantle of authority. It enables me to build "authentic relationships" through a "willingness to be personally forthcoming without being self-centered."[32] In our long-standing partnership with the BSD, we live the work by engaging deeply as a CBPR community.[33] Our weekly research meetings begin with a community-building restorative practices talking circle. We lean into the structured facilitation of relationships, trust, and mutual respect in our research partnership using the very strategies that our educator partners are using with their K–12 students. These very acts of vulnerability and this sharing of ourselves with our school community partners during our opening talking circles make our work more authentic and our partnerships stronger. I still pinch myself that I have the privilege and the honor of working alongside such incredibly thoughtful, fierce, and dedicated school community partners across the hierarchy of the school district, from its central office and leadership to its classroom educators, paraprofessionals, student support staff, and its students themselves.[34]

Explicit Attention to Power and Power Imbalances

In community-engaged research partnerships, I must be steadfast in my commitment to flatten the explicit and implicit power imbalances that are omnipresent in my work. Power can manifest differently in different contexts. I must be critically mindful of my social and organizational power to ensure that the collaborations on which I work are mutually beneficial and foster the assets of all stakeholders. The purpose of working with communities is to produce positive change. This requires an explicit focus on justice and critical theory to produce knowledge, data, and policies that highlight the structural determinants of educational and health inequities in our communities. In my projects on restorative practices implementation with the BSD and on rural community school implementation with the Vermont Agency of Education, my use of data to inform change efforts is the cornerstone of our partnerships. Given that data and "research" often alienates and excludes individuals outside of academia, it is vital that we acknowledge multiple voices and realities and that we share data to tell stories. Equity in data access and ownership is a guiding value of both of these projects, and so is our determination to democratize the knowledge production process so that academic institutions are not the sole bearers of truth and expertise. As our MOU puts it, "This RPP [research-practice-partnership] does not assume that UVM researchers have solutions or that there is information lacking in practical contexts. Instead, the promise of this RPP is that by bringing practitioners into research, research questions will be more relevant to practitioners and the results from this research are more likely to be implemented in real-world contexts (Research + Practice + Collaboration) Science."[35]

Interdisciplinarity and Diplomacy

As no community is static or monolithic, I have found that interdisciplinary and joint thinking can be incredibly helpful in navigating the realities of community-engaged scholarship. Although diplomacy is often discussed as a skill set in the political arena, community-engaged scholars have found it a critical disposition to support strong relationships nested within multiple systems of power. "Diplomacy speaks to the learned capacity of negotiating and dealing with these various forms of community and the often-competing demands that can emerge when working with multiple partners, individuals and stakeholders."[36] Over and over again, our CBPR team has had to deal with tensions such as these within the multiple systems of power present in the K–12 and higher-education contexts. When data from students, parents, and educators diverge, contradict, or misalign, how do we deal with the data discordance? How do we express to our publics our complex and nuanced story of restorative practices implementation? Synergistically supporting a diplomacy orientation is the need to cultivate interdisciplinary and diverse stakeholders for our research teams. Wicked social problems will only be successfully addressed through collaborations and partnership with individuals from across disciplines, sectors, and contexts. One of my greatest joys in and deepest senses of gratitude for my time as a faculty member at UVM has been the availability of interdisciplinary research, teaching, service, and thinking, not just across the academy but within the community and across the state.

Institutional Structures, Supports, and Constraints for Community-Engaged Scholarship

There remain real and significant institutional constraints on and supports for community-engaged scholarship, and they have influenced my professional trajectory. It is important to name them and contend with them if institutions of higher education truly want to pursue community-engaged scholarship beyond superficial recognition and head nods. In addition to institutional constraints and supports, I have discovered that there are also relational supports among colleagues that can inspire and propel community-engaged scholarship forward.

Within a Team of Community-Engaged
Scholarship Colleagues, Be Relationally Available
for Timely Needs of Community Partners

Often the timelines of community partners and academia are disjointed and
not clearly communicated. Over the course of our six-year partnership with
the BSD, I can recall countless examples of community partners sending an
email or calling our cell phones to ask us to meet an immediate need related
to fallout from data presentations, to testify at the state legislature, or to help
with a grant application due within weeks. My deep connections with my
academic faculty colleagues on our scholarship teams has been the heartbeat
of how we approach the work and why I continue to engage in the work.
Because we have showcased vulnerability and shared parts of ourselves with
each other, we are acutely aware of workload capacity and personal needs at
all points in the academic year to ensure that we can pick up someone who
needs to fade out or have the affordances of tenure to "clear our desks" to
respond immediately to a community partner's request or need. This is relational research.

Ensure That Tenure and Promotion Processes Value
and Reward Community-Engaged Scholarship

This could look like explicitly naming various modalities of publication
that count toward academic productivity metrics, including community
dissemination products and recognition of the process of developing and
maintaining community-engaged scholarship research teams.[37] I had the
privilege of having tenure during the early stages of developing a project that
I would not have been able to pursue if I was bound to unrealistic expectations for promotion to tenure, especially given our teaching load. An evaluation of success based solely on the academic currency of the number of
publications—devoid of any acknowledgment of the process by which these
publications came to be, whose voices are represented in them, their societal impact and the ways in which work informs and serves our local and
global communities—disincentivizes faculty engagement in community-
engaged scholarship. My annual performance review during the academic
year 2022–2023 was by far the hardest and most depleting process of my
academic tenure-track career thus far. Despite being tenured and having an

endowed professorship, I have struggled to publish academic peer-reviewed manuscripts since the pandemic. COVID has affected academic women, especially caregiving women, profoundly. As a mother of four young children, I have experienced its differential impact on my scholarly productivity. The burnout is real. I haven't had the energy or mental space for visionary thinking, empirical writing, and manuscript crunching since 2019. A recent article in the *BMJ* validated my own feelings (and frankly my resentment) about the academic assessment process. The biggest loss, say female academics with young children, has been the loss of time to think. "There simply wasn't enough quiet, solitude, or 'bandwidth' to concentrate or be strategic about new innovative ideas for future research."[38] I myself have found little intrinsic motivation to publish "fast food" research. I do not want to do articles based on secondary data analysis of projects that have lapsed or on material connected to writing purely for an academic audience. I seem to always find time for community partner meetings, email responses, new projects, and the dissemination of my work to the community, but I fear that I may never again be able to stir up or dig down deep enough to cultivate the desire to publish for self-serving ambitions for stature and fame that the academy requires. So why do it?

Commit to Epistemic Equity

Elevate the diverse and marginalized knowledges situated within systems of power.[39] Embrace methodological diversity as a powerful way to solve complex social problems. I am a mixed-method methodologist who takes a craft attitude toward my calling. I am comfortable with uncertainty and recognize that research is an act of storytelling, often of nonlinear storytelling. It is inherently messy.[40] The paradigm wars and heated debates over the worth of different methodologies and data-collection processes shape how knowledge production in the academy is valued, at the individual level of faculty advancement, at the interpersonal level of colleagueship and peer support for methodologically diverse approaches, and at the institutional level of methodological courses taught and prioritized in undergraduate and graduate programs. My research has been called "fluffy" by colleagues, because I rely significantly on qualitative methods. I collect stories, narratives, and voices of communities. The community-produced knowledge with which I work is often dismissed as anecdotal, invalid, unscientific, or nongeneralizable, particularly when my data speaks to an issue that requires action or challenges the status quo. This visceral dismissal of qualitative and mixed methods is not confined to academia. In my community-based participatory research, K–12 educators sometimes ask where my "real data" is when I present evidence of students' responses to their experiences couched in the students' own voices. This year, in our restorative practices implementation project, we had a 60 percent response rate to our student survey across eleven different K–12 schools. Despite this remarkable return, some educators refused to reckon with our findings. They argued that our discoveries were not representative of the entire school community, or they assumed (on no evidence) that the students had not taken the survey seriously. My community school partners asked me to provide language that could support their response when questioned about the validity of our student restorative practices data. I created a much-too-long document that outlined various ways to conceptualize and determine validity, but I want to highlight one paragraph from that document:

> We welcome collaborative and constructive conversations related to questioning data, findings, and interpretations. We appreciate thoughtful and intentional spaces designed to rethink and unlearn deeply held assumptions of reality, truth and what is "real data." We want to expand our understanding of reality knowing that multiple truths exist, and multiple truths are influenced by individual and structural power and privilege. We would like to challenge immediate discounts of RP BSD data as being invalid without concerted attention to the various dimensions of validity. By validity, "we mean that a research study, its parts, the conclusions drawn, and the applications based on it can be of high or low quality . . ." AND "research needs to be defensible to the research and practice communities for whom research is produced and used."[41] Poking holes in data is much easier than sitting with the implications and collective and individual action required by the data. We want to challenge adultism manifested as assuming our students do not take surveys seriously. We want to invite curiosity and openness if data presented conflicts with your realities. Finally, a commitment and core value of the BSD RP evaluation team is "democratization of knowledge"—meaning transparent access to BSD RP data by the entire community.[42] This is your district and your data.[43]

Too often, in academia and beyond, we poke holes in data that scares us or challenges us to rethink and unlearn the assumptions of our current ways of doing. We refuse such disturbing data under the guise of questioning the methodological rigor by which it was obtained, all the while prioritizing a singular truth established by a very singular process of inquiry. Community-engaged scholarship and community-based participatory research necessitate mixed methodological approaches "that can provide both the 'stories and statistics' needed to help effect policy change."[44]

Resourcing

Institutions of higher education can incentivize and support community-engaged scholarship through intentional resourcing decisions at many points of inflection:

- cluster hires of interdisciplinary faculty who have methodological synergy in community-engaged scholarship;
- adequately funded university centers on community-engaged scholarship that can serve students, faculty, staff, and the larger community through service-learning courses, university-assisted community schools, and outreach;
- student internships, service-learning courses, and place-based education partnerships such as university-assisted community schools;
- library investments in multiple methodological approaches to scholarship through the procurement of a suitable range of books and journals;
- financial support for statistical, mixed, and qualitative data analysis such as computer software, personnel, and technical assistance;
- internal seed and grant funding competitions that give competitive advantage to proposals that include community-engaged scholarship;
- postdoctoral and graduate fellowships that include significant community-engaged scholarship training, experiences, funding, and mentoring to change the arc of the professoriate and the socialization of faculty;
- showcasing of examples of the institution's commitment to community engagement by highlighting campus resources, faculty

scholarship, student research, and community partners during
faculty orientation;

- and creation of shared spaces on campus for community events,
  at reduced costs, so that the university becomes a community
  asset, providing opportunities for townspeople to engage in
  coursework, attend lectures, and be a part of the vibrancy of a
  "democratic civic university."[45]

Circling Back: What Is My Why?

Despite my awareness that knowledge production is rewarded at the
individual level in the academy,[46] I have an unwavering commitment to
community-based participatory research and community-engaged scholarship. The inner core of my proclivity to CBPR and to community engagement in general stems directly from my undergraduate studies at Penn and
the ABCS courses in which we students, Penn faculty, and local schools
partnered to address the obesity epidemic through localized health promotion activities. I am a team player. As a former Division 1 collegiate
athlete—I played field hockey at Penn—I have always had a collective orientation and the "we before me" mindset that is critical to team success and
cohesion. My athletic identity was crystallizing during my undergraduate
experience. My ABCS courses made the importance of collective and deeply
trusting relationships even more salient to the woman I was becoming and
wanted to be.

When looking for a job after I finished my doctorate in public health, I
was very clear with myself that I wanted to be at an institution that prioritized
undergraduate education. As my own discipline, public health, is often siloed
into graduate education, I searched avidly for an academic home in which I
could engage with undergraduate students. This personal commitment was
driven by my own journey as an overly optimistic and somewhat scattered
undergraduate student. My undergraduate professors made lasting impres-
sions on my life, through their passion, their sense of purpose, and their commitment to social justice.

My experiences in the ABCS curricular scaffolding propelled my thinking
and interest in exploring the roles of schools as organizational contexts for
health promotion and primary prevention of health disparities. They fostered
my focus on food access, food production, and food sovereignty. They have

driven my decades-long professional work in those schools as sites for the promotion of positive youth development, community resilience, and place-based democratic transformation. My time working alongside the staff and community partners of the Food Soldiers program is seared in my memory. Picking the vegetables from the school garden, washing them, and preparing dishes from them following the recipes of Black culture was an unforgettably transformative experience. Although I didn't yet have the language of food sovereignty, culturally responsive nutrition education, health inequities, and other public health terms that I would soak up during my graduate training, it was in those experiences that I was able to start to identify my passion and purpose, which are intertwined personally and professionally. I don't consider my professional career a "job." I consider it a way of being that is reflective of my core values and my unquenched desire to uncover and address long-standing structural inequities that lead to differential outcomes for children and their families in the United States. As my academic journey is far from over, I will conclude with additional burning questions and considerations for sustained transformative community-engaged scholarship across individual and institutional contexts.

Burning Personal, Institutional, and Methodological Questions

- What does it mean for an institution to practice cultural humility? What would it look like for an institution of higher education to embody and practice structural and epistemic humility?[47]
- What would it look like for academic adults to value and reinforce authentic vulnerability as an ethos of our research working culture? How do we counter "the disproportionate value that the academy places on fact-based, rational, and emotionless analysis"?[48] How do we demonstrate vulnerability and expertise through relational research?
- How do university faculty members practice authentic, robust, relationally connected, community-engaged research within the confines and expectations of academic productivity and impact? How do we be real about those tensions when developing and sustaining transformative community-engaged scholarship?
- How do we as university faculty name tensions and competing agendas related to publication pressures and grant-seeking

endeavors that may not align with dissemination strategies of our community-engaged partners?

- How does intense pressure to be an expert seep into our methodological and pedagogical orientations and dispositions? Critical service-learning courses may be an antidote to the normative hubris of academy by centering community knowledge and applied experiences.

- Can the term *community-engaged scholarship* and our collective operationalization of this term be a big enough tent to include a variety of disciplines, particularly outside the social sciences?

- How do I maintain criticality in my community-engaged research and teaching to foster mutually beneficial partnerships with school community partners that decenters my whiteness and academic privileges?

Notes

1. Netter Center for Community Partnerships, "ABCS Courses," accessed July 28, 2023, www.nettercenter.upenn.edu/what-we-do/courses.

2. Fania Davis, *The Little Book of Race and Restorative Justice: Black Lives, Healing, and US Social Transformation* (New York: Good Books, 2019).

3. Melanie Tervalon and Jann Murray-Garcia, "Cultural Humility Versus Cultural Competence: A Critical Distinction in Defining Physician Training Outcomes in Multicultural Education," *Journal of Health Care for the Poor and Underserved* 9, no. 2 (1998): 117–25, quotation on 123.

4. Jennifer Adele Morrison and Jeong-Hee Kim, "Resisting the 'Tyranny of an Expert': A Journey Towards Relational Research," in *Preparing Students for Community-Engaged Scholarship in Higher Education*, ed. Aaron Samuel Zimmerman, 43–60 (Hershey, PA: IGI Global, 2020).

5. Donna M. Mertens, "Transformative Mixed Methods: Addressing Inequities," *American Behavioral Scientist* 56, no. 6 (2012): 802–13, quotation on 806.

6. Jennifer Abe, "Beyond Cultural Competence, Toward Social Transformation: Liberation Psychologies and the Practice of Cultural Humility," *Journal of Social Work Education* 56, no. 4 (2020): 696–707.

7. Dave Zeitlin, "Ode to Ira," *Pennsylvania Gazette* 121, no. 6 (July/Aug. 2023): 32–37, quotation on 34, thepenngazette.com/ode-to-ira/.

8. Alan S. Tinkler, Barri E. Tinkler, Virginia M. Jagla, and Jean R. Strait, eds., *Service-Learning to Advance Social Justice in a Time of Radical Inequality* (Charlotte: Information Age Publishing, 2015).

9. Netter Center, "ABCS Courses."

10. Francis E. Johnston, Ira Harkavy, Frances Barg, Danny Gerber, and Jennifer Rulf, "The Urban Nutrition Initiative: Bringing Academically-Based Community Service to the University of Pennsylvania's Department of Anthropology," *Michigan Journal of Community Service Learning* 10, no. 3 (2004): 100–6.

11. Francis E. Johnston, "The Agatston Urban Nutrition Initiative: Working to Reverse the Obesity Epidemic Through Academically Based Community Service," *New Directions for Youth Development* (Special issue: Universities in Partnership: Strategies for Education, Youth Development, and Community Renewal) 122 (Summer 2009): 61–79.

12. Johnston, "Agatston Urban Nutrition Initiative," 78.

13. Lauren N. Irwin and Zak Foste, "Service-Learning and Racial Capitalism: On the Commodification of People of Color for White Advancement," *Review of Higher Education* 44, no. 4 (2021): 419–46.

14. Irwin and Foste, "Service-Learning."

15. Abe, "Beyond Cultural Competence," 700.

16. Dennis Deturck, Lori Flanagan-Cato, Matt Hartley, John Jackson, Terri Lipman, and John Puckett, *Report of the Ad Hoc Faculty Committee on Community Engaged Scholarship for the Provost of the University of Pennsylvania*, June 22, 2022), 1, www.nettercenter.upenn.edu/sites/default/files/Community_Engaged_Scholarship_report_6-22-22.pdf.

17. Nina Wallerstein, Bonnie Duran, John G. Oetzel, and Meredith Minkler, eds., *Community-Based Participatory Research for Health: Advancing Social and Health Equity*, 3rd ed. (San Francisco: Jossey-Bass, 2017).

18. Irwin and Foste, "Service-Learning."

19. Karen Glanz, Barbara K. Rimer, and K. Viswanath, "Theory, Research, and Practice in Health Behavior and Health Education," in *Health Behavior and Health Education: Theory, Research, and Practice*, 4th ed., ed. Glanz, Rimer, and Viswanath, 23–40 (San Francisco: Jossey-Bass, 2008), quotation on 31.

20. Kurt Lewin, "Psychology and the Process of Group Living," *Journal of Social Psychology* 17, no. 1 (1943): 113–31, quotation on 118.

21. James F. Sallis, Neville Owen, and E. Fisher, "Ecological Models of Health Behavior," in *Health Behavior: Theory, Research, and Practice*, 5th ed., ed. Karen Glanz, Barbara K. Rimer, and K. Viswanath, 43–64 (San Francisco: Jossey-Bass/Wiley, 2015).

22. Jennifer W. Purcell, Andrew Pearl, and Trina Van Schyndel, "Boundary Spanning Leadership Among Community-Engaged Faculty: An Exploratory Study of Faculty Participating in Higher Education Community Engagement," *Engaged Scholar Journal* 6, no. 2 (2020): 1–30.

23. Urie Bronfenbrenner, *The Ecology of Human Development: Experiments by Nature and Design* (Cambridge, MA: Harvard University Press, 1979).

24. David J. Weerts and Lorilee R. Sandmann, "Building a Two-Way Street: Challenges and Opportunities for Community Engagement at Research Universities," *Review of Higher Education* 32, no. 1 (2008): 73–106; Purcell, Pearl, and Van Schyndel, "Boundary Spanning Leadership."

25. Cynthia Gordon da Cruz, "Critical Community-Engaged Scholarship: Communities and Universities Striving for Racial Justice," *Peabody Journal of Education* 92, no. 3 (2017): 363–84.

26. Paulo Freire, *Pedagogy of the Oppressed* (New York: Continuum, 1970).

27. Morrison and Kim, "Resisting the 'Tyranny of an Expert,'" 60.

28. Shawn Wilson, *Research Is Ceremony: Indigenous Research Methods* (Black Point, Nova Scotia: Fernwood, 2020); Bagele Chilisa, *Indigenous Research Methodologies* (Thousand Oaks, CA: Sage, 2019).

29. Julie E. Lucero, Katherine E. Wright, and Abigail Reese, "Trust Development in CBPR Partnerships," in Wallerstein et al., eds., *Community-Based Participatory Research for Health*, 3rd ed., 61–76.

30. Tervalon and Murray-Garcia, "Cultural Humility," 123.

31. Rebecca London and Ronald David Glass, "Toward Equitable Collaboration: Community Partners' Strategic Perspectives on Community-Engaged Research," William T. Grant Foundation, last updated Apr. 4, 2022, wtgrantfoundation.org/toward -equitable-collaboration-community-partners-strategic-perspectives-on-community -engaged-research.

32. Andrew R. Hatala et al., "The Interpersonal Skills of Community-Engaged Scholarship: Insights from Collaborators Working at the University of Saskatchewan's Community Engagement Office," *Journal of Community Engagement and Scholarship* 10, no. 1 (2017): 44–58, quotation on 49.

33. Bernice Raveche Garnett, Lance C. Smith, Colby T. Kervick, Tracy A. Ballysingh, Mika Moore, and Eliaquin Gonell, "The Emancipatory Potential of Transformative Mixed Methods Designs: Informing Youth Participatory Action Research and Restorative Practices Within a District-Wide School Transformation Project," *International Journal of Research & Method in Education* 42, no. 3 (2019): 305–16.

34. Eliaquin Gonell, Lance C. Smith, Bernice Garnett, and Elizabeth Clements, "Practicing Youth Participatory Action Research for School Equity: A Pedagogical Model," *Action Research* 19, no. 4 (2021): 632–55.

35. Memorandum of Understanding Between the University of Vermont's College of Education and Social Services and the Vermont Agency of Education, Sept. 12, 2023.

36. Hatala et al., "Interpersonal Skills," 51.

37. Marissa Bell and Neil Lewis Jr., "Universities Claim to Value Community-Engaged Scholarship: So Why Do They Discourage It?," *Public Understanding of Science* 32, no. 3 (2023): 304–21; Sue DeWine, "Contributions of Engaged Scholarship to the Academic Community," in *Engaging Communication, Transforming Organizations: Scholarship of Engagement in Action*, ed. Jennifer L. Simpson and Pamela Shockley-Zalabak, 191–202 (Cresskill, NJ: Hampton, 2005).

38. Jocalyn Clark, "How Pandemic Publishing Struck a Blow to the Visibility of Women's Expertise," *BMJ (Online)* 381 (Apr. 6, 2023), www-bmj-com=.proxy .library.upenn.edu/content/381/bmj.p788.

39. Bell and Lewis, "Universities Claim."

40. Nozomi Sakata, "Embracing the Messiness in Mixed Methods Research: The Craft Attitude," *Journal of Mixed Methods Research* 17, no. 3 (2023): 288–307.

41. Anthony J. Onwuegbuzie and R. Burke Johnson, "The Validity Issue in Mixed Research," *Research in the Schools* 13, no. 1 (2006): 48–63.

42. Bell and Lewis, "Universities Claim."

43. Project CORE Memo to our Burlington School District partners, May 2023.

44. Meredith Minkler, Analilia P. Garcia, Victor Rubin, and Nina Wallerstein, *Community-Based Participatory Research: A Strategy for Building Healthy Communities and Promoting Health Through Policy Change* (Oakland, CA: PolicyLink, 2012), 22.

45. Ira Harkavy, Sjur Bergan, Tony Gallagher, and Hilligje Van't Land, "Universities Must Help Shape the Post-COVID-19 World," in *Higher Education's Response to the COVID-19 Pandemic: Building a More Sustainable and Democratic Future*, ed. Sjur Bergan, Tony Gallagher, Ira Harkavy, Ronaldo Munck, and Hilligje Van't Land, 21–30 (Strasbourg: Council of Europe, 2021), quotation on 24.

46. Bell and Lewis, "Universities Claim."

47. Victoria M. Parente, Gabriela Nagy, and Kathryn I. Pollak, "Patient- and Family-Centered Hospital Care: The Need for Structural Humility," *JAMA Pediatrics* 177, no. 6 (2023): 553–54.

48. Mika Dashman, Katherine Culberg, David Dean, Anna Lemler, Mikhail Lyubansky, and Julie Shackford-Bradley, "Bringing a Racial Justice Consciousness to the Restorative Justice Movement," in *Listening to the Movement: Essays on New Growth and New Challenges in Restorative Justice*, ed. Carl Stauffer and Ted Lewis, 21–35 (Eugene, OR: Cascade, 2021), quotation on 22.

CHAPTER 8

Local Culture of Global Proportions

Andrew Zitcer

Academically Based Community Service (ABCS) and community-based learning (CBL) are core to my identity as a faculty member at Drexel University. I attribute these commitments to the exposure I had to these traditions while a student at the University of Pennsylvania in the late 1990s and particularly to the experiences I had through the Netter Center for Community Partnerships.

The most impactful of those experiences was the cocreation of the Foundation Community Arts Initiative (later, simply, the Rotunda). This community arts center is still in operation twenty-five years later.

It grew directly out of a paper I cowrote for an honors seminar taught by Lee Benson and Ira Harkavy in the 1998–1999 academic year, and that paper grew directly out of an earlier piece of student work in the seminar. Benson and Harkavy gave me a copy of that prior project to examine: a proposal to site a jazz club on 40th Street, which with Penn's expansion had become the boundary line between Penn's campus and the neighborhoods of West Philadelphia.

At that time, it seemed to me extraordinary to share undergraduate work from one year's students to another, to continue the momentum of promising ideas. But if I had not been exposed to that concept paper, the idea for the Rotunda would not have occurred to me. Now, sharing (with permission) work from one generation of students to the next informs my mentoring of graduate-thesis students at Drexel. I actually require them to read at least two prior theses as inspiration for both the form and content of their own thesis process.

Alas, I cannot replicate another aspect of that honors seminar. Graduate theses, at Drexel and elsewhere, are individual enterprises. All projects in the

Benson-Harkavy seminar were group projects, and I benefited immensely from the opportunity to collaborate with fellow undergraduates Noah Bilenker, Swapnil Shah, and Micah Westerman, who worked with me to refine and advance the vision for the Rotunda.

But back to the concept of a jazz club on 40th Street. Even as a twenty-year-old undergraduate, I knew that the idea would not work. I understood that successful jazz clubs are products of local relationships and national connections. They do not work when they appear out of thin air, just dropped in a place without suitable context or bridge-building to the music communities that surround them. Besides, by the late 1990s, jazz was no longer as popular as it had been in the past, and there were other jazz clubs in West Philadelphia struggling to remain viable.

As our thinking advanced, the idea of a jazz club morphed into a proposal for a community arts center that would promote not only jazz but also a multitude of other forms of musical and cultural expression. It would be a hub and a home for artists in West Philadelphia and beyond. It would take the best of the thriving cultural scenes of the time and amalgamate them in one venue that could be a community gathering place for the promotion of arts and culture.

How did I know that a community arts center would be the right fit for 40th Street? A set of other experiences also influenced my sensibility regarding community engagement while at the University of Pennsylvania.

The first of these was another ABCS course: the Black Bottom Theater Project, led by Professor Billy Yalowitz (who was then working for the Center for Community Partnerships). The Black Bottom is the name of the historic African American neighborhood in Philadelphia that was destroyed by urban renewal in the late 1960s.[1] Despite losing their homes, elders from the Black Bottom continued to form an association—one that exists to this day—and gather periodically to celebrate what once was and mourn what has been lost. Working with undergraduates from the University of Pennsylvania and high school students from University City High School (built in the former Black Bottom and later demolished as part of another renewal scheme in the 2010s), Yalowitz connected with living elders from the Black Bottom. These elders told their stories as oral histories, which were recorded and turned into scenes for a theater production by the Penn students, to be acted out in community performance by the high school students and the elders. These "Black Bottom Sketches" were performed in a local church, not a proscenium theater. This was an important lesson in the practice of community arts. Working on this performance project was a powerful introduction to the depth and resonance of local history in West Philadelphia and to the importance of the arts in revealing other perspectives and counternarratives that need amplification and showcasing in spaces like the Rotunda.

In addition to being part of the Black Bottom performances, Penn offered other key experiences that led to the project at the Rotunda: working at the Kelly Writers House and WXPN during my time as an undergraduate. Both remain important Penn arts institutions. The Kelly Writers House is a home for local, national, and international writers to engage with students and the literary community at Penn; WXPN is Penn's professionally run campus radio station. I was a student worker at the Writers House and a production intern at WXPN for much of my time at Penn. The two entities collaborated on a poetry program called Live at the Writers House that was recorded live to tape during the academic year. I served as an engineer on this program. During the months when Live at the Writers House was on hiatus, I served as a producer and sometime host for its sister program, Dystopia, which featured local musicians in themed episodes (for example, hip-hop, contemporary classical, psychedelic rock) punctuated by poetry interludes. Each of these experiences, in its own way, sensitized me to the power of working collaboratively with communities, either geographically based or funded in common interest. By getting exposed to the rich local arts communities that Philadelphia had to offer, I was falling in love with these forms of cultural expression. My own dreams of heading to New York to pursue a career in arts and culture were starting to shift; Philadelphia had gotten under my skin.

At the end of the semester, I expected to leave the community arts center proposal behind, perhaps to be picked up later by another group of students. After all, that's what happens in universities most of the time. The semester ends, and everybody moves on. This is one of the main frustrations felt by community members about university partnerships. But to my great surprise and delight, Ira Harkavy did not forget about the Rotunda proposal. He showed the seminar paper to Penn's Vice Provost for University Life, Dr. Valarie Swain-Cade McCoullum, and to the Vice President for Facilities and Real Estate, Omar Blaik, and his deputy, Tom Lussenhop. With their enthusiastic endorsement of the idea, we undertook a space search that ultimately led to a Christian Science church that had been sold to Penn a few years before. This space, now dubbed the Rotunda (after its most distinguishing architectural feature), began to host performances and community events in April 1999 and has never looked back. It thrived because the programming decisions were made by a group of artists that handpicked the performers, as opposed to being curated solely by me or by Penn students. And it thrived because of the budgetary support of the university, which paid the performers, maintained the space, purchased a sound system, and more. Today, the Rotunda hosts free events each week and draws from the diversity of Greater Philadelphia's audiences to host one of the widest arrays of programming of any venue in Philadelphia.

Setting up and running the Rotunda was not always easy. I recall cold-calling community representatives such as the heads of the local neighborhood associations, telling them about the idea. One leader from Walnut Hill had harsh words for me, strongly doubting that any Penn undergraduate would follow through on these commitments to the community. She was justified in her wariness and disbelief. The record is littered with unfulfilled promises between Penn and West Philadelphia. Also, the work of setting up the Rotunda was painstaking. In the early days especially, it fell largely to a volunteer crew of undergraduate students who had a host of other academic and cocurricular priorities. And there were times when we got the programming wrong. I recall shows in those early days where the performers outnumbered the audience, even when it was a solo performance! Still, programming grew stronger as time went on, and the Rotunda began to attract a large and dedicated following.

Ira Harkavy's advocacy of the Rotunda and of my role at Penn led to my being appointed to a new position in Penn's Division of Facilities and Real Estate Services. I was now the cultural asset manager, responsible for bringing even more arts and culture onto and around the 40th Street corridor as a cultural component of Penn's West Philadelphia Initiatives.[2] I passed off the daily work of running the Rotunda to Gina Renzi, the incredibly talented director who runs it to this day, and focused on supporting the Slought Foundation (an art gallery and community space), the 40th Street Artist-in-Residency Program, the studio of Argentine American artist Osvaldo Romberg, Scribe Video Center, and more. It was an incredible time for arts and culture in the life of Penn and West Philadelphia. I held this position until 2008, when I left Penn to pursue a PhD in urban planning and public policy from Rutgers University. I was inspired by my work at the Rotunda and wanted to become an activist scholar, like my mentors at Penn. (At Rutgers, I found a mentor in Dr. Robert Lake, who is, like Ira Harkavy, a scholar of John Dewey and his ideas of cities and social justice. I doubt that this was a coincidence.)

Today, I lead the Urban Strategy graduate program at Drexel University's Antoinette Westphal College of Media Arts and Design. The Urban Strategy program, whose curriculum I codesigned and coauthored, has community engagement at its core. One of the required first-year courses is "Civic Engagement and Participatory Methods." I coteach it as a side-by-side course, with West Philadelphia residents enrolled in the course in equal numbers to Drexel students, learning together simultaneously. The focus of the course is how to be a changemaker in local communities, through intercultural dialogue, active listening, advanced group process, analysis of one's leadership style, and exposure to community changemakers who provide examples of their practice. This course has run in partnership with Monumental Baptist Church, the Enterprise Center, and the Drexel Writers Room. In addition to "Civic Engagement and Participatory Methods," I oversee several other CBL courses taught by other faculty in my program, covering areas as diverse as immigration and community codesign for literacy. Throughout my teaching and my research, I think and act carefully regarding the intersections between the university and the community, having learned these lessons early on from Drs. Harkvay and Benson. Currently, I am working on a book entitled *Democracy as Creative Practice: Weaving a Culture of Civic Life*. This effort would never have happened without my exposure to ABCS and the Rotunda. It is in direct lineage with my early exposure to these principles while at Penn.

Luckily, Drexel's commitment to community engagement has supported and bolstered my efforts to become a community-engaged teacher and scholar. Drexel's Lindy Center for Civic Engagement has provided me with training and ongoing support for my goals in CBL. Early in my time at Drexel, I undertook a three-day intensive training in which faculty learned about CBL as a cohort and spent a full day at SCI Graterford Prison, where we had the privilege of learning about engaged pedagogy from incarcerated members of the Inside-Out Think Tank who were trained in such methods. Since then, the development of the Urban Strategy program and its ongoing stewardship has been supported by members of the Lindy Center who have helped me map community engagement goals to the learning goals of the Urban Strategy curriculum and recruit community students to my side-by-side courses. Even in my tenure process, the community-based work that I did was called out for special attention, though such work did not replace traditional scholarly publications. In fact, this Netter retrospective may be the first time I have written about my CBL teaching for publication, though I have considered it in the past.

The ease with which I have been able to pursue CBL teaching and scholarship at Drexel does not mean that the work itself has been easy. CBL and side-by-side teaching take considerably more time, attention, and care than other forms of classroom teaching, without additional compensation for planning time or execution. I have been humbled by the challenges presented by working with neighborhood residents and Drexel students working together in community. One such challenge that I recall involved a prompt to students that active listening in community settings involved making eye contact. A community student explained firmly but with care that eye contact is not a norm in many cultures and may even be a sign of disrespect rather than a sign of communicative engagement. I have also faced challenges recruiting and retaining community students for my courses. It is sometimes tricky to find the right language and imagery (and advertising mechanisms) to entice community students to see the value in the course offerings of the Urban Strategy program.

There are other struggles inherent in this work as well, at least from my vantage point. One struggle relates to my own status as a community-engaged scholar and teacher. There are others around me, at Drexel and beyond, who seem to have forged more consistent and deeper connections with community partners. There are faculty who seem to have a social ease at making contacts beyond the walls of the university and sustaining them through care over time. There are those naturally gifted teachers who have bolstered these natural gifts with intensive study and reflection on community-engaged pedagogy. They understand the most effective and liberatory practices for this work. Relative to them, I often feel like a second-rate activist scholar, a vocal champion of this work who has not been able to invest the time and effort to do this work to its (exhausting) fullest. In a very real sense, this has to do with a very high teaching load, an administrative role running the Urban Strategy program, and the commitments I have made to coparenting my two children. None of these are meant to be excuses; they are just ways I notice others going the extra mile for their CBL work in ways that I would like to do but have not yet been able to do.

Another struggle is the unease I feel in doing community-engaged work in the neoliberal urban university. Despite their partnership rhetoric and their lofty aspirations to mutually beneficial relationships, I see universities doing much harm in the neighborhoods that surround them. Sometimes this harm looks like gentrification and displacement. Sometimes it looks like indicators (health, public safety, education) that seem not to move in a positive direction, even as the universities themselves continue to thrive and grow stronger. Sometimes it takes the form of research fatigue, when members of the surrounding communities are continually asked to participate in faculty and student research without receiving any real benefit that will change the material conditions of their lives. As I watch these disparities and inequities persist and grow—even and especially amid the talk of development without displacement, equitable development, or being the most civically engaged university in the country—I cannot help but think that the university uses our engagement work as a cover for the more pernicious effects of its real estate deals, endowment investments in fossil fuels, and other schemes. It sometimes feels like the university permits us to do this work as a distraction from the real anchor-led exploitation of local communities. I am not naïve enough to think that university administrators see it this way consciously. But the divergent rhetoric and reality can often be hard to ignore, or to swallow.

I can imagine two remedies for this, albeit partial ones (while we wait for a massive redistribution of wealth from the haves to the have-nots!). One is a serious dose of realism. The other is a sustained focus on people's positive capabilities.

A realistic assessment of the possibility of significant change is something that I think the Netter Center (at least when I was a student there) could do a better job of holding as a value and conveying to its students. University faculty and students are not going to be able to solve the problems of racial capitalism and neoliberal urbanism. We will not be able to overturn two centuries and counting of disparity between wealthy anchor institutions and the communities that surround them that struggle to survive and thrive. As much as I endorse Ira Harkavy's vision of a radically transformed urban university,[3] it is important while we wait for this transformation not to mislead faculty and students (particularly undergraduates) about the importance of their contributions in isolation. Sure, they can make meaningful contributions that stand the test of time. (I am thinking of the Agatston Urban Nutrition Initiative, or even the Rotunda, as examples.) But even with successful partnerships, we need to remain realistic about how much we can accomplish in a wildly inequitable urban environment.

A focus on people's ability to do and be what they are destined to do and be—an approach to human thriving pioneered conceptually by Amartya Sen and Martha Nussbaum[4]—can actually be taken as a lesson from the Netter Center's work and from the whole movement for community-engaged scholarship. We need to create the conditions for partnership that allow people the freedom to express what *they* would like to know about their communities, what *they* would like to see researchers focus on, and the ways in which the university can be of service to *their* priorities. This reframing of research, teaching, and partnership would radically recenter the demands and desires of community members and challenge the status quo. I believe the Rotunda has been successful because it is community driven, without an editorial agenda or ideological stance on the part of the university.

Of course, approaches like these are not always possible, especially in this increasingly reactionary and antidemocratic moment in which we find ourselves today. They are reliant on critical approaches that are not always accepted and that are now in some places derided as "woke" and demonized and banned. So, while I am sanguine about my own role in doing this work in Philadelphia over the next many years, I am concerned for my colleagues in conservative areas who must fight not only the issues I raised above but also the broader political climate in which they find themselves working.

Finally, I want to speak to the question of why I do this work. For me, the field of urbanism and urban studies depends on active, sustained, reciprocal engagement with communities of interest or identity and geographic communities. Universities cannot train the next generation of urbanists without engaging in real-world, collective problem-solving. I am familiar from my own training as an urban planner with the form of expertise that generates scads of data which it foists on community representatives to demand that they agree to the terms of engagement set by the planner, architect, city official, or developer on the assumption that the data marshaled by the expert has the force of superior argument. In these interactions, local, embedded knowledge is forsaken; historical oppressions and injustices are swept under the rug; and the mutual cocreation of place is denied. To train urbanists as I have been trained myself through my engagement with the Netter Center is to see multiple forms of knowledge and experience as essential to community development and urban planning. It means teaching students how to know themselves and their strengths and weaknesses so they can equitably engage with others across a power differential and make meaningful strides toward spatial and social justice.

I intend to continue this work as both a scholar and a teacher in the future because I believe the future of our cities depends on this form of dialogic practice. Community engagement has not only enabled me to grow personally in both humility and empathy. It has also taught me more about the

realpolitik of civic process than the idealized but unrealistic theories my professors promoted in grad school, which ignored the needs and desires of local
communities and enabled the whims of the powerful to prevail. These are the
rewards of community-based learning and scholarship as I see them in my
own evolving practice.

Notes

1. Laura Wolf-Powers, *University City: History, Race, and Community in the Era of the
Innovation District* (Philadelphia: University of Pennsylvania Press, 2022); John L. Puckett
and Mark Frazier Lloyd, *Becoming Penn: The Pragmatic American University, 1950–2000,*
Haney Foundation Series (Philadelphia: University of Pennsylvania Press, 2015); Harley F.
Etienne, *Pushing Back the Gates: Neighborhood Perspectives on University-Driven Revital-
ization in West Philadelphia,* repr. ed. (Philadelphia: Temple University Press, 2013).

2. John Kromer and Lucy Kerman, *West Philadelphia Initiatives: A Case Study in Urban
Revitalization,* (Philadelphia: University of Pennsylvania, Fels Institute of Government,
2004); Judith Rodin, *The University and Urban Revival: Out of the Ivory Tower and into the
Streets* (Philadelphia: University of Pennsylvania Press, 2007), philadelphiabattlefields
.org/wp-content/uploads/2020/05/WESTPHILADELPHIAINITIATIVES.pdf.

3. Ira Harkavy, "Dewey, Implementation, and Creating a Democratic Civic University," *Pluralist* 18, no. 1 (Apr. 1, 2023): 49–75, doi.org/10.5406/19446489.18.1.06.

4. Amartya Sen, "Development as Capability Expansion," in *Human Development
and the International Development Strategy for the 1990s,* ed. Keith B. Griffin and John B.
Knight, 41–58 (Basingstoke: Macmillan, 1990); Martha C. Nussbaum, *Creating Capabilities: The Human Development Approach* (Cambridge, MA: Belknap, 2011), site.ebrary
.com/id/10488676; Andrew Zitcer, Julie Hawkins, and Neville Vakharia, "A Capabilities
Approach to Arts and Culture? Theorizing Community Development in West Philadelphia," *Planning Theory & Practice* 17, no. 1 (2016): 35–51.

CHAPTER 9

University-Community Partnerships: How Students Help Cities Tackle Urgent Challenges

David Park and Jiyoung Park

An Unlikely Engineering Thesis
(and Service-Learning Case Study)

I remember the advice Netter Center leaders Dr. Ira Harkavy and Cory Bow-man gave me in 2000, something to the effect of, "David, you're in the School of Engineering and *Applied* Science, it's not just *book knowledge*." What was I, an engineering student, doing with the Netter Center anyway? Everyone else was in sociology, education, or some other noble field to improve the greater good through *social* sciences, not *hard* sciences. And what was I doing with the Netter Center, when I was barely passing my computer science and engineering classes? I did not have time for this. And yet the task at hand was so urgent, I couldn't *not* do it. I felt compelled, *called* to the work. So I threw myself into it and was forever changed.

The Netter Center is an incubator that takes ideas on how to change the world and gives it form—arms, legs, and muscles. You bring the heart and do the work. That's how my idea for the Program to Bridge the Digital Divide was birthed into a living, breathing thing in 2000. It all seemed to come out of nowhere, magically, catching me unaware. But in truth, its origin was quite ordinary: it came out of a storage closet.

In the summer of 1999, I worked in a Penn biomedical research lab using computer simulations to study the effects of anesthetics on brain neurons. My first week, the office manager asked me to clear my desk and set up a new computer station. In the process, I placed old IT equipment in a storage closet down the hall. The closet, an old, converted office, fifteen-by-ten feet with a small window, housed old computers and monitors stacked to the ceiling, along with countless boxes of keyboards, mice, and speakers. Sun-faded blue carpet, a thin layer of dust everywhere. I asked the office manager about the old equipment, and she said it was from prior research grant programs, no longer needed. It got me thinking: *This is a lot of waste, but let me focus on my job.*

A month later, as I helped a new lab mate set up his desk, I again took old computer equipment to the same dusty storage closet down the hall. In a month's time, more equipment had accumulated, outdated but still functional. I thought back to a need for computers I'd seen while tutoring at a West Philadelphia elementary school the prior academic year. The school had a lab with about twenty-five computers, but fewer than ten worked, so large classes had three to four students per machine, taking turns. I asked the office manager if the old equipment in the closet could be donated to the community. She didn't know but would ask around. The answer, a couple months later, was yes.

Out of that closet, my college career took a sharp turn. I learned about the Netter Center from a Penn newsletter and connected with the Center's Isabel Sampson-Mapp. From there, in the Netter Center womb, my idea evolved into the Program to Bridge the Digital Divide in a matter of months. During that time, the Center imprinted DNA for the program by

- advertising across the Penn community for old computers to recycle and volunteers to help;
- finding space on campus to process old, decommissioned computers;
- guiding me to a grant opportunity and supporting development of a SeedCo/AmeriCorps grant application;
- connecting me to the Penn IT roundtable, a group of university administrators who helped me to establish processes for wiping and transporting the computers and to develop and deliver computer-skills training in the community;
- identifying other key stakeholders and allies across Penn with whom to partner; and
- connecting me with community leaders across the city to better assess and help meet the need.

The Netter Center was well-connected across Penn and across the city, particularly in West Philadelphia. One of my first forays into the community was at a faith forum on after-school programs organized by the Netter Center in partnership with local communities of faith, particularly Black churches in West Philadelphia. I leaned into civic engagement as the *applied* component of my academic journey, and this work became my nontraditional engineering thesis: "Building Community Technology Hubs to Foster Partnerships in Education." My thesis adviser and the engineering department took some convincing, requiring several emails and in-person meetings. I remember my adviser asking, "What *technical* challenge are you taking on?" I said something to the effect of, "I'll be learning computer science by teaching it." I'm not sure they were convinced, but they eventually approved it. This was not what they or I had envisioned for my academic path, but it became my calling.

According to the US Census Current Population Survey, in 2000, half of all households nationally had a computer and 40 percent had access to the internet at home. For Black households, in stark contrast, less than one-third of households had a computer and less than one-quarter had internet access.[1] In 2000, three-quarters of West Philadelphia households were Black, and the poverty rate in West Philadelphia was 21 percent,[2] almost double the national rate of 11 percent.[3] Without the necessary computer skills, West Philadelphia residents would have been left behind, as more than half of jobs required the use of a computer.[4]

The Program to Bridge the Digital Divide provided computers, job skills training, and technical assistance to underserved communities across Philadelphia. From 2000 to 2002, we placed more than five hundred computers in over twenty-five underserved schools, recreation centers, and faith communities. We developed and delivered instruction to more than five hundred students across over forty community sites.[5] For high schools, for example, we developed and delivered a geospatial mapping class for ecology students, a digital video and web animation course for art students, and current tech trends and job information for juniors and seniors in a career seminar. For the broader community, we created computer literacy job training for adults, a basic tech skills train-the-trainer course, and other programs. We connected businesses, universities, and health systems to electronics salvaging companies, diverting nearly three tons of electronic waste from landfills. We had over twenty part-time staff and more than forty volunteers. All this was possible because the Netter Center gave life to an idea that came from a dusty closet.

With continued guidance from Netter Center mentors, the program became a national model replicated in six cities across the country. We convened a national conference in 2002, where we provided training to this network of replicated programs. We met a need at a time when computer reuse and recycling programs were emerging and not yet commonplace. Over the years, the program evolved, and its mission and heartbeat currently resides with School of Engineering student projects, while computer recycling now resides with the university's Office of Environmental Health and Radiation Safety. By 2021, the digital divide in West Philadelphia had lessened; 88 percent of households had a computer, tablet, or smartphone, and 78 percent had access to the internet.[6]

The areas of need I witnessed in underresourced West Philadelphia left an impression on me, inspiring me to lean into civic engagement. The Netter Center instilled in me the importance of being civically engaged and gave me the know-how to be civically effective no matter your career field, and that has stuck with me.

Partnerships Tackling the Most Urgent Challenges of Our Time

Fast-forward nearly twenty-five years. "Bridging the divide" has served as a metaphor and motto for my life, from that dusty storage closet that birthed the Program to Bridge the Digital Divide until now. The Netter Center imprinted this mission on my life, no turning back. What are the divides we can bridge today, and how do we do it? How do we break down barriers and build connections across people, organizations, and networks to solve urgent and complex societal problems?

In my work since graduating from Penn, I have seen that a large part of the answer to these questions are university-community partnerships based on the model of the Netter Center and its three founding principles, as described by Dr. Harkavy:

1. Universities and their communities are intertwined.
2. Penn can do a great deal to improve the quality of life in the community as its largest employer, purchaser of goods and services, and landholder. Most importantly, students—idealistic, creative,

caring—and faculty and staff are crucial to improving the quality of life in the city.
3. This work isn't just for the community; it's mutually beneficial. Through it, Penn becomes a greater research university, a greater contributor to knowledge, and more effective in developing better citizens and lifelong contributors to a democratic society.[7]

Of these three founding principles, I have seen foremost in my work the idea that students are crucial to improving the quality of life in the city. In other words, universities embody a vital human resource to help tackle challenges facing cities. I have seen how local academic expertise and resources can help respond to some of the greatest challenges of our time, from natural disasters to the COVID-19 pandemic to poverty. And I can imagine how enriching the experience must be for students, to learn from and contribute to solving such urgent real-world problems.

Much of my career has been with nationally focused nonprofit organizations working alongside government at the local, state, and federal levels. As valuable as our research and advocacy services were, we were not anchored in a local community; that was not our role. Where we collaborated with local higher-education institutions, our work benefited, and where we did not, their absence was felt. Changemaking requires an ecosystem. When localities lack resources to conduct in-depth research and analysis, for example, large research organizations can help at scale. When solutions require additional brainpower or boots on the ground, local universities can and should step in. After all, in Dr. Harkavy's summation, local university-community partnerships serve as real-world learning sites in which community members and academics work together on a complex problem and determine whether the work is making a difference.[8]

More than 1,800 lives lost; more than a million people displaced; and $190 billion (in 2022 dollars) in damage. And that was just the first of two devastating storms when 125-mph winds and torrential rains wreaked havoc along Louisiana's Gulf Coast in 2005.[9] As part of a Brookings Institution team, I worked with the Louisiana Recovery Authority and federal, state, and local partners on economic redevelopment planning after Hurricanes Katrina and Rita. Our focus was building on existing economic strengths of the region, and Louisiana State University students and professors provided critical background on the economic history of southern Louisiana that served as a foundation for our efforts.

When COVID-19 swept around the globe and was declared a pandemic by the World Health Organization, communities scrambled to respond. Globally, there have been more than 760 million confirmed cases of COVID-19 and nearly seven million deaths.[10] While my work at the National League of Cities (NLC) focused on advocating for COVID-19 relief for cities,[11] I encountered stories of how communities benefited from university partnerships. For example, with the University of Maryland Medical Center, John Hopkins Medicine, and a community group, Baltimore City deployed mobile test sites where case rates were high. These teaching hospitals' medical students and residents helped set up tented clinics and drive-through testing,[12] whereas nonteaching hospitals did not have medical students or residents to deploy.

One of the most intractable challenges facing communities is poverty, with nearly 38 million people living in poverty in the United States (11.6 percent of the population).[13] In 2007, while at Brookings, I developed an economic model to assess the benefits of an expanded Earned Income Tax Credit (EITC). The EITC provides substantial support to low- and moderate-income working parents who claim a qualifying child,[14] and my model identified characteristics of benefiting households, such as race, age, and occupation. A Brookings convening disseminated the model,[15] which several cities, states, and research institutions adopted to advance antipoverty initiatives. For example, New York City adopted it in 2008 to identify households for a conditional cash transfer program that lifted 4,800 families out of poverty, prompting them to open bank accounts and save.[16] While no universities directly supported our work, local university partnerships would be invaluable to help cities assess antipoverty programs and determine which approaches are most effective over the long term.

For vulnerable populations, even parking tickets can yield dire outcomes. Consequences of unpaid fines and fees can include driver's license suspension, which can present a significant barrier to employment, child care, or medical appointments; bad credit reports that can impede home rental or purchase; and in some cases, jail time.[17] A 2017 US Commission on Civil Rights report compiles findings of the impact. In California, one in six licenses were suspended for failure to pay a citation, affecting four million drivers. In New Jersey, 42 percent of suspended drivers lost their jobs due to license suspensions. In Benton County, Washington, 25 percent of those jailed for misdemeanors were in for nonpayment of fines and court fees.[18] Such devastating consequences can trigger cycles of debt and poverty. At NLC, I adapted my EITC model to help cities in a pilot program understand the impact of fines and fees. It may be too early for our pilot program to share findings, but it's not too early to appreciate that local universities can support this kind of work in their communities. For example, Georgetown University's Masters in Data Science and Analytics students have begun to assist the Washington, DC, Office of Financial Empowerment and Education in examining the impact of traffic fines and fees on previously incarcerated citizens.

Why Cities Need University-Community Partnerships

Cities need university partnerships not only to meet the most urgent challenges of our time but also to deliver ongoing programs and services that improve the quality of life for all residents. Indeed, university-community partnerships foster the socioeconomic health of the surrounding community and benefit universities themselves (in other words, a healthy environment is critical to the well-being and retention of residents, employees, and students).[19]

According to the Urban Institute, "Anchor institutions can provide the stable backstop needed to change communities over many years, as public officials come and go."[20] I saw this truth in action while advising a Tennessee city on a potential program to create local manufacturing jobs among under-served populations.[21] The mayor's office invited local universities to partner, but the universities declined, half citing a lack of resources, and the initiative lost steam. A civically minded university partner would have bolstered the effort, which we modeled after Portland Made, a program that Portland State University spearheaded and has sustained over a decade and counting.[22] The program has nurtured an ecosystem that created twenty-five thousand manufacturing jobs while other cities saw such jobs decline.[23]

That wouldn't be the last time I encountered missed opportunities. At NLC, I work with local elected officials across the country, whether mayors, council members, or their staff. At a recent conference, I spoke with a professor from a university in New Jersey who said his school was not engaged with its city; I also spoke with a council member for a large city in Nevada who said he and his fellow council members were not engaged with their local university but wished they were. I hear these anecdotes all too often. On a positive note, in recent conversations with St. Louis officials, I learned that Washington University students and faculty have provided program evaluation services to the city. Over the years, I've observed that program evaluation and complex data analyses represent a consistent challenge among cities due to limited resources and staff capacity, so it's heartening to hear Washington University supports St. Louis in this way. I can't imagine a city that would not welcome and benefit from such assistance from local universities.

A tale of two North Carolina cities illustrates my next point, namely, that students can also be an immense resource for cities seeking funding for critical projects and programs. Specifically, grant proposal preapplication work such as background research and project scoping can be a tremendous help. Two North Carolina cities sought federal and state grants to fund parking garage renovations as part of downtown revitalization efforts. One engaged local urban-planning students in the project scoping process, while the other spent scarce funds with a consultant because they didn't have a university partner. Universities represent a large and vital human resource that cities would be remiss not to leverage, and students gain valuable real-world experience in return.

If local universities do not engage their cities in long-term partnerships, cities have much to lose. If they do, cities have much to gain. As summarized by Vanderbilt University's Center for Teaching, community benefits of student engagement include valuable human resources to achieve community goals, new energy and perspectives applied to community work, and enhanced community-university relations.[24] Empirical data from a 2017 Boise State University study offer additional insight about how communities benefit from student engagement. Surveyed community organizations report being satisfied and benefiting from working with students and appreciating the energy, creativity, and enthusiasm students brought to their organizations. For the most part, those organizations used the products, services, and skills the students provided and reported that the student work made a moderate to large impact.[25]

Another indicator of community benefit is the longevity of partner relationships. The Netter Center has maintained strong ties with West Philadelphia organizations over the years. I worked with Metropolitan Baptist Church and the Philadelphia Masjid in the early 2000s, and more than twenty years later, I saw leaders from those congregations at the Netter Center's thirtieth anniversary celebration earlier this year.

Students also have much to gain from service-learning experiences, as I did. University-community partnerships help students as well as the community. A recent St. John's College study found that "service learners acquired knowledge about local and national politics, developed an appreciation of the diverse backgrounds and characteristics of community recipients, and increased their confidence in their ability to make a difference in the community."[26] This rings true for me personally. My Netter Center experience at Penn awakened in me a sociopolitical awareness and civic engagement that I have carried with me throughout my academic, professional, and personal life. Dr. Harkavy captures this idea as he invokes John Dewey: "Democracy must begin at home, and its home is the engaged neighborly college or university and its local community partners."[27]

Finally, service learning can lead to deeper, longer-term community service relationships and perhaps students choosing to stay in the community after graduating. The same St. John's College study showed that students "changed their preconceived notions about the community, learned to interact with people who are culturally different and discovered commonalities, and developed tolerant attitudes toward cultural differences. Students formed relationships with community recipients and sustained these relationships and their involvement beyond the initial service."[28] That was certainly true for me. I stayed in West Philadelphia for two years after I graduated to continue the work, until my graduate education, inspired by my Netter Center experience, took me to Washington, DC, to study public policy.

How Cities and Universities Can Build Partnerships

While much of my personal experience has focused on students engaging in service learning, other parts of the Netter Center's strategic university-community partnership framework also represent significant opportunities to help cities. I would be remiss not to make this broader appeal for their benefit. Universities can make a positive community impact as workforce developer, employer, real estate developer, purchaser, incubator, and adviser–network builder.[29] For example, in the 1980s, what is now the Netter Center started workforce development programs for K–12 students. Penn's efforts expanded to adults in the 1990s. In 2009, adult workforce development programs evolved to provide direct connections to specific opportunities at Penn and Penn's Health System as well as other local anchor institutions through the West Philadelphia Skills Initiative.[30] In my hometown, Johns Hopkins University has invested heavily in its neighborhood's East Baltimore Development Initiative, which focuses on building affordable housing and nurturing local, small minority-owned businesses through procurement and financial assistance.[31] Downstream, universities can strategically repurpose assets, as we did with Penn's computers for the Digital Divide program. The previously cited Portland Made program is an incubating effort out of Portland State University.[32]

While building such comprehensive university-community partnerships may seem like a daunting task, the Netter Center's *Anchor Institutions Toolkit: A Guide for Neighborhood Revitalization* is a useful resource to help universities establish and strengthen partnerships with their cities. (The resources and recommendations referenced in the following section, "How the Netter Center Can Help," also may provide useful insights.) Here are three steps from the *Anchor Institutions Toolkit* that universities can begin today and that cities can encourage their local universities to undertake:

1. Conduct a self-assessment: Universities can review the *Toolkit* and conduct a self-assessment of their assets and capacities to engage with their cities.
2. Reach out to potential collaborators: Though institutions may not have all the necessary resources, they can partner to leverage resources collectively for the greater good of the community. Each potential partner's self-assessment will reveal strengths and resources that can be leveraged.
3. Start small while thinking big: Go for quick wins where you have resources and can demonstrate results and create momentum. All while fleshing out a multi-pronged, holistic, long-term strategy that may evolve over the years.[33]

In Washington, DC, where I've lived for two decades, I believe university-community partnerships face an uphill battle due in large part to the prominence of national and international interests that often overshadow local issues in our nation's capital. Against this backdrop, there's all the more need to collaborate and pool resources to focus on local community issues. Georgetown University, my graduate alma mater, has many notable service-learning programs,[34] such as its widely recognized Prisons and Justice Initiative that empowers incarcerated citizens through degree coursework at the DC jail, where I had the privilege of guest lecturing.[35] Washington's other civically engaged universities include American, Catholic, Gallaudet, George Washington, Howard, Trinity, and the University of the District of Columbia, each with unique assets and capacities to leverage.[36] While helpful, Washington universities' community engagement efforts could amplify with greater collaboration.

As one local university administrator told me in confidence, university efforts in DC are more competitive than collaborative, with each institution in its own lane worrying about its own funding. Other cities facing a similar challenge and opportunity likewise may see fit to prioritize collaboration.

It's through partnering with universities and other anchor institutions that Penn has amplified its efforts, starting small. During my freshman year, Penn's UC Brite initiative repaired streetlamps in West Philadelphia, which had an immediate, tangible impact by making students and neighborhood residents feel safer walking around at night. That was one early component of a multipronged, holistic, and integrated approach that continues today, in partnership with a regional network of anchor institutions.[37] This type of collaboration provides a useful model for Washington, DC, and other cities.[38]

How the Netter Center Can Help

More cities need more models like the Netter Center to shape college students' academic journeys—to captivate students in engineering and related fields like me, to detour and change their lives, to spark passion and purpose. To tap the human resource of service learning for students' academic and life enrichment and the community's benefit. Having lived the experience in Philadelphia, and having lived in and worked with cities with similar community needs and gaps, I humbly offer the following five ideas the Netter Center can consider to help cities successfully replicate its model and create "democratic civic universities"[39] in the future.

First, expand efforts to connect students from across disciplines to the Netter Center's work. Connecting computer-science students with the Netter Center's work intentionally rather than by happenstance (as was my case) could expand the Center's reach across campus and beyond. If more Wharton School business students were involved, imagine the social impact business ideas that might emerge. A mandatory requirement that every Penn undergraduate and graduate student take at least one ABCS course would embed the principles of a "democratic civic university" within each Penn student—as Georgetown University, my graduate alma mater, requires introductory theology and philosophy courses for each undergraduate and graduate student as part of its Jesuit tradition.

Second, continue to capture stories, measure and quantify results, document learnings, and publicize them to expand the Netter Center's reach and impact and grow the movement of democratic civic universities. Perhaps students from Penn's Fels Institute of Government and School of Social Policy and Practice can assist with this effort.

Third, update and repackage the 2008 *Anchor Institutions Toolkit* into a concise, executive-level format that cities and their potential partner institutions can easily navigate to assess their partnership fit and plan a partnership strategy. Perhaps Annenberg School for Communication students can assist with distilling the 125 pages of Philadelphia-centric wisdom into graphic and actionable takeaways, tools, templates, and case studies for a wide, non-academic audience in cities across the country. Developing a companion training program for faculty, students, and staff at universities across the country to replicate the Netter Center work would be an additional valuable resource.

Fourth, actively engage with current students, faculty, and alumni to establish and strengthen partnerships in their hometowns or where they currently live. Formalize and strengthen the Netter Center's alumni network in parallel with or as part of existing Penn Alumni chapters to engage with campus efforts and mobilize in their respective communities. Creating a step-by-step guide for alumni to mobilize interest and resources in their local communities to replicate the Netter Center model would be a valuable tool to assist with alumni efforts.

Finally, partner with civil society organizations such as the National Civic League, International Town and Gown Association, National Governors Association, National Association of Counties, US Conference of Mayors, and National League of Cities (my current employer) to share best practices and help other communities adopt the Netter Center model of building and sustaining partnerships to drive community change. Partnerships with these civil society organizations could be as simple as offering webinars to introduce the model and technical assistance to replicate the model in their communities.

I have returned to the Penn campus over the years to reconnect with the Netter Center's work. It was a seminal part of my undergraduate experience and beyond. My wife of fifteen years once remarked that she never fully understood my passion for civic engagement via service learning until she attended a Center panel with me several years ago. Hearing from other students, alumni, and Dr. Harkavy, she now understands the passion and purpose that the Netter Center nurtured in all of us and the systematic way in which we carried out the work across the city. The power of the Center's collective testimony to ignite and inspire others is palpable. Together with Penn alumni and other civic and academic leaders across the country, I hope we can harness that power and replicate the Netter Center model in Washington, DC, my home, and in many cities beyond. In Dr. Harkavy's words, "If you're going to do this, you can't bring change just in Philadelphia, West Philadelphia, and Penn; you need to . . . share those ideas and spread them to the rest of the country and around the world."[40]

Notes

1. Eric Newburger, US Census Bureau, *Home Computers and Internet Use in the United States: August 2000,* (Washington, DC: US Government Printing Office, Sept. 2001), 3, www.census.gov/content/dam/Census/library/publications/2001/demo/p23 -207.pdf.

2. University of Pennsylvania, West Philadelphia Community History Center, 2000 Census Tracts, accessed Oct. 20, 2023, westphillyhistory.archives.upenn.edu/statistics /census/2000.

3. Joseph Dalaker, US Census Bureau, Current Population Reports, Series P60-214, *Poverty in the United States: 2000* (Washington, DC: US Government Printing Office, Sept. 2001), 1, www2.census.gov/library/publications/2001/demographics/p60-214.pdf.

4. US Bureau of Labor Statistics, "Computer and Internet Use at Work Summary," last modified Aug. 10, 2005, www.bls.gov/news.release/ciuaw.nr0.htm.

5. "University of Pennsylvania's AmeriCorps Program to Bridge the Digital Divide," 2002, accessed Oct. 20, 2023, web.archive.org/web/20021217025322/http://www.upenn .edu/ccp/digitaldivide/.

6. Author's tabulation using 2021 American Community Survey five-year data compiled for West Philadelphia zip codes: 19104, 19131, 19139, 19143, and 19151. See "2017–2021 ACS 5-Year Data Profile," U.S. Census Bureau, accessed Oct. 20, 2023, https://www.census.gov/acs/www/data/data-tables-and-tools/data-profiles/2021/.

7. Dave Zeitlin, "Ode to Ira," *Pennsylvania Gazette* 121, no. 6 (July/Aug. 2023): 32–37, thepenngazette.com/ode-to-ira/.

8. Ira Harkavy, "Dewey, Implementation, and Creating a Democratic Civic University," *Pluralist* 18, no. 1 (Spring 2023), www.nettercenter.upenn.edu/sites/default/files /Harkavy_Dewey_Implementation_Pluralist_2023_0.pdf.

9. National Weather Service, "Hurricane Katrina: A Look Back 15 Years Later," 2020, accessed Oct. 20, 2023, www.weather.gov/lix/katrina_anniversary; The Data Center, "Facts for Features: Katrina Impact," Aug. 26, 2016, www.datacenterresearch.org /data-resources/katrina/facts-for-impact/.

10. As reported by the World Health Organization as of July 19, 2023, covid19 .who.int/.

11. We worked to analyze data and advocate for passage of what became the American Rescue Plan Act that provided direct financial assistance and public health resources to states and local governments.

12. Tina Lee, Brooks Rainwater, and David Park, "Disaggregated Data by Race and Ethnicity Can Help Us Get Closer to Recovery COVID-19," National League of Cities, Aug. 25, 2020, www.nlc.org/article/2020/08/25/disaggregated-data-by-race-and -ethnicity-can-help-us-get-closer-to-recovery-from-covid-19/.

13. John Creamer, Emily A. Shrider, Kalee Burns, and Frances Chen, US Census Bureau, Current Population Reports, P60-277, *Poverty in the United States: 2021* (Washington, DC: US Government Printing Office, Sept. 13, 2022), www.census.gov/library /publications/2022/demo/p60-277.html.

14. Urban-Brookings Tax Policy Center, Briefing Book, accessed Oct. 20, 2023, www.taxpolicycenter.org/briefing-book/what-earned-income-tax-credit.

15. New York City Center for Economic Opportunity, *The CEO Poverty Measure* (Aug. 2008), vi, www.nyc.gov/assets/opportunity/pdf/08_poverty_measure_report.pdf.

16. James Riccio, Nadine Dechausay, Cynthia Miller, Stephen Nuñez, Nandita Verma, and Edith Yang, *Conditional Cash Transfers in New York City: The Continuing Story of the Opportunity NYC–Family Rewards Demonstration* (New York: MDRC, Sept. 2013), iii, www.mdrc.org/sites/default/files/Conditional_Cash_Transfers_FR%202-18-16.pdf.

17. US Commission on Civil Rights, *Targeted Fines and Fees Against Communities of Color: Civil Rights & Constitutional Implications* (Washington, DC: US Commission on Civil Rights, Sept. 2017), 72, www.usccr.gov/files/pubs/docs/Statutory_Enforcement _Report2017.pdf.

18. US Commission on Civil Rights, *Targeted Fines and Fees,* 38.

19. Netter Center for Community Partnerships, *Anchor Institutions Toolkit: A Guide for Neighborhood Revitalization* (Philadelphia: University of Pennsylvania, Mar. 2008), 11, www.nettercenter.upenn.edu/sites/default/files/Anchor_Toolkit6_09.pdf.

20. Brett Theodos, *The East Baltimore Development Initiative: A Long-Term Impact Evaluation of a Comprehensive Community Initiative* (Washington, DC: Urban Institute, Nov. 2022), 48, www.urban.org/sites/default/files/2022-10/The%20East%20Baltimore %20Development%20Initiative.pdf.

21. This advisory work was with the Urban Land Institute, a real estate development and land use network.

22. Greg Schrock and Mark Foggin, *The State of Urban Manufacturing: Portland City Snapshot* (Portland, OR: Urban Manufacturing Alliance and Portland State University, June 18, 2018): 12–16, www.urbanmfg.org/wp-content/uploads/2018/06/UMA -State-of-Urban-Manufacturing-Portland-City-Snapshot.pdf.

23. Author's calculation of Bureau of Labor Statistics data comparing 2018 and 2023 manufacturing jobs.

24. Joe Bandy, "What Is Service Learning or Community Engagement?" Vanderbilt University Center for Teaching, 2011, accessed Oct. 20, 2023, cft.vanderbilt.edu/guides -sub-pages/teaching-through-community-engagement/.

25. Nancy Vizenor, Tasha J. Souza, and Joshua Jordan Ertmer, "Benefits of Participating in Service-Learning, Business-Related Classes: Assessing the Impact on the Community Partners," *Journal of Research in Business Education* 58, no. 1 (2017): 8, scholarworks.boisestate.edu/cgi/viewcontent.cgi?article=1009&context=ctl_teaching.

26. Lori Simons and Beverly Cleary, "The Influence of Service Learning on Students' Personal and Social Development," *College Teaching* 54, no. 4 (2006): 316, www.stjohns.edu/sites/default/files/uploads/asl-influence-on-development.pdf.

27. Harkavy, "Dewey," 57.

28. Simons and Cleary, "Influence," 316.

29. Netter Center, *Anchor Institutions Toolkit*, 18.

30. "About Us," West Philadelphia Skills Initiative, accessed Oct. 20, 2023, philadelphiaskills.org/about/.

31. "Core Values," East Baltimore Development, Inc., accessed Oct. 20, 2023, www.ebdi.org/core_values.

32. Schrock and Foggin, *State of Urban Manufacturing*, 10.

33. Netter Center, *Anchor Institutions Toolkit*, 19, 109, 119.

34. Georgetown University's service-learning engagement includes its Prisons and Justice Initiative; fifty-year-old Street Law program, in which law students teach Washington, DC, high school students practical law; Center for Social Justice, through which my wife, Jiyoung, tutored elementary students; Masters in Data Science and Analytics, which is supporting Washington, DC, to assess the impact of fines and fees on previously incarcerated citizens; McCourt School of Public Policy, which recently began a partnership with Howard University on an environmental data science initiative; and the umbrella Office of Community Engagement.

35. At a national level, the Prisons and Justice Initiative conducts legal research to overturn wrongful convictions.

36. American University has the Center for Community Engagement and Service; Catholic University, its Service and Justice Campus Ministry; George Washington University, the Honey W. Nashman Center for Civic Engagement and Public Service; Howard, its Experiential Learning program; and the University of the District of Columbia, its Community Outreach program. Enrollment across the aforementioned eight universities exceeds eighty-five thousand students—a human resource of remarkable size, comparable to that of a large global corporation. For enrollment figures, see National Center for Education Statistics Search for Schools and Colleges, accessed Oct. 20, 2023, nces.ed.gov/globallocator/.

37. The Netter Center collaborates through the Philadelphia Higher Education Network for Neighborhood Development (PHENND), a thirty-member network founded in 1987 with five universities and colleges. Its mission is to build "capacity of its member institutions to develop mutually beneficial, sustained, and democratic community-based service-learning partnership." PHENND provides technical assistance and training to member institutions and community nonprofits through workshops and one-on-one consultations and serves as a clearinghouse of resources such as grant and partnership

opportunities. See "History," PHENND, accessed Oct. 20, 2023, phennd.org/about /history/.

38. At the national level, universities share best practices and resources via the Campus Compact network, a membership organization focused on student civic and community engagement. Both Penn and Georgetown are members. See "Membership," Campus Compact, accessed Oct. 20, 2023, compact.org/membership.

39. Harkavy, "Dewey," 53.

40. Zeitlin, "Ode to Ira."

CHAPTER 10

Food, Policy, Social Justice, Civic Engagement, and Epidemiology

Tamara Dubowitz

In April 2024, when I was just short of eighteen years at the RAND Corporation, I moved to the University of Pittsburgh School of Public Health as professor and chair of the Department of Epidemiology. After developing and leading large multidisciplinary research projects at RAND for nearly two decades, I was ready to take on a new role in a different environment. At RAND, I dedicated my career to building research, policy, and trans- and multidisciplinary teams, leading projects across research organizations, academic institutions, and communities. My new role is allowing me to share my experience and passion in a setting where I can support my colleagues as well as the next generation of public health scholars and practitioners. But my interests in urban health, health disparities, and policy translation started early on—grounded in issues of justice and civic engagement. It has taken a lifetime of cumulative experiences and training, including my critically important experience at Penn, to bring me to where I am today.

In 1977, when I was three years old, my (white, Eastern European–descended Jewish) parents left an apartheid-ridden South Africa and immigrated to a small coal-mining town in Pennsylvania. How and why we got there is a separate story, but growing up in this small, predominantly rural setting was a critical life experience. Only a small fraction of my high school class continued to a four-year college. The vast majority found jobs in the area or entered military service. Many of my friends were on what were then called food stamps, and a good handful lived in subsidized housing. This experience was juxtaposed with the knowledge that my family had left a country because of its institutionalized racism, which left a great majority of the South African population without basic rights or even the slimmest chance at comfort, let alone prosperity. These formative years of my life introduced me firsthand to issues of social justice and the impact of socio-economic status, race, and geography on individual outcomes, both short term and lifelong.

When I left Pottsville, Pennsylvania (the home of Yuengling Beer and the famous twentieth-century novelist John O'Hara, who parodied the town and its parochial inhabitants in his early work), to attend the University of Pennsylvania, I was met with more juxtapositions as well as my first major urban experience. One of the hardest adjustments was integrating with the population of wealthy and privileged kids from much higher-quality suburban and prep schools, who were at least theoretically my peers. I felt dramatically underprepared for the classroom rigors of Penn, and it took time for me to find my feet. My self-doubt was quickly replaced by growing excitement and confidence once I abandoned the pre-med track for anthropology. Anthropology was an amazing match for me. I was able to situate my own life and experience within a discipline that exists to study the interplay of cultural, social, economic, political, natural, and environmental factors in humans and their communities. My training offered a framework for me to understand my own experiences and allowed me to better understand Pottsville and West Philadelphia, the two places I thought of as home at the time.

My work with the Center for Community Partnerships (what is now the Netter Center) started in 1993, when I enrolled in Professor Frank Johnston's anthropology course, a fairly new Academically Based Community Service (ABCS) course that was involved with running what we called the Turner Nutritional Awareness Program. The course aimed to understand how and why the nutrition and diet of residents and especially of kids in urban neighborhoods were substandard. At the time, Frank would have Penn undergraduates visit Turner Middle School and teach nutrition to sixth graders. For my nineteen-year-old self, teaching nutrition to West Philadelphia middle school students quickly turned into a learning opportunity in and of itself. I knew very little about diet and nutrition and was teaching it to kids who lived a different life in a different world than mine. There was a convenience store across the street from Turner Middle School where many of the kids would stop on their way to and from school. What was the Penn student providing nutrition education doing? Who was benefiting? Was any of it changing the behavior of middle school students?

Alas, at the time, I concluded that the greatest value coming out of this ABCS class was that Penn students were being exposed to a different community and world. And thus began my educational journey to think much more deeply about structural inequities of food and nutrition access and about potential solutions. I realized that low-resource conditions, whether they be in urban areas like West Philly or in areas like rural Pennsylvania, shared commonalities. I was challenged to think deeply about how conditions were baked into people's lives and how solutions required addressing the root causes of inequities.

It didn't take too much longer for my friend and fellow undergraduate at the time, Danny Gerber, and I to write an application for a five-hundred-dollar grant from Penn to branch off and start what is now the Agatston Urban Nutrition Initiative at the Netter Center. At the time, we proposed that this money kick-start a youth-centered entrepreneurial arrangement where Turner Middle School students designed and implemented an after-school fruit and vegetable business, Fruits 'R Us (and Vegetables, Too). Our goal was to create a business led, directed, and run by the middle school students themselves that would change access to healthy after-school options. We envisioned this as a way to provide an alternative to the junk food that Turner students were buying on their way to and from school, and we hypothesized that the more involved the Turner students were in the effort, the more successful it would be with sales. In the event, our hypothesis was evaluated by undergraduates taking ABCS classes. As part of her senior thesis in 2000, Anna Schwartz found that Turner Middle School students involved with fruit-stand activities were significantly more likely to make at least one purchase from the stand and that their parents were more likely to know about the fruit stand.[1] This new approach was one that sought to create systemic change in what Turner Middle School students were learning and in how they were acting with respect to diet. The "fruit stand" was operated after school and on weekends for students, staff, parents, and members of the community. During the next few years, the Urban Nutrition Initiative began the process of linking the class to external activities in an integrated curriculum of health promotion designed to change behavior and improve community nutrition and health status.

Over time, the Urban Nutrition Initiative evolved into a multifaceted program with school gardens, a community fitness program, a thematic curriculum, summer programs, and urban agriculture and microbusiness development. Today, the Agatston Urban Nutrition Initiative (AUNI) has taken a much larger and more comprehensive shape. It has funding from the Pennsylvania Supplemental Nutrition Assistance Program Education program and offers hands-on school-day, after-school, and summer learning opportunities for nearly six thousand students and their families at more than a dozen Philadelphia public and charter schools. Cooking and gardening clubs and youth-run fruit stands connect school-day and after-school learning activities for K–12 students and incorporate the academic work of Penn students and faculty. Another evaluation by university students of AUNI found that twelfth-grade high school students who were part of the program consumed twice as many fruit and vegetable servings daily as ninth graders who were in the beginning of their participation in the program.[2]

This involvement with the ABCS course "world" and what is now the Netter Center also inspired me to pick up an additional major, in Urban Studies. Adding that new focus allowed me to dive into issues including housing, transportation, food systems, greenspace, and education. I learned about the history of housing policies and racial segregation in the United States and about urban health and income inequality. I was introduced to the power of policy and was challenged to think about social change and justice in settings ranging from neighborhoods to cities to states to the nation itself. I was part of Ira Harkavy and Lee Benson's famous small seminar series in 1993 in the Castle, which housed one of the first living learning programs at Penn—the Community Service Living Learning Program. Together, our house of twenty-two engaged questions concerning community service, activism, and social change. In 1995, during my senior year at Penn, eight of us lived together in an off-campus house that we fancied a hub of civic engagement. Danny Gerber and I started a group to try to get Penn students to better understand their West Philadelphia neighborhood and to meet their West Philly neighbors.

I knew that when I finished at Penn, there was more learning to do, and I wanted the opportunity for a hands-on experience. Much to my parents' dismay at the time, I decided to apply for the Peace Corps to learn more about poverty, income inequality, community, health, and the world outside of the communities that I had come to know during the early part of my life. Perhaps naively, I also thought I could make a difference in the lives of people in the community where I would be placed. I like to think that I always knew that it would be me who learned and grew and changed so much more than any of the people with whose lives mine intersected. So, after West Philly, I spent two-and-a-half years in Burkina Faso, West Africa.

In Burkina Faso, I lived in a tiny, remote village on a dirt road in the middle of two towns in the south of the country. Lokosso was 141 kilometers east of Banfora, a relatively large town in the mid-1990s, and 58 kilometers west of a smaller town at the time, Gaoua, to the east. I was a health extension volunteer and was assigned to work with the village midwife in our health clinic, a one-room concrete structure with a refrigerator that held vaccinations when we were able to get propane gas. I learned how latrines were constructed (since when I arrived, I did not have one), was taught how to live on a scarce supply of water (that we had to travel a kilometer to pump into a bucket), and aligned my schedule with the sun and the seasons. I worked with the women in my village to construct a new building (made from adobe bricks and not concrete) that housed a grain mill that ran with diesel. Running of the mill was by the women for the women, and the building became a small entrepreneurial center where the villagers also made and sold soap. Even though I was meant to be a health volunteer, my efforts were centered on creating more agency and empowerment for the women within the village. I learned quickly that this was, in fact, an issue of health.

I returned to the United States after the Peace Corps in 1998 and decided to go back to West Philadelphia. I wanted to apply the knowledge I gained in Burkina Faso to kids and schools I had gotten to know as an undergraduate. I contacted Frank Johnston, and he welcomed me back with open arms. This time I got an interdisciplinary master's degree, started working at Civic House (as the associate director to David Grossman), and with Danny Gerber wrote my first true proposal, to the US Department of Agriculture to help grow the Urban Nutrition Initiative (UNI). During this time, Danny and I started a school garden at University City High School and thus began UNI's expansion. During these years, Danny would spend his days weeding and tilling garden soil with University City High School students, while I organized Penn students involved with the program and worked on the logistics of trying to situate the program within the high school without creating an undue burden for teachers. Danny was the hands-on, "in the weeds" worker and visionary, and I helped make the trains run on time! I stayed in Philly for two more years before leaving to pursue my doctorate at the Harvard School of Public Health.

I set out to understand how to address and improve health on a population level and to learn how to measure whether such improvement did, in fact, happen. When I began graduate school, I had visions of working for an organization like World Food Program or UNICEF either in Washington,

DC, or abroad. Alas, life sometimes intervenes and plans change. While doing my doctoral work at Harvard, I met my future husband, who was finishing his dissertation and getting ready to do a postdoc at the Kennedy School. He was offered a faculty job at Carnegie Mellon University after his postdoc and off we went to Pittsburgh, where we have lived for the past twenty years! It turned out to be not so bad after all. I went to work at RAND, which had recently opened up a large new office in town to take advantage of the graduates coming out of Carnegie Mellon and the University of Pittsburgh. Even more important, the city of Pittsburgh had low housing costs and a high quality of life. As I did during my time at Penn, I decided to focus my research on my own community, which I have been doing for the past eighteen years.

RAND is a research organization whose mission is to develop solutions to public policy challenges and help make communities throughout the world safer and more secure, healthier and more prosperous. Researchers are trained in sociology, demography, epidemiology, statistics, psychology, economics, organizational behavior, mathematics, and many other disciplines. It is a soft-money environment, which means that as a researcher, you are responsible for either writing (and leading) your own grants or finding other researchers who are looking for coinvestigators to contribute to their grants. When I joined RAND in 2006, I came equipped and ready to help design studies that could examine whether and how neighborhood features were associated with individual health behavior and health outcomes. I became part of RAND's Center for Population Health and Health Disparities, which was funded by the National Cancer Institute (NCI). I worked on projects related to the center as well as other opportunities that came up related to health disparities.

I had been spending time getting to know the city since we moved there in 2004. In 2009, inquiring about gardening projects happening across the city, I learned that the Hill District, a historically Black neighborhood and the cultural center of Black history in Pittsburgh, hadn't seen a full-service supermarket in more than three decades but was finally going to get one. The supermarket was being funded, in part, by Healthy Food Financing Initiative Funds as part of a broader policy to incentivize supermarkets to locate in food deserts. The theory behind getting supermarkets into food deserts was plausible enough. Without access to healthy foods, residents of such food deserts were forced to buy processed, packaged, and unhealthy foods from convenience stores, which contributed to the poor diet and high rates of overweight, obesity, diabetes, and hypertension in neighborhoods like the Hill District. I saw this planned new supermarket as an opportunity to test by natural experiment whether this theory was indeed true. I immediately got to work on my National Institutes of Health (NIH) proposal.

My first large grant from the NIH/NCI was awarded in April 2010. We called the study "Pittsburgh Hill/Homewood Research on Eating, Shopping, and Health," and the acronym PHRESH was adopted. With this grant, we recruited a random cohort of households from the Hill District (where the supermarket would eventually open in 2013) and from a comparison neighborhood in Pittsburgh called Homewood, which was sociodemographically similar but remained a food desert without a full-service supermarket for the duration of the study and remains one in 2024. The main research was whether access to a new full-service supermarket would change resident diet. Our study found that after the supermarket had been open for a year, residents in the Hill District did improve many components of their diet, especially in comparison to residents of Homewood. But our findings were far more surprising than the mere confirmation of the theory that they seemed to present. These dietary shifts in the Hill District were not related to whether the residents we followed used the supermarket.[3]

This initial grant turned into a larger suite of studies, part of the research program Pittsburgh Hill/Homewood Research on Neighborhood Change and Health. We realized that neighborhood developments like supermarket openings do not happen in isolation. Neighborhood change is dynamic. For more than a decade now, we have followed this cohort of households in the Hill District and Homewood, systematically collecting place-based data on the changing built and social environment in these communities. Our research has built on a natural experiment design, using changes and developments in these Pittsburgh neighborhoods to better understand the impact of place-based investments on resident health and health behavior. Since this suite of studies started, I have brought in nearly $30 million—mostly through grants from NIH—to grow this research in Pittsburgh. Our team has published dozens of papers highlighting features of neighborhoods that matter for resident health. We have found that, despite perceptions to the contrary, neither Hill District nor Homewood residents rely on convenience stores for major food shopping. We have shown the ways that neighborhood crime and perception of safety gets under the skin and is associated with overweight and obesity.[4] We've discovered that residents living in the neighborhood with more investments had better sleep.[5] But perhaps the biggest question that remains is to what extent resident involvement and agency in community redevelopment processes may be related to their health outcome changes.

Science works in interesting ways. Although my goal has always been to answer questions that can impact policy, I have learned that publishing in scientific journals and disseminating information to impact policy are sometimes two different things. Our team showed that efforts from the healthy food financing initiative did seem to have positive results.[6] We demonstrated that food insecurity spiked during the initial phases of the COVID-19 pandemic.[7] And community organizations have been able to use the data collected through our efforts to advocate for future investments. Yet our findings have not provided groundbreaking revelations for policymakers and government officials about empowering disinvested communities.

I am coming to realize that my scientific contributions to policy are a small part of what I'm interested in doing. I have learned that I am driven and energized by learning from the world around me and by supporting and encouraging others. When I first saw the job description of the new chair in epidemiology at the University of Pittsburgh, I was struck by its call for someone who could contribute directly to a new era in epidemiology by expanding the scope of the department. I am fueled by the possibilities of merging real-life experience with classroom and scientific learning. I am committed to being able to do science and community engagement concurrently. To me, this is all a commitment to social justice. It is part of a larger process of building a more just and fair society by allowing people the opportunity to be exposed to different people and different experiences and grow to be more understanding and adopt more responsibility. I am excited about growing social epidemiology within the University of Pittsburgh's Department of Epidemiology, and I look forward to teaching methods that draw on rigorous scientific design and integration of community-centered questions. I am happy to be surrounded by the next generation, who can infuse new energy and ideas into my own experiences.

It's important to note a few things about the work I did at RAND with PHRESH. First, its heart and soul were in the community. At the start of this work in 2011, we opened a field office in one of the two neighborhoods where we work, with a field coordinator who grew up in the neighborhood, and hired data collectors from the neighborhood. We collaborated with a community partner for a new Research to Action coordinator and have disseminated findings through community-based outreach, recognizing the importance of research reciprocity. Our approach was not participatory action research (see the earlier discussion of NIH funding—that's another story). But it has centered community partnerships, and it lives by those premises.

This work, without a doubt, was grounded in my days at Penn nearly thirty years ago. When I was at the university between 1992 and 1996, the Netter Center was in its relative infancy. It was merely the Center for Community Partnerships, since the Netters had not yet provided it their generous support, and we undergraduates were part of WEPIC, or the West Philadelphia Improvement Corps (which evolved into the Netter Center's university-assisted community school strategy). There were just a small handful of ABCS courses. Yet it was enough to give me the foundation to continue to study and learn about participatory action research, social justice, and the real meaning of engaging communities in research.

The University of Pittsburgh's School of Public Health is giving me the opportunity to work directly with educating the next generation of public health scholars and practitioners. I am relishing the opportunity to grow my department's commitment to social epidemiology, including place-based approaches, complex systems, natural experiments and policy, and urban planning, design, and health. Even though I am at the beginning of my tenure at Pitt, I am thrilled to be growing the areas near and dear to by heart, focusing on social epidemiology, climate change, urban health, neighborhoods, and turning epidemiology into action.

My next major career goal is to help train the next generation. I want to empower and involve historically underrepresented scholars and to involve community organizations and leaders in understanding the value of their knowledge and lived experience. My ultimate goal is to produce knowledge for action and to do science that can impact policy and what I think of as "structural" levers of change.

I'm excited to be in an academic setting again, and I really feel like I've come full circle from my Penn days more than a quarter-century ago. I don't think I would ever have imagined, arriving at Penn in 1992, that the ABCS classes and work with the West Philadelphia Improvement Corps would become a part of who I am. I don't think I ever would have predicted that UNI would become the Agatston Urban Nutrition Initiative, serving as a central component of Netter's university-assisted community schools, with some eighteen full-time Netter staff and hundreds of Penn students in ABCS courses and volunteer and internship activities supporting nutrition education, gardening, and physical health. UNI's growth and evolution has been nothing short of phenomenal and has really mirrored what the Netter Center has done since its 1992 version of the Center for Community Partnerships.

I'm also thrilled to be at the University of Pittsburgh, whose Office of Engagement and Community Affairs has made place-based commitments in the very two neighborhoods where the PHRESH research that I have grown is located. Their community engagement centers in the Hill District and Homewood neighborhoods are an opportunity for me to continue my own commitment to engaged scholarship, learning, capacity-building, and economic inclusion.

As I take this next step in my career, it has given me the chance to think about how the lessons from my days at Penn with Ira Harkavy, Lee Benson, Frank Johnston, and others can help me in my new academic home. First, don't try to come up with better course titles than Ira Harkavy's, which are something like "Universities and the Future of Humanity: University-Assisted Community Schools as a Case Study for a Post-Modern Neighborly Utopia, Beyond the Ivory Tower and Fully Realizing the Dreams of John Dewey." Next, remember to place the "civic" front and center and continue to press, challenge, and reflect on who you are within the context of social justice—race, color, religion, national origin, sexual orientation, gender, gender identity, disability, and so on. Finally, don't be afraid to talk about the elephant in the room. In a recent paper sent to me by Ira, "Dewey, Implementation, and Creating a Democratic Civic University," he noted a 2017 *New York Times* study revealing that thirty-eight elite universities in the United States, including Penn and four other Ivy League institutions, enrolled more students from the top 1 percent of the income scale than from the entire bottom 60 percent.[8] I think we all know this, but this status makes achieving true democracy a challenge.

Alas, nothing is perfect, and we are faced with challenges, juxtapositions, and contradictions in everything we do. One step at a time, with a heavy dose of civic awareness. Thank you, Penn, and thank you, Netter Center, for promoting education of Penn students (and I'm quoting this from Lee Benson): to be ethical, empathetic, engaged, democratic citizens, and advance knowledge for the continuous betterment of the human condition.[9]

Notes

1. Francis E. Johnston, Ira Harkavy, Frances Barg, Danny Gerber, and Jennifer Rulf, "The Urban Nutrition Initiative: Bringing Academically-Based Community Service to the University of Pennsylvania's Department of Anthropology," *Michigan Journal of Community Service Learning* 10, no. 3 (Summer 2004): 100–6, data on 104.

2. Francis E. Johnston, "The Agatston Urban Nutrition Initiative: Working to Reverse the Obesity Epidemic Through Academically Based Community Service," *New Directions for Youth Development* (Special issue: Universities in Partnership: Strategies for Education, Youth Development, and Community Renewal) 122 (Summer 2009): 61–79, data on 77. See also Francis E. Johnston and Ira Harkavy, *The Obesity Culture: Strategies for Change—Public Health and University–Community Partnerships* (St. Ives, UK: Smith-Gordon, 2009).

3. Tamara Dubowitz et al., "Diet and Perceptions Change with Supermarket Introduction in a Food Desert, but Not Because of Supermarket Use," *Health Affairs (Project Hope)* 34, no. 11 (Nov. 2015): 1858–68, doi.org/10.1377/hlthaff.2015.0667.

4. Andrea S. Richardson et al., "Pathways Through Which Higher Neighborhood Crime Is Longitudinally Associated with Greater Body Mass Index," *International Journal of Behavioral Nutrition and Physical Activity* 14, no. 1 (Nov. 2017): article 155, doi.org/10.1186/s12966-017-0611-y.

5. Tamara Dubowitz et al., "Does Investing in Low-Income Urban Neighborhoods Improve Sleep?" *Sleep* 44, no. 66 (June 2021): zsaa292, doi: 10.1093/sleep/zsaa292, PMID: 33417708; PMCID: PMC8193558.

6. Tamara Dubowitz et al., "Community Investments and Diet-Related Outcomes: A Longitudinal Study of Residents of Two Urban Neighborhoods," *American Journal of Preventative Medicine* (Nov. 14, 2023): S0749-3797(23)00463-4, doi: 10.1016/j.amepre.2023.11.005, Epub ahead of print, PMID: 37972799.

7. Tamara Dubowitz et al., "Food Insecurity in a Low-Income, Predominantly African American Cohort Following the COVID-19 Pandemic," *American Journal of Public Health* 111, no. 3 (Mar. 2021): 494–97, doi: 10.2105/AJPH.2020.306041, Epub 2021 Jan 21, PMID: 33476228; PMCID: PMC7893363.

8. Gregor Aisch, Larry Buchanan, Amanda Cox, and Kevin Quealy, "Some Colleges Have More Students from the Top 1 Percent Than the Bottom 60: Find Yours," *New York Times*, Jan. 18, 2017, A3, cited in Ira Harkavy, "Dewey, Implementation, and Creating a Democratic Civic University," *Pluralist* 18, no. 1 (2023): 49–75.

9. For more details on Benson's and colleagues' view of the purposes of higher education, see Lee Benson, Ira Harkavy, John Puckett, Matthew Hartley, Rita A. Hodges, Francis E. Johnston, and Joann Weeks, *Knowledge for Social Change: Bacon, Dewey, and the Revolutionary Transformation of Research Universities in the Twenty-First Century* (Philadelphia: Temple University Press, 2017).

CHAPTER 11

The Power of Connected Learning

Christina Cantrill

> Without the ability to think about yourself, to reflect on
> your life, there's really no awareness, no consciousness.
> Consciousness doesn't come automatically; it comes
> through being alive, awake, curious, and often furious.
>
> —Maxine Greene

At one point in my schooling, I got pretty good at playing the game of education. Taking tests, responding to abstract ideas that I only vaguely understood, and playing the role of a "good student"—it clicked into place for me and seemed to work, at least for a while. But as grades and scores started to matter more than what it all really meant, I felt myself disengaging from a larger sense of purpose in my learning. I was going to school, doing well in school, but year by year losing track of "why" school in the first place.

By sophomore year at Penn, it was catching up to me. I was confused and overwhelmed, unsure what I was doing or even why I was there. When I look back at my transcript, I can see that I was jumping from one thing to another. Without a "why" for learning, I felt lost. Asking for advice was not my strong suit back then, so I just kind of kept shifting from this to that to this again as I tried to find a place of connection to help me make sense of it all.

My attempts to connect included volunteering at Turner Middle School. As a kid, I had gone to a similar middle school in another part of Philadelphia and was happy to have an excuse to wander beyond campus and reconnect with what was familiar to me. It was not the first time I tried volunteering while at Penn, but this time was different at Turner. I found something that *connected back.* These connections helped me to begin to make sense of my undergraduate education, of myself, and of the possibilities within.

By the spring of 1991, I was enrolled in the Urban University-Community Partnerships honors course taught by Ira Harkavy and Lee Benson. I was in my third year, and suddenly here I was, doing something I cared about. I was assisting in the art room at Turner every Saturday, while researching during the rest of the week what it meant to be a volunteer. These were the days of George Bush Senior and his "thousand points of light" agenda, so the topic was available to me as an inquiry. It was part of public discussion, and this allowed me to start to notice what I was doing and take a more critical stance toward interrogating "the why" and "for what" of it all.

That experience reawakened the learner in me—the kid inside that was always curious and eager to try new things and make connections—by reengaging my sense of place and ultimately of purpose. It clarified the complexities of feelings I had as I shifted between local schools and the university. And it opened me to the power that thoughtful and critical questioning, alongside real-world experience and relationships, can make for one's own understanding of self, history, place, and the possibilities of the imagination.

Now, as a professional educator looking back at that experience, I can see what made the difference for me: my learning felt connected. It was part of something I was interested in and that was meaningful to me; it involved real people that gave me input and feedback; and the relationships I formed led to more opportunities to learn and develop. In research on learning, investigating the ways that youth are able to direct their own pathways in richly networked environments, this is described as "Connected Learning."[1] It is this kind of learning experience that I seek to reproduce now as a teacher and learning designer myself, in and across a range of contexts and communities.

*   *   *

At the turn of the twenty-first century, educator Maxine Greene wrote about the power of the imagination to support active learning and the ability to see what is possible. She explored and documented the role that encounters with the arts, specifically, play in provoking "the growth of individuals who reach out to one another as they seek clearings in their experience and try to live more ardently in the world."[2]

Even in my early twenties, Greene's words resonated with me. As I kept an eye out for opportunities after graduation, I was moved by my recent experiences at Turner and with the Center for Community Partnerships to attempt to live more ardently. And it was through these attempts that I connected with two organizations that embraced similar values and ideas. First, I met and got a job with the teachers of the Philadelphia Writing Project, a Penn-based teacher professional development organization affiliated with the National Writing Project. Soon after, I started volunteering with Spiral Q Puppet Theater, a West Philly–based, nonprofit creative arts and social justice organization.

Sometimes I joke that after I finished my undergraduate degree, I went to do my graduate work at the "schools" of Spiral Q and the Writing Project. This is because both these spaces turned out to be more than just jobs or casual pastimes. Rather, the writing project was a place where I could learn alongside teachers and continue to develop the sense of purpose in learning that the Center for Community Partnerships (now the Netter Center) had begun to foster in me. And Spiral Q, or "the Q" for short, was an alternative space and place for me to creatively engage with others and to explore the intersections of identity, interests, and participatory world-building.

* * *

The Philadelphia Writing Project is—like the Netter Center—designed as a university-community partnership. The idea is to bring together educators—across schools and university, K–16—to write and to inquire into the teaching of writing as practitioners and scholars alike. In this way, the art of teaching writing moves from being a solo and behind-the-door practice to one that is deeply theorized, examined, and shared. School is not conceived of as an isolated place of learning but instead as one node in the connected web of a learner's life. And, through exercising voice and agency as teachers-researchers-writers themselves, writing project educators begin to be able to support their students in taking up their own agency in their learning and literacy.

The writing project started as an idea and a summer convening of teachers and professors at the University of California–Berkeley in the early 1970s.[3] Its ways of working—across grades and disciplines, bridging scholarship and practice in support of local communities—were so popular that other endeavors like it got started at universities and colleges across the country. In the early 1990s, a 501c3 was formed to connect these local sites and to further build a network "in reach of all teachers." This national nonprofit is called the National Writing Project (NWP). After working for a few years at the

Philadelphia Writing Project, exploring the early internet and its possibilities for learning and for teaching alongside my writing project colleagues and their students, I was hired by the NWP to help further design and foster this work on the national level. I continue to work there today.

At the NWP, I strive to support and to design programs that are connected—back and forward—like the Netter Center's work. Using various frameworks for learning, including the framework of Connected Learning,[4] I've been most interested in designing participatory spaces that fall in between schools and outside-of-school learning. A couple of projects we have run that fall into these categories include an online professional development started in 2015 called CLMOOC, or the Connected Learning Massively Open Online Collaboration, and a more recent project that is in its sixth year called Write Out, which manifests as an annual event and is part of a larger partnership between the NWP and the National Park Service.

*   *   *

CLMOOC was an online professional development experience designed as an openly networked, production-centered, participatory learning collaboration for educators. It was the NWP's response to the excitement about "MOOCs" in education, but our focus was to design a MOOC whose "C" shifted from a "course" to a "collaboration." This collaboration, which had the support of the MacArthur Foundation's Digital Media and Learning initiative, ran for three summers and engaged thousands of teachers in composing and sharing multimodal artifacts online while exploring implications of the Connected Learning research on teaching and learning. CLMOOC's design was based on the framework of Connected Learning research while also reflecting the core beliefs and established social practices of the National Writing Project. It was led by teachers for teachers, and it engaged writing and the teaching of writing situated in social contexts around shared interests. In these ways, we were able to surface, for ourselves as teachers, the transformative possibilities of openly networked, web-mediated professional learning.[5]

Learning from the CLMOOC experience, we continue to leverage these possibilities in the design of other professional learning opportunities such as our current Write Out project. Write Out is a free two-week celebration of writing, making, and sharing inspired by the great outdoors. It is designed as a public invitation to get out and create that is supported with a series of online activities. The goal is to connect and learn through place-based writing and sharing, using the common hashtag #writeout. Write Out runs every October and includes Indigenous People's Day and the National Day of Writing.

While Write Out works to support teachers in schools in designing their own opportunities to bring kids outdoors to write and create each October, it is an open participatory event that supports writing and creating outdoors by any interested individual or community. Therefore, we develop our professional practices together, as educators, while we engage our communities in a fun, creative, and place-based activity. Over time we have partnered with groups such as Outdoor Afro and Latino Outdoors that support expanded representation and access to outdoor opportunities. And we've explored various themes—from STEM to poetry-writing to history and storytelling—to engage different aspects of what is possible when you take your writing outside and connect to public spaces and places in your community.

*   *   *

My experience with these kinds of open participatory designs actually got honed many years before, on the Q side of things, which operates not online but in the streets of West Philadelphia, using recycled materials like cardboard and house paint. It was in the late 1990s that I got involved with the then-nascent parade and pageant organized by Spiral Q called Peoplehood. Now almost twenty-five years old, Peoplehood is described as a "giant puppet spectacle" envisioned as an opportunity to bring people and organizations together who have been involved in Q programming over the previous years.

Through partnerships and local alliance-building, Peoplehood kicks off every year at the Paul Robeson House at 50th and Walnut Streets and parades south, wending its way through residential streets, and ending up at Clark Park, a municipal park whose prominent feature is a former pond now known as the "bowl." Neither the parade nor the pageant is meant simply to be watched. Instead, the city is invited to help create the affair or even to jump in at the last minute. This happens via public "build" days that are scheduled and announced publicly; all who show up are invited to help with something already in process or to create something of their own.

The narrative within the pageant, which is often visible within the parade itself, is collaboratively composed during the public build days and by those organizations involved in that year's event. The details of the story have shifted over time, but the arc of the story is often essentially the same; topics of the day and of importance to the participants bring a focus to the story.

Struggles within these topics have included school closures, lack of afford-able housing, gun violence in the community, and recovery from addiction. The puppet objects carried by community members form the details of the narrative as they move and dance and interact with one another—a kind of cultural remix.

My experience with the Q—jumping in, leading small groups, working to help build, and ultimately cochairing the nonprofit's Board of Directors—further created the kind of "clearings" in my experience that Maxine Green wrote about. And these clearings supported me to expand what I imagined was possible while it provided regular places and creative spaces to practice social learning, participatory design, and public collaborations.

*   *   *

When we can shift the attention to learning, instead of focusing only on "schooling," we can bring more attention to the interests, relationships, and opportunities that foster learning and think more clearly about the possibili-ties. For example, taking this time to think back over my experience with university-community partnerships, I find myself playing with the words to imagine what might be possible if the phrasing of this work was shifted the other way, that is, community-university partnerships. Or what if the words were part of a circle, instead of a line, and maybe written on sheets of card-board and paraded around a public park instead?! What interests show up here? What relationships are being connected and fostered? What opportu-nities are connected or are enabled?

partnerships

community   university

In creating more space around these ideas and thinking about the role of Connected Learning in the mix, I start to wonder not just about the partner-ship between the community and the university but also about all the part-nerships that exist within and around the community and university overall. This makes me think of partnerships not as a line connecting university with community but as an ecosystem. Connected Learning research shows that, despite our conventional understanding of learning as a straight shot through a "pipeline" of traditional educational structures, the path for success is most often not linear at all. It is instead a complex landscape where learners are surrounded by all kinds of support from mentors, brokers, family members, networks, clubs, and more. The research also points to the fact that this larger ecosystem is much less visible in our normal ways of thinking about schooling and education, often obscuring key factors, such as how privilege, demographics, and inequitable access to opportunities play out in continuing disparities.[6]

Thirty years later, I look back and see the influence of my experience at Turner Middle School. The design for learning supported through the Netter Center for Community Partnerships helped me to connect important dots for my younger self. I see this in the ways that the city of Philadelphia itself became a partner in my learning at the time and in the ways that I was supported to reflect on my lived experience while connecting with research, community leaders, and other learners (at both Turner and Penn). And I see it in how it fostered my commitment to participation centered on inquiry, social learning, and asset-based, community-focused design.

When designing for Connected Learning today, I focus my attention on learners' interests and on processes that support social learning and relationship building within a larger ecosystem. I work to connect learning to real-world opportunities beyond any particular class or learning situation. I also work to embrace the values of social, participatory, and equitable learning that ground Connected Learning, concentrating on creating healthy learning ecosystems designed for each specific context. My goal is to balance and leverage these various pieces, imagining—like a biological ecosystem described by Marijke Hecht and Kevin Crowley[7]—how learning design can embrace diversity and change in order to stay connected. These are the approaches and values I strive to design for all learners, whether they are based at a middle school in Philadelphia or at an elite higher-educational institution, whether they are adults engaging in professional development, or families, friends, and strangers spending time together in public parks and shared community spaces.

Notes

1. Mizuko Ito et al., *Connected Learning: An Agenda for Research and Design* (Irvine, CA: Digital Media and Learning Research Hub, 2013).

2. Maxine Greene, "Art and Imagination: Reclaiming the Sense of Possibility," *Phi Delta Kappan* 76, no. 5 (1995): 378–82, quotation on 382.

3. James Gray, *Teachers at the Center: A Memoir of the Early Years of the National Writing Project* (Berkeley, CA: National Writing Project, 2000).

4. "Connected Learning Alliance," accessed Oct. 26, 2023, clalliance.org/about-connected-learning/.

5. Anna Smith, Stephanie West-Puckett, Christina Cantrill, and Mia Zamora, "Remix as Professional Learning: Educators' Iterative Literacy Practice in CLMOOC," *Education Sciences* 6, no. 1 (2016): 12, doi.org/10.3390/educsci6010012

6. Mimo Ito, "Connected Learning Explained," Keynote for Concord Consortium Presents: Designing 2030 Summit, Connected Learning Alliance, Dec. 20, 2018, recorded presentation, 18:14, www.youtube.com/watch?v=HacgaDN971Y.

7. Marijke Hecht and Kevin Crowley, "Unpacking the Learning Ecosystems Framework: Lessons from the Adaptive Management of Biological Ecosystems," *Journal of the Learning Sciences* 29, no. 2 (2020): 264–84.

CHAPTER 12

A Reflection on Creating My Own ABCS
Course Around Participatory Design

Jason Yip

Introduction

"I quit." I didn't think I would ever say those words, but they came out of me in 1998 after a rough spring semester in pre-med. I felt defeated. I hadn't enjoyed my STEM courses the way I wanted to. I decided to give up medicine and change over to education, with a newfound intention of becoming a chemistry and mathematics teacher. While at the University of Pennsylvania, I wanted to find ways to use a STEM degree that could benefit the local and greater community of Philadelphia.

In the summer of 2000, during my transition to education, I took a seminar through the Center for Community Partnerships with Dr. Ira Harkavy, an Academically Based Community Service (ABCS) course about Philadelphia and civic engagement. We undergraduates all lived together in a fraternity house to develop relationships with each other. In the mornings, we did tutoring work at John Turner Middle School. In the afternoons, we would meet together at the Center for Community Partnerships working on ideas for ABCS courses. I was hooked. In the first semester of my senior year, the fall of 2000, I began spending time developing ABCS curriculum in STEM settings for the Center. I loved this time and ended up devoting much of my senior year researching ways in which the Chemistry Department at the University of Pennsylvania could integrate ABCS into its curriculum offerings.

At the time, the Chemistry Department was not interested in ABCS. But the Math Department had considered it. So, during spring 2001, I worked to develop Penn's MATH 123 as an ABCS course alongside Theresa Simmonds, who was, at the time, a teacher and the small learning community coordinator at University City High School. I did some preliminary curriculum design and conducted interviews with teachers and students. Eventually, I wrote a senior thesis on MATH 123, what it could look like as an ABCS course, and what would be needed to get it off the ground for the Math Department. I was quite happy to see that MATH 123 did take off after I left, and I was also thrilled to see that the Chemistry Department did eventually embrace the idea of ABCS with its CHEM 010 course.

Life After Graduation

I graduated from the University of Pennsylvania in the spring of 2002 with a dual degree, a bachelor's in chemistry and a master's in education (science, mathematics). I was on my way. I became a chemistry and mathematics teacher at an independent school from 2002 to 2006 and then at a large suburban public school from 2006 to 2008. Over the course of those six formative years, I did more than merely teach biology, chemistry, geometry, and algebra. I learned how to design new lesson plans, activities, and curricula and how to integrate educational technologies into my practice. I did simulations in geometry design, used molecular simulations to teach chemistry, and incorporated video clips of animations such as *The Simpsons* into my pedagogy. Life as a teacher was good through those years.

However, by about 2008, the world of K–12 education was shifting. Policies such as No Child Left Behind started to push many school districts to adopt high-stakes standardized testing to assess students. As a result, those districts sought standardized curricula for subjects such as chemistry. In my school, we received a handbook full of schedules, worksheets, standards, and assessments. The district no longer wanted us each to design an individual curriculum; it wanted us all to use the same curriculum, no matter the high school where we taught. This meant a lot less autonomy and a lot more following of district rules.

By 2008, then, I thought it best to take off and start a PhD at the University of Maryland College of Education, where I studied Curriculum and Instruction (Science Education). In truth, I wanted to return to the sorts of experiences I'd had at the University of Pennsylvania, where I did curriculum design work in ABCS classes and independent studies. During my time at the University of Maryland, I learned much about curriculum, instructional design, theories of learning, and design work.

In my third year, I found myself transitioning to working at the College of Information Studies, learning about a concept called participatory design, a method that allows stakeholders and designers to work together in a democratic fashion to negotiate and collaborate about designs and particularly about designs for the stakeholder. One of my advisers, Allison Druin, started a program at Maryland called Kidsteam. Kidsteam (or KidsTeam) is an intergenerational participatory design group of children and design researchers coming together to design. Druin encapsulated the philosophy of Kidsteam in the term "cooperative inquiry," which embodied the aspiration to have children and adults act as design partners in an equal and equitable fashion.[1]

In Kidsteam, children ages seven to eleven came to our design labs twice a week after school to work together in codesigning new technologies, learning activities, and curricula for other children. Kidsteam was the place for me to start putting together new ideas, not only around designing new learning technologies for children but also curriculum and activities. I finished my PhD in 2014 and spent a year at the Sesame Workshop at the Joan Ganz Cooney Center to learn how to think about families and technology use with children. Then, in the winter of 2015, I accepted a position at the Information School of the University of Washington as an assistant professor in digital youth.

The Behind-the-Scenes Thinking About ABCS and Participatory Design at the University of Washington

I arrived at the University of Washington (UW) with a lot on my mind as a young, novice researcher. My main questions were all about how families and children collaborate and learn together around new technologies. I wanted to build new technologies, codesign with children, and study the taking up of new technologies in the home. At the same time, questions informed by my prior work at the University of Pennsylvania (ABCS) and the University of Maryland (Kidsteam) were swirling in my mind:

- Question 1: I knew that at some point I wanted to do design work with public libraries and families. I wanted to consider more informal learning, especially having dealt with some of the difficulties of standardized curricula and testing. I wanted participatory design with adults and children to be at the forefront of the creation of this course. How would participatory design fit into an ABCS course?

- Question 2: Similarly, I needed to spend time with community-based organizations that worked closely with youth and families. I knew that building an ABCS course would not happen overnight. It would be a multiyear process built on developing relationships with community groups. I wanted to focus particularly on libraries integrating participatory design in their programs. Who would be the community players? What kind of neighborhoods and youth could benefit?
- Question 3: Finally, I had to think closely about how university students could take part in this course. What would they gain from learning about participatory design? How could I integrate design into their learning?

With these questions in my mind, I knew I had to get started developing community relationships and research partnerships and collaborations. I began by reaching out to Juan Rubio, the digital media and learning program manager at the Seattle Public Library. He oversaw education technology and managed programs for nondominant youth for all the branches of the Seattle Public Library system. In the winter of 2015, I met with Juan to get to know how youth programming worked at the library.

At the same time, I was also planning my KidsTeam UW group.[2] This intergenerational codesign group would take principles and foundations from the original University of Maryland team (Kidsteam) but focus more on the potential of families and digital technologies integration. As soon as our Institutional Review Board application was approved, I began outreach to the UW community to invite children. I started this team in the fall of 2015, with a small group of eight children (ages seven to eleven), four master's and undergraduate volunteers, and one doctoral student. Once the fall 2015 term began, I immediately invited Juan Rubio to come to our sessions to see what KidsTeam UW was all about. I was very lucky that he had time to come visit our group, since he had to travel from downtown Seattle to the UW campus. Every time he came, he helped to solidify our development of design potential for the Seattle Public Library.

Over the course of the next year, from fall 2015 to spring 2016, Juan began to bring us education technology projects he had considered, such as toy robots, e-textile play circuits, and programming tools online. Through Kids-Team UW, we successfully created new learning activities using these digital educational technologies for youth in the Seattle Public Library.[3] As we were able to successfully create more activities and try out new technologies from Juan, he continued to bring us more education technology projects—in robotics, coding, paper circuits, digital storytelling, and hardware circuitry.

As Juan worked on creating these activities with children's codesign, he started to develop design relationships with our team.[4] He observed that children in KidsTeam UW came to our group consistently, always wanting to design and always coming up with great ideas for other Seattle youth. By 2016, we were starting to talk about the possibilities of setting up a KidsTeam group at the library.

To do that, however, we had to address a number of logistical questions. Who from UW could travel to a branch of the Seattle Public Library to work with children? Which library branch could host? How would we integrate youth, librarians, and university students together? It soon became clear to me that this could be the right time to come back to the idea of piloting an ABCS course.

Piloting an ABCS Course

In the spring of 2016, I wrote up the first proposal for an ABCS course. Taking KidsTeam UW as a model and offering the Columbia City branch of the Seattle Public Library as the first test site, I proposed a small, fifteen-person, graduate-level course for our Master's in Library and Information Science (MLIS) program. In that proposal, I argued that training librarians in traditional educational technology was no longer effective. Instead, I suggested that the integration of digital literacy and digital technologies is now an essential part of youth librarianship and that design epistemology, the knowledge generated in the process of design, is a necessary part of training future librarians.

First and foremost, I proposed to develop KidsTeam SPL (Seattle Public Library). As with our KidsTeam UW, we would recruit children from the neighborhood (ages seven to eleven) to come and codesign new digital activities for the other branches. Those local children would work with MLIS students and the branch librarians to test new educational technologies and to develop learning activities.[5] MLIS students would also have an opportunity to run their own design sessions to try out new technologies they thought might be effective for youth and public libraries.

On Mondays, we would reflect on the work of the prior week, discuss theories of participatory design, and plan for Wednesday codesign sessions. On Wednesdays, we would travel to the Seattle Public Library branch—located about thirty minutes from the UW campus— by car, bus, or train. We would arrive at 3:15 p.m. to start with Snack Time, a time to hang out and play with the children and enjoy some food together. At around 3:45, we would get started with Circle Time, an introductory moment where children and adults answer the Question of the Day. This question always primed the children to think about the codesign we were going to engage in. During Circle Time, we would present the design goals of the session and get everyone into smaller groups of MLIS students and children. By 4:00, we would be ready for the main event: Design Time. For about three-quarters of an hour, children and MLIS students would engage together in the specific codesign task. To help design partners work together, we paired each task with a specific design technique.[6] For example, in an early-stage design, we used a Bags of Stuff technique, in which children and adults have a bag of art supplies, craft materials, and junk to engage in low-fidelity prototyping. In later-stage testing, we tried a technique called Likes, Dislikes, and Design Ideas, where children implement a design and then write out on sticky notes what they liked and disliked and what improvements they wanted. After Design Time, we would all return to the larger group for Discussion Time. Here, main ideas and larger themes came together. Children presented their ideas, and adults helped them communicate and synthesize what they had to say.

Once the sessions were completed, MLIS students went back home to write up their reflections in analytic memos, connect their ideas of the session to the readings, and come up with design principles we might use in the following week. Design researchers on the team analyzed the memos and the video of the session to write up design guidelines and produce designs (for example, technologies, activities, curricula) for future work with libraries. Once fall-term sessions were completed, we often worked with MLIS students to develop capstone projects for those who wanted to engage further in codesign in the winter and spring terms.

The Highs and Lows of Running ABCS in Librarianship

Since our first sessions in 2017–2018, we have run KidsTeam SPL every year but the one we lost to COVID. Since its inception, we have had a lot of highs and met a lot of challenges in running an ABCS course independently.[7]

One of the major opportunities that ABCS affords is integrating design problems into librarianship. I argue that using design problems through participatory design invites everyone (stakeholders, children, patrons, librarians, university students, among others) to the table and stimulates their broader participation in their communities. Children work together with university students and librarians, and their collaboration fosters different dialogues. Instead of children being the recipients of services, children and librarians confront design challenges together.

A crucial benefit of running an ABCS course with design and librarianship at its core is that it allows people to reflect together. By using different design techniques[8] and partnership perspectives,[9] different people can find different ways to be heard. Nothing like this is happening in schools today, where real community issues concerning design are suppressed by "professional" determinations of the methods and approaches that can be used to address problems. In our ABCS course, MLIS students learn to be librarians who are not sole experts in design but participants in much wider community conversations about community issues.

All that said, I must also confess that after running KidsTeam SPL for six years I have observed a number of challenges. Conflicts and group dynamic tensions do surface. Trying to go through participatory design with children who may have a hard time concentrating and connecting with the problem can be hard for adults. Children can have difficulties with executive function, emotional reactions, and behavior management. Librarians and MLIS students have to figure out how to work with problematic behaviors. Sometimes groups do not have enough children. Sometimes they have too many children who do not work well due to personality conflicts.[10] Working with the community can be quite challenging, especially since the MLIS students are themselves diverse in age, upbringing, motivation, cognitive ability, and socioemotional regulation. Several of them experienced working with children as anxiety-provoking. They wanted to run perfect codesign sessions, and they especially wanted to motivate children and families to participate in their community libraries. They had difficulty dealing with the unpredictability of children's behavior, which is the challenge of working with neighborhood children in participatory design.

While participatory design and ABCS can allow people a space to engage one another, having so many stakeholders in the process can also present challenges. Under those circumstances, ideas are often both abundant and divergent. Some MLIS students have had a hard time helping the group converge on ideas on which to concentrate. The process of participatory design can be enjoyable for the community, but it is also difficult to build out an excess of ideas for future work. There are also challenges in collaborating with children and figuring out how to make sense of their ideas.

Lessons Learned

Developing an ABCS course from scratch took me almost twenty years, from 1998 to 2017. Over the course of these two decades, I have learned a lot about the range of people's interests and the diverse roles requisite to creating and implementing such a course.

The Role of the Librarian and Community Organizer

Juan Rubio and a number of local librarians were indispensable in the takeoff of the class. Juan played the role of advocate for us with the leadership of the Seattle Public Library. He had to convince his own leadership team that codesign and working with the university was going to be a positive influence for the community and his librarians, and he had to make this pitch despite the fact that we had no funding in the early days of the project. Similarly, local librarians played an advocacy role for us in their neighborhoods. Once we got buy-in from the Seattle Public Library leadership, local librarians had to recruit children in the community for the design sessions. They had to convince families that it is worth their time to bring children to the library to design together with adults who were not their coaches or teachers. The connections that both community organizers and librarians made were crucial to setting up an ABCS course in libraries. Those connections could not have been made by the University of Washington. They depended on trust that had to exist already because children and families had to commit their own time and resources to come and work with us. Librarians and community organizers are always going to be the advocates for marginalized communities, especially those that may be distrustful of universities on account of poor prior relationships. However, not all libraries have librarians who can take the time to connect with leadership and patrons, and not all libraries have librarians sympathetic to ABCS models, which do not provide traditional services to the community but instead seek to work closely with patrons on a more even playing field.

The Role of Researcher and Instructor

Building a course syllabus and curriculum structure is already difficult, but doing so with an ABCS model in mind is even more taxing. Doing an ABCS course with participatory design as the core can be exceedingly challenging. A class structured on MLIS students engaging in participatory design with children and communities means that lots of discussion and inquiry takes place around how to solve problems in the community. While many ABCS courses focus on community empowerment through design, an ABCS course with participatory design at the center entails a dual focus. Researchers and instructors must help their university students balance between design theories and design practice. While university faculty need to teach and support university students, librarians need to make sure that the design sessions are engaging for their communities. This is especially important for librarians, for whom patron engagement in programming is important for community development and relationship-building. Instructors designing ABCS courses built on participatory design are constantly caught in this duality: supporting their own students while simultaneously making sure that library patrons and librarians are getting their own benefits as well.

The Role of the Stakeholders

Tensions can arise between stakeholders (librarians, children, MLIS students) as they codesign, and all the more sharply when those stakeholders hold tightly to what they perceive as their core roles and goals. Graduate students may be too concerned about their class requirements. Librarians may need to follow what is expected of them from the library. Children may think of themselves only as followers of adults. Tensions such as these are difficult to ignore. Librarians and MLIS students do have real workplace and academic constraints. Children and their parents might not understand (or care) exactly what ABCS is. Overall, we find that it is important to make an effort to have open communication about these tensions and to make all participants' roles as clear as possible in the context of ABCS and participatory design.

Conclusion

Since 2015, I have attempted to build and run a library and information science class integrating participatory design and ABCS with children, librarians, and university students. Looking back, I now see that putting together such an ABCS course from scratch required more than just the motivation to build a curriculum. Creating this course did not start, as I used to suppose, in 2015. The seeds of my endeavor were planted in my time at the University of Pennsylvania in 1998. Much of what I have done at the University of Washington is the culmination of my time in ABCS at the University of Pennsylvania, my participatory design work in graduate school at the University of Maryland, and my experience with community-based design. To offer this ABCS course, I partnered with local librarians and community leaders and first spent years building these relationships. It also took me years to learn the method of participatory design and figure out how to weave it into my pedagogical practice. Even after all those years of building and learning, I still experience tensions constantly rearing their demanding heads between stakeholders and the university.

Despite these challenges, doing this work has been a chance of a lifetime. We have begun the work now of getting teenagers at the library to lead and facilitate codesign sessions.[11] As I reflect on the more mature version of this class, I will have to consider the next phase, which is how the ABCS course will eventually have to be transferred over to someone else to take leadership.

Notes

1. Allison Druin, "The Role of Children in the Design of New Technology," *Behaviour and Information Technology* 21, no. 1 (2002): 1–25; Jason C. Yip, Kiley Sobel, Caroline Pitt, Kung Jin Lee, Sijin Chen, Kari Nasu, and Laura R. Pina, "Examining Adult-Child

Interactions in Intergenerational Participatory Design," paper presented at CHI Conference on Human Factors in Computing Systems, Denver, May 2017, 5742–54, doi.org/10.1145/3025453.3025787

2. Yip et al., "Examining Adult-Child Interactions."

3. Jason C. Yip, Kung Jin Lee, and Jin Ha Lee, "Design Partnerships for Participatory Librarianship: A Conceptual Model for Understanding Librarians Co-Designing with Digital Youth," *Journal of the Association for Information Science and Technology* 71, no. 10 (2019): 1242–56, doi.org/10.1002/asi.24320.

4. Yip et al., "Design Partnerships"; Jason C. Yip and Kung Jin Lee, "The Design of Digital Learning Activities for Libraries Through Participatory Design," in *Reconceptualizing Libraries: Perspectives from the Information and the Learning Sciences*, ed. Victor Lee and Abigail Phillips, 203–16 (New York: Routledge, 2018).

5. Kung Jin Lee, YooJung Kim, Wendy Roldan, Jin Ha Lee, and Jason C. Yip, "Caring for the Community: An Academically Based Community Service Course in LIS," *Journal of Librarianship and Information Science* 55, no. 1 (2022): 232–45, doi.org/10.1177/09610006221132276.

6. Greg Walsh, Elizabeth Foss, Jason C. Yip, and Allison Druin, "FACIT PD: Framework for Analysis and Creation of Intergenerational Techniques for Participatory Design," paper presented at SIGCHI Conference on Human Factors in Computing Systems, Paris, Apr. 2013), 2893–902, doi.org/10.1145/2470654.2481400.

7. Lee et al., "Caring for the Community."

8. Walsh et al., "FACIT PD."

9. Yip et al., "Examining Adult-Child Interactions."

10. Lee et al., "Caring for the Community."

11. Wendy Roldan, Kung Jin Lee, Kevin Nguyen, Lia Berhe, and Jason C. Yip, "Disrupting Informal Computing Education: Teen-Led Co-design in Libraries," *ACM on Transactions on Computing Education* 22, no. 3 (2022): 1–33, doi.org/10.1145/3484494; Jason C. Yip et al., "Children Initiating and Leading Cooperative Inquiry Sessions," paper presented at Twelfth International Conference on Interaction Design and Children, New York, June 2013), 293–96, doi.org/10.1145/2485760.2485796.

CHAPTER 13

Weaving Civic Engagement into the Fabric of Scientific Inquiry

Kim Van Naarden Braun

"If we are to achieve things never before accomplished, we must employ methods never before attempted." I was introduced to Francis Bacon's words by Dr. Ira Harkavy in 1991, during my first-semester freshman year. *Epidemiology* was not a word or field I had heard of in high school or as I entered Penn. There was no such course, major, or minor in the catalogue. As I immersed myself in participatory action research (PAR), I created my own major, Public Health Policy, an intersection between Dr. Harkavy's Urban Studies and Dr. Frank Johnston's Medical Anthropology. Fast-forward thirty-two years: I start my days deep in translational epidemiology at a large pharmaceutical company. Many of my impressive fellow alumni who are contributing to this collection of narratives reside in academia. I have never worked at a university or college. I have spent twenty years in government followed by almost five years in industry. Was it an unlikely turn? By the standards of liberal assumptions, probably yes. I would argue, absolutely not. My work at the Centers for Disease Control and Prevention (CDC) and now in the pharmaceutical industry have been deeply informed and even driven by my early experiences with PAR, Turner Middle School, and what has grown to be the Netter Center.

As an eighteen-year-old passionate about social justice and investigative journalism, I came to Penn in the summer of 1991 to participate in Penn-CORP to build houses in West Philadelphia. The neighborhood we worked in was distinct from the North Philadelphia streets I had walked in high school when I was trying to understand the issues and advocacy work of Philadelphia's homeless population. In my senior year of high school, my friend and

I filmed a documentary on Philadelphia's homeless situation with requisite research and interviews. I conducted several clothing drives and participated in soup kitchens, but there was no line of sight that allowed moving the needle in any way toward change other than to build awareness of the issue in our school and contribute goods at certain cross-sections in the calendar. Our donations and efforts were always appreciated, but I was frustrated. I felt that I had a superficial understanding of the issue and no accessible mechanism to dive deeper, let alone effect systemic change. PennCORP felt familiar and productive, handling Philadelphia's housing insecurity problem with a spirit of hard labor, but then I moved into my freshman dorm to start the academic year, activity completed.

Serendipity struck with my first-semester seminar, "Strategies in Revitalizing West Philadelphia: Case Study—Turner Middle School." This was my introduction to Dr. Harkavy's vision for PAR and university-assisted community schools. The seminar was focused on health issues in West Philadelphia, reflecting concerns voiced by the Turner Middle School community. The conceptual framework of our course readings and classroom discussions resonated strongly with me. I clearly recall another Bacon quote—"Knowledge is power"—and delving into John Dewey's powerful proposition that Bacon's theory of societal progress may only be realized through advancement of scientific learning and only be truly transformative through participatory democracy.[1] I felt that a path was forming, somehow bridging the thinking, the doing, and the potential for impact. I was intrigued by the notion of systemic social change grounded by the stability and longevity of its link to the university.

I began to engage with the West Philadelphia community by volunteering at Turner's Saturday School program to learn more about the neighborhood. The difference between this volunteer work and what I'd done before was that it was now tied to my academics in a way that was both structured and agile, leaving room for creativity and trial and error in forging relationships and forming programs. The following two summers, I participated in the Summer Institute program at Turner, teaching and mentoring on a variety of health issues centered on nutrition. As I continued creating and teaching hands-on classes on vegetarian cooking–chemistry and nutrition at Saturday School, I worked with other undergraduate and graduate students to pilot a range of lesson plans. A Ford Foundation grant enabled me to publish those lesson plans as a textbook that was at once culturally sensitive to the Turner environment and available for use more widely. An anthropology course with Dr. Frank Johnston, a PAR course titled "Human Adaptability and Biomedical Science," allowed me to continue this work and extend it. Implementation of the lesson plans was integral to the course, and so was data collection for an assessment of the health status of the Turner community. The current Agatston Urban Nutrition Initiative (AUNI) at the Netter Center is the outgrowth of Dr. Johnston's course. Now, thirty-two years later, it continues to help build and sustain healthy communities through nutrition education and food access with hands-on school-day and after-school programs in the form of cooking and gardening clubs, student-run produce stands, summer learning, and job training, as well as adult senior nutrition. The literal seeds planted by Dr. Johnston, the eventual Netter Center, consistent student-community engagement, and university support have resulted in multifaceted sustainable impact. I could not have imagined this evolution and growth. I had not experienced anything of its kind before reaching Penn. From my freshman seminar, I felt the Academically Based Community Service (ABCS) and university-assisted community schools (UACS) efforts were laying down cobblestones on a path leading toward systematic change, and AUNI is evidence that this has been the case.

While teaching the chemistry–nutrition lessons my first two-and-a-half years at Turner, I constantly wondered whether the problem of adolescent obesity, prevalent in the Turner community, was as common in other communities and how environmental factors influenced nutrition and eating habits differentially in an inner-city ecology. But my ruminations were not, at the time, grounded in a scientific hypothesis or potential intervention to test. During my years at Penn (1991–1995), epidemiology was not a commonly referenced field of study in undergraduate circles, and independent research projects were not something that many college students led. Yet the multidisciplinary, experiential learning that I was immersed in, through ABCS, UACS, and the accessible visions and active dialogues with Drs. Harkavy and Johnston, encouraged me to formulate a research question based on my real-world experiences. As I did, I learned about study design, systematic data collection, analysis, inferences, and translating empirical evidence into actionable insights. Acknowledging that my work was an epidemiologic study, Dr. Harkavy, Dr. Johnston, Dr. Penny Gordon Larsen (a graduate student at the time), and I worked together to develop my research project and senior thesis, "An Ecological Study of Adolescent Nutrition Behavior Case Study: John P. Turner Middle School vs. Murray Avenue Middle School." (Murray Avenue was my middle school in suburban Philadelphia.) Their grounding of my work in epidemiology led me to explore the field and pursue my master's and subsequent PhD in epidemiology.

My journey into public health began in Dr. Harkavy's classroom and beyond Penn's ivory tower through the Center for Community Partnerships and work at Turner Middle School. The juxtaposition of my suburban, well-resourced middle school and Turner was enlightening on many fronts. As I continued in the pursuit of my master's and doctorate, I carried with me the importance of social determinants of health, disparities in individual and community health due to a myriad of contextual influences, and the need to understand deeply the interaction effects of multiple risk and protective factors. If I ask myself how much impact my senior thesis made on the broader landscape of the challenges of obesity in the underserved populations of West Philadelphia, my answer is likely little to none. Yet, if it even contributed a modicum of evidence to support funding of AUNI; ignited a single Turner Middle School student's interest in science, nutrition, or both; or simply sounded intriguing to another undergraduate student to serve as impetus to enroll in an ABCS course or work with the Netter Center, then I deem it as a positive step toward change. Even if none of these came to fruition, the exposure, skills, and hands-on experience of participating in this work was invaluable and shaped me as a scientist, collaborator, and analytic problem-solver.

During my master's and doctoral studies, I began working at the CDC, where I spent twenty years focused on the surveillance and epidemiology of neurodevelopmental disabilities and congenital defects. My work ranged from providing empirical evidence for passage of universal newborn hearing screening[2] to setting up a national surveillance system for monitoring the prevalence and risk factors for autism spectrum disorders;[3] examining the association between lower birth weight, cerebral palsy, and racial-ethnic disparities;[4] and developing a systematic approach to monitoring the impact of universal screening for critical congenital heart defects in New Jersey.[5] And during the COVID-19 pandemic, I was asked by the National Medical Committee of the Ramah Camping Movement to provide assistance in creating protocols to safely mitigate the introduction and transmission of SARS CoV-2 in congregate settings. Working with an extraordinary set of medical providers, I helped develop multicomponent mitigation protocols. After these protocols were implemented, there were no secondary transmissions identified in camp during the 2021 summer sessions of nine overnight camps serving approximately 7,200 campers and staff from 50 states and 13 countries. With the collective foresight of the medical committee, we quickly designed a study to prospectively evaluate these mitigation strategies and partnered with the CDC to publish the findings to inform other organizations struggling with developing methods to keep their children and staff healthy during the pandemic.[6] Each of these studies required analytic problem-solving of difficult public health issues, and each in some way built on my foundational multidisciplinary ABCS and UACS involvement.

During my tenure at the CDC, a significant portion of my time was invested in building the Metropolitan Atlanta Developmental Disabilities Surveillance Program (MADDSP), conceived and created by my very special mentor, Dr. Marshalyn Yeargin-Allsopp, and then developing its larger replica, the Autism and Developmental Disabilities Monitoring (ADDM) Network. MADDSP was established in 1991 as the first multiple-source surveillance system for developmental disabilities. The aim was to estimate the number of children who had one or more of four developmental disabilities—intellectual disability, cerebral palsy, hearing loss, and vision impairment—in metropolitan Atlanta. In 1996, autism spectrum disorder (ASD) was added as a fifth developmental disability.[7] Prevalence estimates are released every two years along with the detailed descriptive characteristics of the cohorts. With the passage of the Children's Health Act in 2000, funding was directed to replicate the MADDSP model to conduct ASD surveillance across multiple sites in the United States: the resultant ADDM Network. The data produced from these surveillance programs are consistently referenced as the population-based prevalence in the United States for ASD and are the pool for numerous research studies working to further our understanding of these complex neurodevelopmental conditions. From the programs' inceptions, community partnerships have been key to the MADDSP and ADDM methods of identifying children with ASD and other developmental disabilities. Ascertainment of children with ASD relies on identifying places in the community that educate, diagnose, treat, and provide services to children with ASD. Once these sites are identified, they enter into a memorandum of agreement with their ADDM site to appoint the ADDM site as their public health representative for confidential record review. This review includes a group of trained abstractors who identify behaviors consistent with ASD documented in children's records. Scientists analyze the collected data and return findings to the community to improve the care of children with ASD.[8] As the principal investigator for MADDSP, I made it a priority not only to ensure the scientific rigor of our methods but also to cultivate and maintain trustworthy relationships with our partners at the Georgia Departments of Education and Health, at the many local special education departments, and at public and private health care providers. As in my experiences with the Turner Middle School community, partnerships grounded in trust and strong communication enabled us to work toward the common goal of moving science forward to help children and their families.

I was and am deeply proud of my CDC work, and I still hold the relationships that I made during that time close to my heart. But after twenty years, I needed a new professional challenge. I was recruited to pharma many times over my years at the CDC, but the work wasn't what I wanted to do. When presented with the opportunity to leverage real-world observational data to support a new space—the creation of synthetic control arms for single-arm clinical trials—I was both intrigued and energized at the prospect of bringing new therapies to very sick patients with few or no options. An epidemiologist in research and development was quite new and unique to pharma, so I was drawn to be at the beginning of a formative wave. As it turned out, the technical skills required in my CDC work and my new venture were not worlds apart. This made the technical transition smooth. More important, there was and is a cultural understanding in research and development that our goal is to advance drugs for patient benefit, not to make the company money per se. New analytic challenges coupled with this shared sense of purpose quickly diffused the warnings that a few friends voiced about my jump to pharma. I could tell you story upon story about how novel drugs have saved lives in populations of patients with truly unmet medical needs. As I get older, I see ever more illness around me. Living through the pandemic, I truly appreciate the impact of innovative drug development, and I now see how very hard it is to accomplish. The work I do accelerates and targets the drug development process. This, I feel, is a good thing. Despite what many may think, pharma is actually not the "dark side," from my perspective.

I dove into industry to create two synthetic comparator arms to match two single-arm trials. Our aim was to quantify the efficacy of two chimeric antigen receptor T cellular therapies for large B-cell lymphoma and multiple myeloma, respectively, bringing them both to regulatory approval.[9] Since then, my remit has expanded to translational epidemiology within early research. My current work leverages observational real-world multimodal data—linked patient-level clinical, genomic, transcriptomic, imaging (radiologic and immunohistologic), and electrophysiologic data—to identify new therapeutic targets for drug development. Our efforts are laser-focused on bringing the right drug to the right patient at the right time. How does my work now relate to that of the Netter Center? To me it is rather clear. It is the ability to think critically about scientific questions, whether at the bench, bedside, or community school setting, and to work collaboratively and creatively across functions to innovate and iterate toward improving the health of the public and all of its populations.

Is there a place for the pharmaceutical industry within the Netter ethos of ABCS courses and UACS? Private enterprises such as drug companies always have their financial priorities. They are, by definition, unbound by the accountabilities of public-private entities receiving federal funding. Their conceptions of community engagement and partnerships are inevitably different from those of entities anchored in the Netter Center's framework. Yet it is worth noting that pharmaceutical companies, too, contribute to social welfare in its widest sense. They pioneer new therapeutics and devices in areas of high unmet medical need for both very broad and select patient populations, improving health as they do. They make sizable charitable contributions, launch fundraising and health education and awareness campaigns that give back to their communities. They invest in hands-on civic engagement projects, work to increase diversity in clinical trial recruitment, and donate therapeutics to help eradicate preventable communicable diseases in developing countries as well as improve access to medicines globally.[10] Is meaningful improvement on these efforts necessary? Most definitely. Where I see parallels in the pharmaceutical industry to my early career development is the industry's support for future cohorts of scientists. Offering individual students opportunities for intellectual growth and paving the way for potential professional paths tracks with what Netter did for me. I have found that the tenets of the Netter Center's approach to creative problem-solving are easily transferable to the industry's research setting. Creating cross-functional, multidisciplinary scientific teams and work streams that are both structured and agile enough to move innovation forward are crucial and highly reflective of how progress is made in the Netter Center communities.

As I have spent my career in a field of counting, I could not help but quantify the reach of the Netter Center since its founding in 1992: from 4 ABCS courses and 100 students led by 3 faculty members in the 1991–1992 academic year to 73 such courses with over 1,850 students and 69 faculty members in 2019–2020. The growth of the reach of the Netter Center has been exponential over the past three decades.[11] The replication of the UACS framework has occurred in various regions nationally and globally. Yet the field of counting—epidemiology—goes far beyond determining prevalence and incidence. Understanding the predictive and prognostic factors that mediate or modify the correlations and causal mechanisms in human health is both crucial and complicated. It is an appreciation for the complexities of identifying and working to solve real-world problems that I see impacting students in ABCS classes and those participating in UACS partnerships. Through both identifying the problem and working toward change, the experiential learning and accessible community dialogue afforded by ABCS coursework and UACS programs develop analytic problem-solving skills widely applicable beyond the specific gains of a given semester.

Just as counting and understanding the multifactorial nature of disease processes are part and parcel of epidemiology, so too are the concept and practice of measurement. The emphasis I place on methodological issues surrounding study design, such as the various forms of bias, measurement error, and data missingness, has grown over time. In my senior thesis at Penn, conducting anthropometric measurement of our study sample of middle school children was straightforward. Making multiple measurements to ensure validity was also feasible, as was collecting documentation of the school lunch program over the study period. But collection of socioeconomic data through surveys and interviews proved to be more variable and less informative than I had hoped in my undergraduate endeavor. This was my entry into the importance of thoughtful measurement design. Can I measure the construct well with the tools and data that I have? If not, what is the impact of measurement error on my analysis and how can we mitigate inaccurate and inappropriate inferences? My concern over measurement error recurred in nearly every study and analysis I have led. From varying denominator definitions for measuring prevalence to the impact of changes in diagnostic criteria on case ascertainment, a keen focus on specifying the measures of interest proved crucial.[12] This continued to be true in the pharmaceutical context, where we used observational, electronic health care data to create a cohort of patients receiving standard of care in real-world practice settings to serve as the control group matched with subjects who meet strict eligibility criteria for enrollment in a clinical trial. To rigorously match the real-world patient controls with subjects from the clinical trial for regulatory purposes, the data elements essential for propensity score matching needed to be ascertained and derived from standard of care as comparably as possible to those collected as a part of the trial. Further, the study design needed to account for the inherent differences between the prospective design of a clinical trial and the retrospective, observational data collection of real-world data. I can attribute my fascination and constant struggle with measurement in data collection and analysis to my early days in ABCS and UACS.

Though I have remained professionally and personally outside academia through my entire career, the multidisciplinary analytic toolkit that I amassed from my years with the Netter Center has been readily and easily transferable across professional sectors and has empowered me at each step in my professional journey. The other absolute truth constant in each experience has been the invaluable role of trusted partnerships. Partnerships can take and have taken many shapes, but each has been an essential thread in weaving the fabric of productive science together.

While my fellow contributors, most based in academic settings, are tied in some ways more directly to the work of the Netter Center than I am in my current role in industry, I see my work in translational epidemiology within early research as well as my previous work at the CDC as highly reflective of the methods and skills at the heart of the Netter Center's initiatives. I identify problems, I appreciate their deep contexts, and I work collaboratively across disciplines to uncover innovative solutions. I work daily to identify the right data to meet a given research question, develop methods to appropriately measure and statistically test hypotheses, and in the end support drug development to bring better treatment options to patients. I am constantly struck by the many parallels between my undergraduate problem-solving around adolescent obesity and need for creativity in developing hands-on chemistry-nutrition lesson plans and my professional efforts to understand racial-ethnic disparities in the risk for cerebral palsy among low-birthweight babies and to validate a predictive biomarker for a specific treatment for colorectal cancer.

I dug out my senior thesis, and I would like to share what I found on page 24, the end of the introduction, written in spring semester my senior year in 1995:

> At this stage of my participation with the participatory research model, I believe as a young researcher that I have not fully articulated the multi-dimensional and comprehensive aspects which the participatory research model provides at all levels of the interactive spectrum. I have seen a continual building of growth and

empowerment within the Turner community over the past 3½ years as well as the university's relationship with West Philadelphia. This same growth has enriched me personally as a researcher and citizen in ways I will not be able to fully appreciate until later in my career. I feel that this model enables its participants on all levels to approach an environment with real-world problem solving as a continual "work in progress" toward the betterment of society whatever path that may be. Ultimately it is both the process and the goal which equally impact the individual and community. As each researcher in the participatory research model process moves onward in life it is this framework which links social responsibility with practical theory and experiential learning that can be applied to the solving of any scientific research question.[13]

Over the years, when asked about the influences on my professional trajectory, I have replied that my exposure to and work with Drs. Harkavy and Johnston and what is now the Netter Center fostered my analytic skills to creatively solve real-world problems. I honestly did not realize until I read my own words from twenty-eight years ago that as a college student I somehow felt that my experience had a larger impact than that moment in my life. The influence of ABCS and the Netter Center's work, regardless of the field of study, have inspired so many to tackle hard real-world problems with a civic-minded, innovative, collaborative, critical, and thoughtful approach. I have been very fortunate. I have had extraordinary mentors and satisfying professional opportunities at each step in my journey. I have followed and will continue to follow new challenges, hard problems, and my intellectual curiosity, always in the context of wanting to help others and advance science. My experience as a college student with Dr. Harkavy and the Netter Center truly shaped my approach as a quantitative scientist spanning multiple sectors over the course of the last thirty-two years, and for this I am sincerely grateful.

Notes

1. Lee Benson, Ira Harkavy, John Puckett, Matthew Hartley, Rita A. Hodges, Francis E. Johnston, and Joann Weeks, *Knowledge for Social Change: Bacon, Dewey and the Revolutionary Transformation of Research Universities in the Twenty-First Century* (Philadelphia: Temple University Press, 2017), xi–xiii.

2. Kim Van Naarden, Pierre Decoufle, and Kimberly Caldwell, "Prevalence and Characteristics of Children with Serious Hearing Impairment in Metropolitan Atlanta, 1991–1993," *Pediatrics* 103, no. 3 (Mar. 1999): 570–75, doi.org/10.1542/peds.103.3.570.

3. Kim Van Naarden Braun, Daisy Christensen, Nancy Doernberg, Laura Schieve, Catherine Rice, Lisa Wiggins, Diana Schendel, and Marshalyn Yeargin-Allsopp, "Trends in the Prevalence of Autism Spectrum Disorder, Cerebral Palsy, Hearing Loss, Intellectual Disability, and Vision Impairment, Metropolitan Atlanta, 1991–2010," *PLoS One* 10, no. 4 (2015): e0124120, doi.org/10.1371/journal.pone.0124120; Kim Van Naarden Braun, "Tracking Methods for Autism and Developmental Disabilities Monitoring (ADDM) Network," www.cdc.gov/autism/addm-network/.

4. Kim Van Naarden Braun, Nancy Doernberg, Laura Schieve, Deborah Christensen, Alyson Goodman, and Marshalyn Yeargin-Allsopp, "Birth Prevalence of Cerebral Palsy: A Population-Based Study," *Pediatrics* 137, no. 1 (Jan. 2016): 1–9, doi.org/10.1542/peds.2015-2872.

5. Lori Freed Garg, Kim Van Naarden Braun, and Mary Knapp, "Results from the New Jersey Statewide Critical Congenital Heart Defects Screening Program," *Pediatrics* 132, no. 2 (Aug. 2013): e314–23, doi.org/10.1542/peds.2013-0269.

6. Kim Van Naarden Braun et al., "Multicomponent Strategies to Prevent SARS-CoV-2 Transmission—Nine Overnight Youth Summer Camps, United States, June–August 2021," *Morbidity and Mortality Weekly Report (MMWR)* 70, no. 40 (Oct. 8, 2021): 1420–24, dx.doi.org/10.15585/mmwr.mm7040e1.

7. Van Naarden Braun et al., "Trends in the Prevalence."

8. Van Naarden Braun, "Tracking Methods."

9. Hoa Van Le, Kim Van Naarden Braun, and George Nowakowski, "Use of a Real-World Synthetic Control Arm for Direct Comparison of Liso-Cabtagene Maraleucel and Conventional Therapy in Relapsed/Refractory Large B-Cell Lymphoma," *Leukemia & Lymphoma* 64, no. 3 (Mar. 2023): 573–85, doi.org/10.1080/10428194.2022.2160200; Sundar Jagannath et al., "KarMMa-RW: Comparison of Idecabtagene Vicleucel with Real-World Outcomes in Relapsed and Refractory Multiple Myeloma," *Blood Cancer Journal* 11, no. 6 (June 2021): 116, doi.org/10.1038/s41408-021-00507-2.

10. E. Muniz Pereira Urias, "The Contribution of the Pharmaceutical Industry to the Health Status of the Developing World," in *Multinational Enterprises and Sustainable Development* (International Business and Management, vol. 33), ed. Xiaolan Fu, Pervez N. Gharui, and Juha Väätänen (Leeds: Emerald Group Publishing, 2017), 41–67, doi.org/10.1108/S1876-066X20170000033003.

11. "Course History," Netter Center for Community Partnerships, accessed Oct. 16, 2023, www.nettercenter.upenn.edu/what-we-do/abcs-courses/course-history.

12. Lisa Wiggins, Daisy Christensen, and Kim Van Naarden Braun, "Comparison of Autism Spectrum Disorder Surveillance Status Based on Two Different Diagnostic Schemes: Findings from the Metropolitan Atlanta Developmental Disabilities Surveillance Program, 2012," *PLoS One* 13, no. 11 (2018): e0208079, doi.org/10.1371/journal.pone.0208079; Kim Van Naarden Braun, Matthew Maenner, and Daisy Christensen,

"The Role of Migration and Choice of Denominator on Prevalence of Cerebral Palsy," *Developmental Medicine & Child Neurology* 55, no. 6 (June 2013): 520–26, doi.org /10.1111/dmcn.12095.

13. Kim Van Naarden, "An Ecological Study of Adolescent Nutrition Behavior Case Study: John P. Turner Middle School vs. Murray Avenue Middle School," unpublished senior thesis, University of Pennsylvania, Philadelphia, 1995, 24.

CHAPTER 14

Reflections on Bursting the Bubble

Michael Zuckerman

We tell ourselves that the college years are times of transformations. Our students enter as adolescents and emerge as young adults. They acquire new analytic tools and new critical perspectives. They encounter new worlds and experience new powers. More than that, they become better citizens and better people. They develop a sense of civic responsibility, an openness to new ideas, a capacity to take the perspective of others. Whether we view them with the optimists as wondrously awakened or with contemporary conservatives as pathetically "woke," we see their years on campus as years of metamorphosis.

And yet there is remarkably little evidence for our conventional wisdom. Study after unnerving study has sought to specify the substance of these transformations, and most of them have come up empty. From the first comprehensive reconnaissance in the literature, almost three-quarters of a century ago, a succession of pedagogues and social scientists have tracked students across their college days. Most of them have come to the same unsettling conclusion: students leave college largely as they come. If they change at all, they don't change much. Their values, convictions, attachments, and antipathies don't even shift in any momentous way, let alone turn topsy-turvy.

The 1950s collegians surveyed in Philip Jacob's classic reconnaissance came to campus as materialistic, self-centered careerists and graduated four years later as materialistic, self-centered careerists. They arrived as conformists and departed marginally more inclined to conform; fewer seniors than first-year students expressed views that deviated from peer norms. As Jacob observed, their responses confirmed the slackness of their very modest moral compass.

Compared to the population at large, collegians were a little more tolerant, a little less antagonistic to "radical" ideas and unconventional people, a
little less prejudiced toward minority groups than their fellow Americans. But
these divergences, marginal as they were, did not develop during their college
days. Young people who chose to pursue higher education were already a tad
more tolerant before they ever matriculated. They did not need professors to
teach them what they'd learned from family and friends. Indeed, Jacob discovered that professors were virtually powerless to affect ethics. The effects
of the content of the curriculum, the quality of teaching, and the methods of
instruction on value outcomes were all negligible.[1]

Later collegians surveyed in later studies have held different views and
values, though always in conformity with the prevailing views and values of
their own cultural moment. Some of those studies have even documented
statistically significant changes in undergraduates' outlooks that could actually be attributed to their college experience. But those changes have, almost
without exception, been small and peripheral. They have touched very little
on the grander life lessons that are often credited to the collegiate experience,
such as a maturing of judgment, an emergent sense of social responsibility,
and a blossoming perspicacity of understanding of self and others. And even
those studies have failed utterly to find that the changes that could be demonstrated could be claimed for the classroom.[2]

It is not hard to see why it has been so difficult to discover changing values
in college. Higher education in modern America has been, on the whole, an
extension of the schooling that comes before it and a prefiguration of what
comes next. As Jacob said seventy years ago, "No sharp break seems to occur
in the continuity of the main patterns of value which the students bring with
them" and carry away with them.[3] Collegians experience their alma mater—
and their alma mater carries itself—as an educational organization that they
churn through in order to get a credential and move on. The four years after
high school are just four more years of school.

Even at places like Penn, undergraduate classes are a lot like secondary school classes in deep essence. To those who take them, they represent
another stretch of the long preparation for and preoccupation with career
success. The term papers and final exams figure mainly as markers in a seem-
ingly endless succession of tests that define the meritocratic gauntlet that the
students run so well and that they appreciate full well goes on beyond the BA.
Long before they celebrate their commencement, they recognize that more
meritocratic sorting awaits them. Their transcripts and scores and letters of

recommendation will help determine their admission to graduate and professional programs of all sorts and their landing of lucrative jobs. And still the struggle will not be over. They will continue in competition, for clerkships and residencies, postdocs and partnerships, at least until they approach meritocratic midlife. Certainly, so long as they remain in school, students have scant reason to rethink the path on which their privileged parents set them years before they came to Penn.

*   *   *

All that said, the life stories in this collection are tales of transformation. How can we account for that? What might we learn from it?

The research suggests that so long as they stay within the bubble that is Penn, students are unlikely to experience anything that will profoundly challenge their assumptions and values or rattle their life goals. But the students who tell their stories here ventured outside that bubble. Not to the chic bars and restaurants—or the dives—of Center City. Not to the concert venues of South Philadelphia and Northern Liberties. But to the mean streets and neglected schools of West Philadelphia west of 40th Street and north of Market. All the stories in this book share that intrepid quest beyond the bounds that Penn warned its students were the outer limits of their safety. All these then-young seekers took what Robert Frost called the road less traveled, and that, as he said it would, made all the difference.

The same studies that fail to find momentous change across four years of formal study do find other ways in which college life does touch students. Researchers speak of these as "high-impact practices," or "HIPs." Some of them, such as first-year seminars, collaborative projects, and capstone courses, are campus-based. Others, such as study away, internships, and service learning, are community-based. All of them are more efficacious than conventional classroom work in altering mindsets and dispositions, in expanding personal and social responsibility, in fostering intrapersonal development and intercultural awareness, and even in pushing young people toward rethinking their career plans. And service learning is the most efficacious of them all.[4]

I experienced these impacts vividly in the Academically Based Community Service (ABCS) course that I taught from 1990 till I retired in 2010. In that course, my students spent two or three hours every week in the schools of West Philadelphia. They encountered more execrable conditions than they could have imagined, but they also got to know a fair number of students in those schools. And when they came to make meaning of what they'd seen, in their final papers, they came to one conclusion more than any other: there, but for the grace of God, go I.

Penn students are victors in the struggle for meritocratic survival. They think very well of themselves. You could call them arrogant. But in those inner-city classrooms, they learned things they'd never learned in their own affluent schools.

The African American high schoolers they'd become close to couldn't read very well, and some could scarcely write at all. They had trouble with sentences and paragraphs, sequences and transitions, spelling and grammar. To my students, none of those failings mattered much. They were the givens of poverty and an underfunded school system. They were at once shocking and perfectly predictable.

The discovery that did matter usually took time to emerge. But time and again, more often than not, it came. My students resisted it at first. They were too confident of their place at the pinnacle. Yet the evidence before their eyes and ears and minds was too strong to deny, and they owned up to it in their final papers for the course. Many of those kids, they wrote, were quick and sharp. As quick and sharp—and as resourceful and thoughtful—as they themselves were. Numbers of them were, if anything, wittier and more incisive. And almost all of them were braver. Almost all of them were coping with challenges—hunger, danger, family responsibilities, and more—that my Penn students believed beyond their own capacity to manage.

My Penn students continued convinced that they deserved their successes insofar as they competed with others equally advantaged. But they did come to see that merit had little or nothing to do with the successes that would be theirs in comparison to the West Philly high schoolers. In their final papers, they wrote of their realization that those young people were headed for poverty, prison, and perhaps an untimely death not so much because of their personal failings as because of the accident of their birth. Weighing themselves against the teens they'd come to know, my students concluded that they were not even their equals. For all their intellectual gifts, they could not see themselves handling daunting difficulties as courageously, as creatively, as powerfully—or as intelligently—as those beleaguered youngsters did.

These recognitions were as routine as they were revolutionary. They turned up year after year, in final paper after final paper. They marked the power of in-your-face experience—of gross inequity in the world beyond campus and classroom—to overturn ideology. Week after week, my ABCS students encountered disparities that they could not slough off as the righteous result of differential aptitudes and abilities. By the end of the semester, they simply could not credit the rationale that underpins their privilege, the conviction that inequalities are ultimately rooted in unequal merit.

Not nearly so routine was the time my ABCS students assaulted me. It only happened once, but I've never forgotten it. The occasion was the first class after spring break. As we chatted before taking up the day's topic, one of the students said, with some acerbity, that I had caused her uncomfortable moments with her family. Another pitched in to the same effect, and another. Half the class joined the attack. My brainwashing had caused them grief at their Easter dinners, Passover seders, and all manner of other family gatherings.

As my classes usually did, that class ran the political gamut. There were red diaper babies, San Diego conservatives, and a half-dozen sitings on the spectrum in between. But one way or another they'd all found themselves on the outs with their parents and aunts and uncles over issues of racial justice. One way or another, they'd all become too radical for kin with whom they'd never before been anything but cordial. And I was responsible for their radicalization.

I pointed out to them, defensively, that I'd done my damnedest not to indoctrinate. No doubt I had my biases, and no doubt they were savvy readers of their professors. But for every reading on our syllabus that was Left there was another that was Right. I could continue to teach the class, I confessed, because I couldn't even resolve those tensions for myself, let alone for them. I still saw intriguing, even revelatory, arguments on many sides.

We went round and round on this for a while—a lot of them had a lot at stake—until one thoughtful young woman suggested that there was a way out, a way between my claims of clean hands and her classmates' experiences of pain. It was not I who had moved them in more radical directions, nor any of the readings I'd assigned. It was the time they'd spent in the classrooms of West Philadelphia. They'd all developed sufficient skill to resist the arguments of professors and books. What they couldn't resist was the force of their own extended exposure to the immediate realities of injustice. They'd seen for themselves the intelligence, the dauntlessness, the caring, and the capacity for coping of the kids they mentored. They'd seen too the abysmal failure of the schools to bring out any of their kids' gifts. When they heard their parents or grandparents pronounce dismissively or derisively on the students they'd come to know so differently, they'd felt compelled to speak up.

She was just one voice, and just a speculative one at that. But before she'd even finished laying out her idea, a couple of others were shaking their heads in excited agreement and waving their hands wildly to chime in. Others soon added their anecdotes of concurrence. They had not engaged—and enraged—their family conclaves as smart-ass Ivy Leaguers. They had simply spoken what seemed to them the plain truths of their hard-won knowledge.

We ditched discussion of the day's reading and spent the rest of the hour wondering how to make those plain truths more palatable to others still protected by their privilege and how to propel others—especially other Penn students—beyond their bubble of ideologized innocence.

I've been wondering ever since.

*   *   *

As a historian, I sometimes turn to the past when I wonder about the present. I think, then, of how different college life once was. Student days may not be times of transformation now, but they might well have been in the more distant past. In the nineteenth century, when Victorian norms kept most middle-class adolescents virginal, colleges were often sites of sexual initiation. Today, more than half of all teens make their sexual debut before they turn eighteen. In the first half of the twentieth century, when most men married before twenty-five and most women before twenty-two, colleges were unabashed marriage marts. Today, college men and women alike defer matrimony till later in their twenties, and few undergraduates feel any urgency about finding a life partner while still in school.

Through the first three-quarters of the nineteenth century, even large colleges were little larger than the small learning communities that contemporary progressives count among the high-impact practices that stimulate deep change in students. Small colleges—the vast majority of American colleges—simply *were* small learning communities. In 1847, when it was the largest seat of higher learning in America, Yale enrolled fewer than six hundred students. Thirty years later, Harvard matriculated a freshman class of two hundred for the first time.

Even at the turn of the twentieth century, a bare 2 or 3 percent of American youth went to college at all. A man could no longer be a doctor if he worked a few cures, called himself a doctor, and attracted patients, but he could still become a lawyer by apprenticing himself to a lawyer for a few months and learning his craft. He didn't need so much as a BA, let alone an MBA, to run a railroad or organize the greatest oil combine in the world. Universities were still generations away from becoming a part of the corporate colossus that is the modern United States of America.

In 1900, Penn itself was just a small speck on the Philadelphia landscape. It occupied just a few brief blocks of its modest Victorian suburb, and it had far too few faculty and staff to count among the consequential employers of the city. Today, it sprawls across an acreage greater than all of Philadelphia did at the time of the American Revolution, and its payroll is the largest in the city. It is a cosmos quite unto itself, bright and bustling, teeming with stuff and styles and ideas at the cutting edge of cosmopolitan American life. Its very brilliance raises questions.

How do we draw students out of that exciting, satisfying cocoon of privilege? How do we entice them toward a more immersive exposure to the worlds of poverty and privation, and resilience and resourcefulness, that surround the university, where they might widen their own world as the authors of the essays in this book did?

As a historian (and, I confess with pride, as my student during his undergraduate days), Ira Harkavy loves to look to the past when he confronts tough questions in the present. He loves especially to look to Ben Franklin for inspiration. But Franklin would not seem to promise much help here. Though his Philadelphia may have been the most populous place in the new American nation, and its political, economic, and cultural capital besides, it was still a very small place. Its settled space ran just six blocks west from the Delaware and eight blocks from its northern to its southern bounds. It simply did not confront the questions that we do. In that cramped compound, no deliberate effort was needed to spur social sympathy or expose citizens to the plights and privileges of others unlike themselves. Rich and poor encountered one another daily on shared streets and in crowded taverns and markets. No class could set itself apart spatially. All had an inkling—if not a very good idea—of how the other half lived.

Yet even in that city, Franklin did provide a pattern. Even in a milieu that afforded the affluent no sustained refuge from unwanted encounters with those they thought dirty or dangerous, Franklin planned to push the students of his fledging college out of their comfort zone. In his *Proposals Relating to the Education of Youth in Pensilvania*—the blueprint for the school that eventually became the University of Pennsylvania—his visionary curriculum included regular trips to the farms that surrounded the city. Though he envisioned commercial careers for the students of his imagined college, he was adamant that they enlarge their horizons. Expulsion from the pleasures of their classrooms and the cozy company of their classmates was, for him, an imperative part of their education.

Today, Penn provides abundantly for such expulsions. Study abroad, semester in DC, summer internships, and many more offer extraordinary opportunities off campus and wondrously worthy enhancements of the undergraduate experience. But almost all of them are continuous in crucial ways with that undergraduate experience. Almost all of them are competitive, performance-graded, and open primarily to the privileged. Almost all of them confer elite merit badges. Almost all of them allow students a taste of power and prepare them for more power.

In short, all of them are cooked. Few if any of them are even as raw as the grubbing in the soil that Franklin recommended for his conjectural collegians, let alone as raw as the close encounters with poverty that the contributors to this volume describe. Few if any of them have the transformative potential that work in West Philadelphia schools, or any other work in any other communities of disprivilege, does. Few if any of them have the power to change lives as profoundly as that work does. Few if any of them are even jarring enough to shake students out of their complacently aspiring lives and push them to develop in new directions: to understand perspectives other than their own, to collaborate as partners with people poorer and less powerful than they are, to grasp the democratic imperative of humility, to care as much for their communities as they do for their own self-interest.

How do we persuade our students that their lives will be richer if they risk that rupture? How do we entice them out of their exhilarating cocoon by the banks of the Schuylkill and get them to go west of 40th Street? How do we break them of their illusions of invulnerability and prepare them for the rude shocks that life brings us all? How do we gift them the resiliency that they will need at those times and the personal growth and public healing that we all need so urgently at this present pass? How do we bring them to see that we can all do better when we can all do better?

* * *

Or do I ask too many questions? Is it too much to ask for more than the marvelous life stories we have here? Might it be enough to rejoice in the many triumphs—most modest, some mighty—that course through these narratives? Might it be sufficient to state the obvious, that every one of these tales, each in its own right, tantalizes?

Though they do not answer my questions, they do testify to the transformative power of experience beyond the bubble. They do show that civic engagement can be a path, not an impediment, to personal and professional success. Their trajectories may be as varied as their voices, but they converge in their common commitments to collaborative problem-solving, participatory democracy, and respect for community knowledge. More than that, they do chart a multitude of ways of coming of age and crafting careers as creative and compassionate citizens who contribute significantly to the welfare of others.

In doing so, they do more than merely vindicate Ira Harkavy's confidence that pursuing solutions to local problems in cooperation with the locals can both alleviate community ills and grow scholarly knowledge. They also mark the maturing of a second generation of community-engaged professors and practitioners, and they model that practice for the third generation that will follow. In sharing their stories and tracing the setbacks and successes they encountered, our authors alert that rising generation to the twists and turns, the frustrations and the splendid surprises that await.

And make no mistake. A third generation is on its way. A veritable movement is now evident in higher education all across America. Colleges and universities everywhere are recognizing the importance of civic engagement, supporting measures to educate their students for democratic citizenship, and creating mutually beneficial partnerships with the communities around them to improve the quality of life in those communities.[5]

The Netter Center has been at the forefront of this movement, and the Netter alumni who have contributed to this collection have been significant contributors to the Center's work. But they are just a very few among the many—literally, thousands—who have taken ABCS classes and participated in Center projects. Netter alumni are everywhere, all of them touched by their experience beyond the bubble.

Even the tiny company who are represented here are almost everywhere. Though they are scarcely more than a baker's dozen, they are based in northern New England and Southern California, in the Pacific Northwest and the South, and across the Midwest as well. They work in large and small state universities, in Fortune 500 companies, in established and emergent NGOs, and in an astonishing array of fields: Africana Studies, anthropology, arts administration, data analytics, education, health care, history, information science, law, marketing, museum leadership, pharmaceuticals, philosophy, and public policy, to take merely the most obvious. In all those places and in all that work, they teach their students and train their successors. In the classroom, on the job, and out in the community, they pass along the values that they took from their time in West Philadelphia. As they do, they multiply the ranks of young people struggling for social justice.

*   *   *

There is a conventional wisdom that is cousin to the conventional wisdom that the college years are times of transformation. In its most colorful version, it moralizes that if you're young and conservative, you have no heart; if you're old and liberal, you have no brain. In less dogmatic versions, it simply holds that we are more radical in our youth, more conventional in our older age.

Of course, there is no more evidence for this conventional wisdom than for that one. And every one of the lives chronicled in the collection gives it the lie. Without exception, these Netter alumni have carried their youthful convictions into satisfying adult lives.

From my perspective, teaching an ABCS class for a couple of decades, their steadfastness is far from remarkable. They have simply remained true to their experience beyond the bubble, because the truths of that experience were so compelling. Like my own students, they discovered that they had something to teach and much to learn in West Philadelphia.

The mutuality and humility that pervade these autobiographical accounts are the core of the democratic aspiration to which the Netter Center is and has always been dedicated. It is the mutuality and humility to which their authors call their students and their colleagues. They still see what they saw as undergraduates, that working for and with others enlarges the self as well as improving the world. They still embrace the realization to which they came those many years ago that there are grander adventures beyond than within the bubble of their privilege. They still think and act in the spirit of Ishmael's revelatory insight into the ethic of his unlikely friend Queequeg in Melville's epic *Moby Dick*. "It's a mutual joint-stock world in all meridians. We cannibals must help these Christians."

Notes

1. Philip Jacob, *Changing Values in College: An Exploratory Study of the Impact of College Teaching* (New York: Harper, 1957).

2. Ernest Pascarella and Patrick Terenzini, *How College Affects Students: A Third Decade of Research* (San Francisco: Jossey-Bass, 2005).

3. Jacob, *Changing Values*, 4.

4. "'High Impact Practices' Increase Students' Civic Engagement," *Higher Education Today*, blog by American Council on Education, Oct. 7, 2022, www.higheredtoday.org /2022/10/07/high-impact-practices-increase-students-civic-engagement/.

5. Lee Benson, Ira Harkavy, John Puckett, Matthew Hartley, Rita A. Hodges, Francis E. Johnston, and Joann Weeks, *Knowledge for Social Change: Bacon, Dewey, and the Revolutionary Transformation of Research Universities in the Twenty-First Century* (Philadelphia: Temple University Press, 2017); Ira Harkavy, Rita A. Hodges, and Joann Weeks, "Towards Creating the Truly Engaged, Responsive University: Penn's Partnership with the West Philadelphia Community as an Experiment in Progress," in *The Responsive University and the Crisis in South Africa*, ed. Chris Brink, 47–77 (Leiden: Koninklijke Brill, 2021).

1981

- Penn Program for Public Service Summer Internship begins, involving a select group of undergraduates in local internships, a research seminar taught by historians Ira Harkavy and Lee Benson, and a common residential experience.

1983

- Office of Community-Oriented Policy Studies (OCOPS) is created by Penn School of Arts and Sciences, and Harkavy is named director.

1984

- Undergraduate in Public Service Summer Internship focuses her research paper on West Philadelphia schools, and significant interest of other interns in her topic leads Benson and Harkavy to focus their seminars on West Philadelphia, particularly its public schools.

1985

- Harkavy, Benson, and Penn President Sheldon Hackney teach first Academically Based Community Service (ABCS) course.
- The West Philadelphia Improvement Corps (WEPIC) begins as a youth corps model in West Philadelphia, based on the proposal of four students in the course cotaught by Benson, Harkavy, and Hackney. Work begins at Bryant Elementary School.

1986

- WEPIC programs expand to West Philadelphia High School and Lea Elementary School.

1987

- US Department of Labor supports WEPIC program involving high school students in housing construction and neighborhood improvement as a national Youth Employment and Demonstration Project.

- WEPIC programs expand to Turner Middle School, which serves as the flagship for many years under leadership of teacher partner Marie Bogle.
- Philadelphia Higher Education Network for Neighborhood Development (PHENND) is cofounded by Benson and Harkavy at Penn with partners at two other local universities, Temple and La Salle.

1988

- Penn Program for Public Service (PPPS) is formed by the School of Arts and Sciences, replacing OCOPS.
- The German Marshall Fund of the United States supports PPPS staff and teachers working with WEPIC and local policymakers to travel to Sweden, West Germany, France, and Great Britain to discuss innovations in school-based training and community revitalization programs. Five cases, including WEPIC, are featured in a book called *SchoolWorks: Reinventing Public Schools to Create the Workforce of the Future* (Brookings Institution, 1989).

1989

- WEPIC school-based programs expand, and Turner and West Philadelphia High School are named "University-Assisted Community Schools" (UACS).
- State funding is added to local and federal monies to develop UACS, initiating an approach that integrates funding streams across all levels of government with private and university sources to support university-community-school partnerships.
- *Universities and Community Schools* journal helps to establish a network of academics and practitioners working to increase the contributions universities make to the development and effectiveness of community schools.

1990

- During the kickoff of Penn's 250th Anniversary celebration, Penn President Sheldon Hackney proposes a universitywide center for community partnerships.
- WEPIC serves as a model for Learn and Serve America's higher-education component, a program under the National and Community Service Act of 1990.

1991

- Professor Francis (Frank) Johnston converts his anthropology course to ABCS; he and his students lay the foundation for school-based health and nutrition programming called the Turner Nutritional Awareness Program.

1992

- The Center for Community Partnerships (now known as the Netter Center) is established as a universitywide center, and Harkavy is appointed as founding director.
- Community Advisory Board of the Center is formed, followed by a Faculty Advisory Board.

1993

- With a planning grant from the Wallace Foundation (then the DeWitt Wallace–Reader's Digest Fund), the Center develops a strategy for WEPIC Replication, to support other colleges and universities in adapting its UACS model.

1994

- Judith Rodin becomes Penn president, increases the university's focus on improving West Philadelphia, and highlights ABCS as a core component of undergraduate education.
- First implementation grant is awarded for WEPIC Replication, which funds three replication sites for initial three years.

1995

- Turner Nutritional Awareness Program evolves to become the Urban Nutrition Initiative (later the Agatston Urban Nutrition Initiative, or AUNI).
- Harkavy is contributor to the essay *The University and the Urban Challenge* by US Department of Housing and Urban Development Secretary Henry Cisneros, indicating the necessity for colleges and universities to contribute to cities as "great anchoring institutions" with "formidable intellectual and economic resources."

1996

- Twenty ABCS courses are taught, engaging approximately five hundred Penn students in the community.
- The Office of University Partnerships through the US Department of Housing and Urban Development (HUD) funds the Center as a Community Outreach Partnership Center.

- Center for Community Partnerships establishes an associate director position to lead Penn Volunteers in Public Service (Penn VIPS), providing a vehicle for staff, faculty, alumni, and West Philadelphia residents to work together on community service activities and events.

1997

- Harkavy cofounds the Coalition for Community Schools and is named chair (position held until 2012).

1998

- Jessie Ball duPont Fund supports work with communities of faith in West Philadelphia, leading to long-term partnerships with faith-based communities and religious leaders.
- With funding from the W. K. Kellogg Foundation, the Center initiates the Nonprofit Institute, offering free workshops for members of local nonprofits and faith-based communities.
- Grants from the Wallace Foundation and the Corporation for National and Community Service's Learn and Service America program expand WEPIC Replication, with twenty-three UACS programs funded across the country through 2004.

1999

- The Center spearheads the creation of the International Consortium for Higher Education, Civic Responsibility, and Democracy to work in collaboration with the Council of Europe; Harkavy initially becomes cochair and soon after chair.
- Undergraduate proposal in Benson and Harkavy's seminar leads to creation of the Foundation Community Arts Initiative, now known as the Rotunda, which hosts performances and community events on 40th Street.
- Access Science (now Moelis Access Science) launches with initial funding from the National Science Foundation.

2000

- The Center receives the Best Practices/Outstanding Achievement Award from HUD's Office of Policy Development and Research.
- National Advisory Board is formed.
- The Mott Foundation funds the Center to work with seventy-five sites on higher education-community-school partnerships.

- Program to Bridge the Digital Divide is developed by a Penn engineering student to recycle and refurbish old university computers as well as provide computer skills training to the community.

2001

- Student Advisory Board is formed.

2002

- Thirty-eight ABCS courses engage approximately nine hundred Penn students in the community.

2003

- The National Academies awards the W. T. Grant Foundation Youth Development Prize to the UACS program for the outstanding, high-quality, evidence-based collaborative that generates significant advances in knowledge while increasing opportunities for young people.
- The Robert Wood Johnson Foundation cites Urban Nutrition Initiative as one of four promising models for improving health and nutrition among US children.

2004

- In her inaugural address, President Amy Gutmann proposes the "Penn Compact," with local engagement as a central tenet, to propel the university forward in its core endeavors of teaching, research, and service.

2005

- Campus Compact recognizes Agatston Urban Nutrition Initiative as one of eight exemplary Campus Community Partnerships in the United States.
- Penn, represented by the Center, is invited to serve as the exemplar private research university to help pilot the Carnegie Foundation's new Community Engagement Classification.

2006

- The International Consortium and the Council of Europe host the first Global Forum in Strasbourg on "Higher Education for Democratic Culture, Citizenship, Human Rights and Sustainability."

2007

- The Center is renamed the Barbara and Edward Netter Center for Community Partnerships in recognition of an extraordinarily

generous commitment from Penn parents and supporters Barbara
Netter and Edward Netter (C53).

- Community School National Award for Excellence is presented
  to Sayre High School and Netter Center partners by the Coalition
  for Community Schools.
- Three Netter Center colleagues author *Dewey's Dream: Universities and Democracies in an Age of Education Reform.*

2008

- University of Oklahoma–Tulsa is selected to develop the first
  regional training center on UACS.
- Netter Center publishes *Anchor Institutions Toolkit: A Guide for
  Neighborhood Revitalization.*
- Penn receives the Presidential Award in the President's Higher
  Education Community Service Honor Roll.

2009

- The Anchors Institutions Task Force (AITF) is created following
  a report by a committee chaired by Harkavy to the Secretary of
  the US Department of Housing and Urban Development, and
  committee members ask Harkavy to serve as AITF chair.
- Penn ties for number-one "Best Neighbor" University by the
  national *Saviors of Our Cities: Survey of Best College and University Civic Partnerships.*

2010

- Netter Center plays catalytic role in University City District's
  development of the West Philadelphia Skills Initiative, which connects local residents to jobs at anchor institutions in University City.

2011

- Indiana University–Purdue University Indianapolis is selected to
  develop the second regional training center on UACS.

2012

- Emerson Fellows program is created, engaging recent Penn grad-
  uates in policy and practice to advance UACS.
- Young Quakers Community Athletics program launches as a
  partnership between the Netter Center, Penn Athletics, and local
  schools.
- Penn receives second Presidential Award of the President's Higher
  Education Community Service Honor Roll in the focus area of
  Summer Learning.

2013

- "August Wilson and Beyond" ABCS course taught by Herman Beavers and Suzana Berger begins in partnership with the West Philadelphia Cultural Alliance (WPCA)–Paul Robeson House and Museum, a Netter Center partner since WPCA's founding in 1984.

2014

- University of Connecticut is selected to develop the third regional training center on UACS.

2015

- University-Assisted Community Schools National Network is formed in collaboration with the Coalition for Community Schools to share resources and best practices to advance UACS policy and practice.
- Penn receives the 2015 Carnegie Foundation's Community Engagement Classification—after receiving the classification originally in 2006—based on its examples of institutionalized practices of community engagement that showed alignment among mission, culture, leadership, resources, and practices.

2016

- Inaugural Netter Center Faculty–Community Partnership Award is presented.

2017

- Seven Netter Center colleagues author *Knowledge for Social Change: Bacon, Dewey and the Revolutionary Transformation of Research Universities in the Twenty-First Century.*
- University of California–Los Angeles is selected to develop the fourth regional training center on UACS.

2018

- Penn Leads the Vote (PLTV)—a student-run, nonpartisan program that increases voter engagement and voting while advancing Penn's role of supporting the democratic and civic engagement of Penn students—is reestablished in 2018 as part of the Netter Center.

2019

- Inaugural cohort of the Provost's Graduate Academic Engagement Fellowship at the Netter Center (PGAEF@NC), a two-year fellowship designed to support graduate students whose work centers on ABCS and other forms of community-engaged scholarship, as well as to elevate the education and training of the next generation of academics, begins.

- First jointly sponsored Provost–Netter Center Faculty–Community Partnership Award is presented.

2020

- Binghamton University is selected to develop fifth regional training center on UACS.
- Partnership is launched with Children's Hospital of Philadelphia (CHOP) and its Healthier Together Initiative to develop a place-based comprehensive approach to social, emotional, and mental wellness in UACS.
- Report of the ad hoc ABCS Faculty Committee for the Provost of the University of Pennsylvania is produced to help advance ABCS research, teaching, and learning.

2021

- Provost's Graduate Community-Engaged Research Mentorship (PGCERM) is created to introduce and engage more graduate students and faculty in community-engaged scholarship.

2022

- Sixth Global Forum is hosted in Dublin on "Higher Education Leadership for Democracy, Sustainability, and Social Justice" by the Global Cooperation for the Democratic Mission of Higher Education, composed of the International Consortium for Higher Education, Civic Responsibility, and Democracy (housed at the Center); the Council of Europe; the International Association of Universities; and the Organization of American States.
- Report of the ad hoc Faculty Committee on community-engaged scholarship for the Provost is produced, providing a definition of community-engaged scholarship at and for Penn.

2023

- Thirtieth Anniversary culminating events are hosted in the community and on campus, including Alumni Symposium on Community-Engaged Scholarship.
- Duke University, North Carolina Central University, and East Carolina University are selected as the site of the sixth regional training center on UACS.

- University's new strategic framework, *In Principle and Practice*, emphasizes Penn's core principles of being an anchored and engaged university and highlights goals to foster service-minded leadership and deepen engagement with West Philadelphia neighbors.
- Provost's Advisory Committee on Community Engaged Scholarship is appointed to advise the Provost's Office on how to further advance community-engaged scholarship at Penn.

2024

- Eight-two ABCS courses are taught, enrolling approximately 1,950 Penn students. More than 425 paid work-study students and interns and over 400 volunteers are also engaged with schools and other partners in West Philadelphia through the Netter Center.
- Anonymous endowment establishes the faculty director as a permanent position to be known as the Barbara and Edward Netter Director of the Netter Center.

CONTRIBUTORS

University of Pennsylvania school degrees: **C**: College (bachelor's); **CGS**: master's, College of General Studies; **ENG**: Engineering and Applied Science (bachelor's); **G**: master's, Arts and Sciences; **GCP**: master's, City Planning; **GED**: master's, Education; **GR**: doctorate; **GRD**: doctorate, Education; **GRW**: doctorate, Wharton; **WEV**: Wharton Evening School

H. Samy Alim (Penn C99) is the David O. Sears Presidential Endowed Chair in the Social Sciences at UCLA. He has written about language, race, youth culture, and education for more than twenty-five years. His books include *Articulate While Black: Barack Obama, Language, and Race in the U.S.* (Oxford University Press, 2012, with Geneva Smitherman), *Raciolinguistics: How Language Shapes Our Ideas About Race* (Oxford University Press, 2016, with John Rickford and Arnetha Ball), *Culturally Sustaining Pedagogies: Teaching and Learning for Justice in a Changing World* (Teachers College Press, 2017, with Django Paris), and *Freedom Moves: Hip Hop Knowledges, Pedagogies, and Futures* (University of California Press, 2023, with Jeff Chang and Casey Wong).

Jeff Camarillo (Penn C01) is the Assistant Director of Secondary Education at the Stanford Teacher Education Program (STEP). Prior to his current leadership role at STEP, Camarillo was a charter high school leader and founding principal of two of the Bay Area's newest and most innovative educational models, Lodestar High in East Oakland and the Luis Valdez Leadership Academy in East San Jose. He was also an assistant principal at the East Palo Alto Academy, a charter school founded by Stanford's Graduate School of Education. Before leading and founding charter high schools throughout the Bay Area, Camarillo was a middle and high school history teacher and coach in his father's hometown of Compton and in San Francisco.

Christina Cantrill (Penn C92) works as Director of Community Partnerships for the National Writing Project, known to be the nation's leading professional development network for teachers of writing. As an enthusiastic learner, she has spent years working alongside writing project teachers and their students to explore the emerging possibilities of new technologies and Connected Learning. She also instructs at the graduate level, with a focus on teaching and learning that connects both in and out of school, as well as digital writing and multimodal composition. She is currently an instructor at Penn's Graduate School of Education. Cantrill brings to her work a background in curriculum studies, puppet arts, and participatory practice.

Tamara Dubowitz (Penn C96, G00) is Professor and Chair in the Department of Epidemiology at the University of Pittsburgh School of Public Health. Her work focuses on the role of neighborhoods, or "place," in shaping health and health behaviors particularly among marginalized and historically oppressed populations. Before this, Dubowitz was a senior policy researcher and faculty at the Pardee RAND Graduate School for nearly eighteen years. Dubowitz received her ScM and ScD degrees from Harvard School of Public Health, where she studied social epidemiology, with concentrations in public health nutrition and maternal and child health. Dubowitz majored in Urban Studies and anthropology at the University of Pennsylvania and obtained an MSc in anthropology at Penn following her service with the US Peace Corps in Burkina Faso, West Africa.

Bernice Garnett (Penn C05) is the Adam and Abigail Burack Green and Gold Associate Professor of Education in the College of Education and Social Service at the University of Vermont. Garnett is an interdisciplinary public health scholar interested in community schools, food security, school climate, and positive youth development. Garnett uses community-based participatory research to address health and educational equity. She earned her doctorate (ScD) in social and behavioral sciences from Harvard School of Public Health; an MPH from Mailman School of Public Health, Columbia University; and her BA in health and society from the University of Pennsylvania.

Rita Axelroth Hodges (Penn C05, GED15, GRD24) is an Associate Director of the Netter Center for Community Partnerships at the University of Pennsylvania. She is coauthor of *The Road Half Traveled: University Engagement at a Crossroads* (Michigan State University Press, 2012, with Steve Dubb); and

Knowledge for Social Change: Bacon, Dewey and the Revolutionary Transformation of Research Universities in the Twenty-First Century (Temple University Press, 2017, with Netter colleagues). Hodges serves as executive secretary of the International Consortium for Higher Education, Civic Responsibility and Democracy, and is a member of the Philadelphia Higher Education Network for Neighborhood Development (PHENND) steering committee. She received her BA in psychology and her MSEd and Doctorate in education (EdD) from Penn.

John L. Jackson Jr. is Provost and Richard Perry University Professor at the University of Pennsylvania. A pioneering scholar of urban anthropology, visual culture, and critical race theory, he is the author of *Thin Description: Ethnography and the African Hebrew Israelites of Jerusalem* (Harvard University Press, 2013); *Racial Paranoia: The Unintended Consequences of Political Correctness* (Civitas, 2008); *Real Black: Adventures in Racial Sincerity* (University of Chicago Press, 2005); and *Harlemworld: Doing Race and Class in Contemporary Black America* (University of Chicago Press, 2001). He is also a producer and/or director of ten films that have been screened at dozens of international film festivals, including the multi-award-winning *Making Sweet Tea* and the widely screened and taught *Bad Friday: Rastafari After Coral Gardens.*

Jacqueline Kraemer (Penn C87) is Director of Policy Analysis and Development at the National Center on Education and the Economy (NCEE). She studies the policies and practices of successful education systems globally to draw lessons, ideas, and inspiration for reform in US states and districts. Kraemer directs comparative research projects, writes policy and research briefs, and serves as a consultant for state commissions and projects focused on the redesign of education systems. Before working at NCEE, she worked on workforce development policy and directed university-assisted community school programs in West Philadelphia schools.

David Park (Penn ENG01) serves as Director of Data and Business Analytics at the National League of Cities, leading organizational strategy to support data-informed policy- and decision-making across its network of 19,000 municipalities around the country. He has over two decades of experience across the public and private sectors and served in roles at the Brookings Institution, PricewaterhouseCoopers, and the Urban Land Institute. Park holds a master's of public policy from Georgetown University's McCourt School and a bachelor's of applied science in computer and cognitive science from the University of Pennsylvania's School of Engineering.

Jiyoung Park is a freelance writer and substitute teacher with Washington, DC, Public Schools, where she partnered with Georgetown University's Street Law and Penn State's Social Justice programs. She spent twenty years in management consulting, federal and District of Columbia governments, and nonprofit management. Park holds a master's in organizational development from George Mason University's Schar School of Government and Policy and a bachelor's degree in English and Spanish literature from Georgetown University.

Wendell Pritchett (Penn GR97) is the James S. Riepe Presidential Professor of Law and Education at the University of Pennsylvania. Pritchett served as provost of the university from 2017 to 2022 and briefly as the interim university president in 2022. Pritchett is the author of *Brownsville, Brooklyn: Blacks, Jews and the Changing Face of the Ghetto* (University of Chicago Press, 2002) and *Robert Clifton Weaver and the American City: The Life and Times of an Urban Reformer* (University of Chicago Press, 2008). Most recently, Pritchett, along with Penn colleagues Susan Wachter and Vincent Reina, published the edited volume *Perspectives on Fair Housing* (University of Pennsylvania Press, 2020).

Eric Schwartz (Penn C08, GRW13) is Associate Professor of Marketing in the University of Michigan Ross School of Business. His research in customer analytics applies machine learning and statistics to topics including A/B testing, native advertising, streaming media, valuing customers, and sequential resource allocation for public health. Schwartz is the cofounder of BlueConduit, a social venture based on work with Flint, Michigan, that works with cities to help them find their lead water pipes. He earned his PhD in marketing from the Wharton School and a BA in mathematics and Hispanic Studies, all from the University of Pennsylvania.

Margo Shea (Penn C95) is an Associate Professor of History at Salem State University and director of SSU's Graduate Certificate in Public History. She is the author of *Derry City: Memory and Political Struggle in Northern Ireland* as well as many chapters and articles on memory, heritage, and the democratic potential of participatory history projects. Her teaching, research, and public history work engage creatively and critically the potential of the past for meaning-making and action in the present and for the future. She lives in western Massachusetts with her husband and a retinue of once-stray creatures.

Salamishah Tillet (Penn C96) is the Henry Rutgers Professor of Africana Studies and Creative Writing and the director of Express Newark, a center for socially engaged art and design at Rutgers University–Newark. She is the cofounder of the nonprofit organization A Long Walk Home. She is the author of *Sites of Slavery: Citizenship and Racial Democracy in the Post-Civil Rights Imagination* (Duke University Press, 2012) and *In Search of "The Color Purple": A Story of an American Masterpiece* (Harry N. Abrams, 2021). Tillet won the Pulitzer Prize for Criticism in 2022 for her writing in the *New York Times* for "learned and stylish writing about Black stories in art and popular culture—work that successfully bridges academic and nonacademic critical discourse."

Kim Van Naarden Braun (Penn C95) has over twenty-five years of experience across federal and state government, hospital systems, academia, and industry. She currently serves as the Senior Director within Translational Epidemiology at Bristol Myers Squibb. Before this, Van Naarden Braun worked for twenty years at the Centers for Disease Control and Prevention and in tandem, for six years, at the New Jersey Department of Health. Before diving into industry, she led the Population Health Analytics team at Hackensack Meridian Health and served on faculty at the Hackensack Meridian School of Medicine. She received her PhD and MPH in epidemiology from Columbia University and BA in public health policy from the University of Pennsylvania under the valued mentorship of Dr. Ira Harkavy and Dr. Frank Johnston.

Michael Vazquez (Penn GR20) is Teaching Assistant Professor and Director of Outreach in the Department of Philosophy and the Parr Center for Ethics at the University of North Carolina–Chapel Hill. He received his PhD in philosophy from the University of Pennsylvania in May 2020 and completed the post-baccalaureate program in Classical Studies at the University of Pennsylvania in 2015. At Penn he was awarded the inaugural Provost's Graduate Academic Engagement Fellowship at the Netter Center to design and teach a new Academically Based Community Service course on public philosophy and civic engagement. Since completing his doctorate, he has continued to serve as a lecturer in the Mid-Career Doctoral Program in Educational Leadership at Penn Graduate School of Education.

Jason Yip (Penn C02, GED02) is an Associate Professor at the Information School and an adjunct Assistant Professor in the Department of Human-Centered Design and Engineering at the University of Washington. His research examines how technologies can support parents and children learning together. He is a senior research fellow at the Joan Ganz Cooney Center at Sesame Workshop. He holds a BA in chemistry and MSEd in science and math education from the University of Pennsylvania, and a PhD in curriculum and instruction from the University of Maryland.

Andrew Zitcer (Penn C00, GCP04, CGS07, WEV07, WEV08) is an Associate Professor of Arts Administration and Museum Leadership at Drexel University's Antoinette Westphal College of Media Arts and Design, where he directs the urban strategy graduate program. His research explores economic and cultural democracy. His book *Practicing Cooperation: Mutual Aid Beyond Capitalism* was published by the University of Minnesota Press in 2021. A coedited volume, *Democracy as Creative Practice: Weaving a Culture of Civic Life*, was published by Routledge in 2024.

Michael Zuckerman (Penn C61) is Professor Emeritus of History at the University of Pennsylvania. He completed his BA at Penn and PhD at Harvard. He has held fellowships from the Social Science Research Council, National Endowment for the Humanities, Guggenheim, American Council of Learned Societies, Rockefeller, Fulbright, Bellagio, Netherlands Institute for Advanced Studies, among others. His first book, *Peaceable Kingdoms*, helped inaugurate what was known for a while as the New Social History. His subsequent books and articles have ranged in such areas as American identity, popular culture, and the history of childhood and the family. Zuckerman began teaching Academically Based Community Service courses in the early 1990s and is a longstanding member of the Netter Center's Faculty Advisory Board.

INDEX

198 Index

Netter Center (*continued*)
impact and lessons of, 26–30, 40, 54,
58–65, 73–76, 80–83, 87, 117, 158, 163–
64; Netter Center–Turner Middle School
summer program, 34; Penn Program
for Public Service Internship of, 33–34;
possibility of change in, 106; and the Philadelphia Higher Education Network for
Neighborhood Development (PHENND),
123–24n37; Provost's Graduate Academic
Engagement Fellowship (PGAEF) of, 7,
20, 21–23, 25–28; reach of, 161–62; time-
line of, 179–87; workforce development
program of for K-12 students, 117; *See
also* Center for Community Partnerships
(later the Netter Center)
Newark community, 6, 8 10–11. *See also*
Express Newark; Newark Free School;
Rutgers-Newark
Newark Free School, 6
North Carolina Department of Public Safety
(NCDPS), 27–28
Northern Ireland. *See* Shea, Margo, commu-
nity engagement in Northern Ireland
Nussbaum, Martha, 106

"Oakland Ebonics Controversy," 37
Oakland Unified School District, 37
Office of Community Oriented-Policy Stud-
ies (OCOPS) at Penn, 14, 15

Paris, Django, 35, 38, 39
Park, David, 109–10; creation of the
Program to Bridge the Digital Divide,
109–12; engineering thesis of, 111; on
how cities and universities can build partnerships, 117–119; work on alleviating
poverty, 114–15; work with the Metropolitan Baptist Church and the Philadelphia
Masjid, 116; work at the National League
of Cities, 114–15
Parr Center (UNC-Chapel Hill), 26; signature outreach program of, 29
participatory action research (PAR), 155,
156, 157. *See also* community-based
participatory research (CBPR)
Paul Robeson House, 140
Penn Compact, 22–23, 25
Pennsylvania Supplemental Nutrition Assistance Program Education, 128

Pepper, Griffin, 22
Perna, Laura, 61
Philadelphia, 4, 16, 21, 59, 102, 111, 120,
142, 144, 155–56, 173. *See also* Southwest
Philadelphia; West Philadelphia
Philadelphia Regional Ethics Bowl, 22
Philadelphia Writing Project, 138–39
philosophy: appeal of philosophical
reflection, 25; civic function of university philosophy departments, 27–28; of
education, 30; uselessness of, 25. *See also*
philosophy, public
philosophy, public, 26–27; guiding principles of (distributed expertise, social
reasoning, universal access), 23; transformative impact of, 29
Philosophy Club at Philadelphia Futures, 21
Pittsburgh: Hill District gardening projects
of, 130–31; Homewood neighborhood
of, 131
Pittsburgh Hill/Homewood Research on
Eating, Shopping, and Health (PHRESH),
131, 132
Pittsburgh Hill/Homewood Research on
Neighborhood Change and Health, 131
Plato, 24–25, 27
Political Participation Center (PPC), 12
Portland Made, 115, 118
poverty, 12–13, 47, 83, 111, 113–14, 128,
170, 173–174
Prisons and Justice Initiative, 123n35
Pritchett, Wendell: community philosophy
of as chancellor at Rutgers-Camden, 5–6;
and creation of the Provost's Graduate
Academic Engagement Fellowship at the
Netter Center, 7; dialogue with Salamishah
Tillet, 1–2; discovery of community-based
scholarship by, 2; on engagement with
ABCS as a doctoral student, 2; full text of
the dialogue, 2–11; on Penn's engagement
with West Philadelphia, 4–5, 7–8; at Turner
Middle School, 3; on work with the Netter
Center as provost, 7
Project for Philosophy for the Young (Penn),
21
*Proposals Relating to the Education of Youth
in Pennsylvania* (Franklin), 173–74
public health, 70, 78–85, 94–95, 125, 133,
155, 158–59
public history/historians, 48–49, 50

Renzi, Gina, 103
Robertson, Tyrone, 44
Rockefeller Foundation, 65, 66
Rodin, Judith, 4, 181
Romberg, Osvaldo, 103
Ross School of Business (Michigan Ross):
 Business+Impact initiative of, 71–72;
 "Multidisciplinary Action Program
 (MAP) of, 71, 72
Rotunda, the: 100, 101, 102–4, 106–7; advo-
 cacy for, 103
Rubio, Juan, 147, 148, 151
Rutgers-Camden, 5–6
Rutgers-Newark, 8, 10; civic engagement
 and community-based scholarship at, 6–7

Sadie Tanner Mossell Alexander University
 of Pennsylvania Partnership School, 22
Sampson-Mapp, Isabel, 110
Sayre High School, 56, 61
Schwartz, Anna, 127
Schwartz, Eric: academic interests in
 marketing, 56–57; experiences with the
 Netter Center, 57, 58, 60, 63, 70, 73–74;
 partnership with the Flint Action and
 Sustainability Team (FAST), 63–64;
 Student Committee on Undergraduate
 Education (SCUE) initiative of, 75–76;
 as tenured professor at The Ross School
 of Business (Michigan Ross), 57, 71–72;
 work of in Academically Based Commu-
 nity Service (ABCS), 57–58; work of with
 the Environmental Protection Agency
 (EPA), 57. See also BlueConduit; Flint
 water crisis, lessons of
Seattle Public Library, 147, 148, 151–52
Sen, Amartya, 106
Shea, Margo: community engagement in
 Northern Ireland, 48–49, 51–52; as coordinator of the federal Learn and Serve
 America Higher Education grant, 47–48;
 engagement with the Center for Community Partnerships and Ira Harkavy, 43,
 44, 46, 54; experiences at Turner Middle
 School, 44–45; interest in public history,
 48–49; as Mellon fellow at Sewanee: The
 University of the South, 52–53; position
 at the Walt Whitman Center for Culture
 and Politics (Rutgers University), 47; as
 professor at Salem State, 53–54; on the

realities of racism faced by, 43–44; at the
 University of Pennsylvania, 42–43, 44
Seligsohn, Andrew, 6
Simmonds, Theresa, 145
Smitherman, Geneva, 38
Socrates, 21
Southwest Philadelphia, 34–35
Spiral Q project (Peoplehood), 140–41
St. John's College, study of on service learn-
 ers, 116–17
Stoicism/Stoics: altruism of, 24; opposition
 of to escapism, 24; tradition of egalitari-
 anism in, 23–24

Tillet, Salamishah: dialogue with Wendell
 Pritchett, 1–2; discovery of community-
 based scholarship, 2–3; on engagement
 with the Netter Center and Turner Middle
 School as an undergraduate, 2–4; on
 experience as faculty at Rutgers-Newark,
 4, 6, 8–9; full text of the dialogue, 2–11;
 influence of Dewey on, 3; on metrics of
 success for community collaborations
 with Penn and Rutgers-Newark, 9–10; on
 relationship of universities to their cities
 and communities, 4; on third space(s)
 that bridge campus and community, 6,
 9; see also Express Newark; Newark Free
 School
Turner Middle School, 2, 3, 15, 36, 38,
 44–45, 126, 127, 136, 137, 138, 142,
 144, 155, 156, 157–58, 160, 164; Netter
 Center–Turner Middle School summer
 program, 34–35; Turner Nutritional
 Awareness Program, 126

United States, mass education system of, 16
university-assisted community schools
 (UACS), 14–15, 17–19, 21–22, 48, 93, 133,
 156–57, 161, 162
University City High School, 81, 83, 101,
 129, 145
University of Michigan, relationship with
 Flint, Michigan, 61–62
University of Michigan–Flint, 67, 69
University of Pennsylvania, 1, 4, 10, 12,
 22, 26, 59, 84, 100–101, 126, 144, 153,
 173–74; anthropology department of,
 81; chemistry department of, 144–45;
 extraordinary resources of, 15; as a

www.ingramcontent.com/pod-product-compliance
Lightning Source LLC
Chambersburg PA
CBHW031132270326
41929CB00011B/1596